WHAT IS CATHOLICISM?

Hard Questions – Straight Answers

JOHN REDFORD

Foreword by Avery Dulles, S.J.

Our Sunday Visitor Publishing Division
Our Sunday Visitor, Inc.
Huntington, Indiana 46750

Nihil Obstat: Rev. Anton Cowan, Censor Librorum
Imprimatur: Rev. David Norris, Vicar General
Westminster, June 20, 1996

First published by Geoffrey Chapman, an imprint of Cassell plc, London, in 1997. This edition published by arrangement with the original publisher.

ISBN: 0-87973-587-2
LCCCN: 99-70514

Cover design by Tyler Ottinger
PRINTED IN THE UNITED STATES OF AMERICA

587

Dedication

This book was written in the latter part of 1995 in the presbytery of St. Dunstan's Church, Hersden, Canterbury. St. Dunstan was Archbishop of Canterbury from 960 to 988, at a time when the whole of Europe was united in one visible Catholic Church. In 961, as was the custom for each elected Archbishop of Canterbury, Dunstan went to Rome to receive the pallium, a stole that was the insignia of his acceptance of the authority of the Bishop of Rome, the successor of Peter. He came back from that hazardous journey with the additional bonus of having been made a papal legate. He was a great reforming archbishop, renewing the life not only of the Church but of the English nation as a whole.

The name of St. Dunstan also revives the happiest memories for me of Dom Dunstan Pontifex, O.S.B., who instructed me in the Catholic faith at Downside Abbey in 1960. He was an ecumenist well before the Second Vatican Council, and was a historian, an expert on St. Dunstan's life, and encouraged my devotion to the saint. The following work is written in honor of St. Dunstan and of all great English Christians past and present, at home or overseas, who lived and died for the Catholic faith, asking them to join us in prayer for that fullness of visible unity in the body of Christ for which we all pray.

Rev. John Redford

"Still, who can doubt that the Church of Rome is the head of all the churches, the source of all Catholic teaching? Who does not know that the keys of the kingdom of heaven were given to Peter? Is not the whole structure of the Church built up on Peter's faith and teaching, so to grow until we meet Christ as one perfect man, united in faith and in our recognition of him as Son of God?"

St. Thomas Becket*

---

* Letter no. 74, quoted in *The Divine Office: The Liturgy of the Hours According to the Roman Rite as Renewed in the Decree of the Second Vatican Council, and Promulgated by the Authority of Pope Paul VI* (London: Collins, 1974), p. 70. (St. Thomas Becket, Archbishop of Canterbury from 1162 to 1170, was martyred in Canterbury Cathedral for defending the rights of the Church, struck down by four Knights of the Realm, at the instigation of King Henry II.)

Contents

Abbreviations

AAS: *Acta Apostolicae Sedis* ("Acts of the Apostolic See," i.e., official documentation from the Vatican issued and published on an ongoing basis).

CCC: *Catechism of the Catholic Church* (London: Geoffrey Chapman, 1994).

CCCC: Michael J. Walsh (ed.), *Commentary on the Catechism of the Catholic Church* (London: Geoffrey Chapman, 1994).

CCL: *The Code of Canon Law in English Translation* (Latin original: *Codex Iuris Canonici*), prepared by the Canon Law Society of Great Britain and Ireland in association with The Canon Law Society of Australia and New Zealand and The Canadian Law Society (London: Collins, 1983).

CTD: K. Rahner and H. Vorgrimler (eds.), *Concise Theological Dictionary* (London: Burns and Oates, 1965).

DFT: René Latourelle and Rino Fischella (eds.), *Dictionary of Fundamental Theology* (Slough: St. Pauls, 1994).

DS: H. Denzinger, rev. A. Schönmetzer, *Enchiridion Symbolorum Definitionum et Declarationum de Rebus Fidei et Morum* ("Compendium of Symbols, Definitions and Declarations Concerning Matters of Faith and Morals") (Barcelona: Herder, 1958).

DV: *Dei Verbum* ("The Word of God"). Dogmatic Constitution on Divine Revelation of the Second Vatican Council: Tanner, II, pp. 971-981.

LG: *Lumen Gentium* ("The Light of the Nations"). Dogmatic Constitution on the Church of the Second Vatican Council: Tanner, II, pp. 849-900.

ND: J. Neuner and J. Dupuis (eds.), *The Christian Faith in the Doctrinal Documents of the Catholic Church* (revised edition) (London: Collins, 1982).

NDCE: J. Macquarrie and J. Childress (eds.), *A New Dictionary of Christian Ethics* (London: SCM Press, 1967).

NJB: H. Wansbrough (ed.), *The New Jerusalem Bible* (London: Darton, Longman and Todd, 1985).

NJBC: Raymond E. Brown, Joseph A. Fitzmyer, and Roland E. Murphy (eds.), *The New Jerome Biblical Commentary* (Englewood Cliffs, NJ: Prentice Hall/London: Geoffrey Chapman, 1989).

ODCC: F. L. Cross and E. A. Livingstone (eds.), *Oxford Dictionary of the Christian Church* (second edition) (Oxford: Oxford University Press, 1983).

PG: *Patrologia Graeca,* J.-P. Migne (ed.).

PO: *Presbyterorum Ordinis* ("Of the Order of Priests"), Decree on the Ministry and Life of Priests of the Second Vatican Council: Tanner, II, pp. 1042-1069.

ST: St. Thomas Aquinas, *Summa Theologica* (Madrid: Biblioteca de Autores Cristianos, 1965).

Tanner: N. P. Tanner (ed.), *Decrees of the Ecumenical Councils* (two volumes; from the original text by Istituto per le scienze religiose, Bologna) (London: Sheed and Ward, 1990).

UR: *Unitatis Redintegratio* ("The Restoration of Unity"). Decree on Ecumenism of the Second Vatican Council: Tanner, II, pp. 908-920.

Foreword

My interest in the present book dates back to the fall of 1997, when I was invited to give a lecture at the Maryvale Institute, Birmingham, England, where the author of this book is on the staff as Director of the Divinity degree program. My first reaction, which I communicated to Father John Redford, was that this work, *What Is Catholicism? Hard Questions — Straight Answers,* spoke to issues that were at least as vital in the United States as in England, and that the book, if published on this side of the Atlantic, would fill a notable gap in the existing literature.

Father Redford, to be sure, is writing in reply to difficulties raised by a clergyman of the Church of England. Besides, he probably has in mind the questions that would have concerned him when he left the Anglican communion to become a Roman Catholic. But most of the issues discussed in this volume are not peculiarly Anglican. Protestants in a country such as our own pose similar, if not identical, questions.

The similarity is in part explained by history. The "Founding Fathers" of the American Republic were for the most part raised either in the Anglican Establishment, which engendered our Protestant Episcopal Church, or in Anglican dissent, which gave rise to New England Puritanism and Congregationalism. Methodism originated as a movement within the Anglican communion. American Presbyterians and Baptists had British forebears who interacted for centuries with Anglicans in their homeland.

Lutherans, to be sure, are much more numerous in the United States than in Britain. But Luther's own theology had an immense impact on all other branches of Protestantism, including the English churches already mentioned. Although Lutheranism is in some ways closer to Catholicism than other Protestant denominations, Luther had difficulties against Rome that have become part of the general Protestant patrimony, so that in replying to other Protestants one is also answering difficulties that would arise from the Lutheran perspective.

To be accurate, this work of Father Redford's is directed not simply against Protestant difficulties. In many respects it is a defense of normative Christianity against modern infidelity. Articles of belief such as the existence of God, the divinity of Christ, the inspiration of Holy Scripture, and the importance of sacramental worship — all treated in these pages — are parts of the common Christian heritage. Father Redford's positions on these matters will be welcomed by all who continue to adhere to the essentials of the faith handed down from the apostles.

These essentials of the faith are under assault nearly everywhere. Like their Protestant neighbors, American Catholic readers are easily infected by the doubts and disbelief that are pervasive in our culture. They are tempted to wonder whether it is still possible to believe in God, in the divinity of Christ, in miracles, inspiration, and the like. For this reason Father Redford's explanations of Catholic doctrine can help Catholic readers to grow in their own faith.

Concern for the vigor and integrity of the faith is a high priority among Catholics who, like Father Redford and myself, have come to the Church as adults, by a deliberate choice. Having entered the Catholic communion before Vatican II, we are troubled by the impression that Catholics today are not as eager in their defense of the faith as were their predecessors before the Council. Although Vatican II had many positive effects, it seems to have weakened the apostolic zeal and self-confidence of the Catholic community. A glance back into history can throw light on this negative phenomenon.

In the sixteenth century, Catholics rushed to the defense of their faith against Protestant objections. Authors such as St. Peter Canisius and St. Robert Bellarmine wrote catechisms and polemical tracts to counteract those of the Protestant Reformers. Bellarmine's masterful *Disputationes de controversiis christianae fidei adversus hujus temporis haereticos* (1586-1593) set the pattern for the pamphlets and manuals of the next three and a half centuries, right down to the time of Vatican II. Catholics were thoroughly drilled in "ready answers" to all the standard objections, especially those coming from Protestants. Popular apologetic literature tended to focus on the errors of Protestants and (unlike Bellarmine's massive work) to present the Catholic answers in rather simplistic style.

Vatican II sounded a different note. After centuries of deploring modern infidelity and disparaging Protestant errors, Catholics were summoned to recognize all that was good and healthy not only in the modern world but more specifically in other Christian traditions — Protestant, Anglican, and Orthodox. In their zeal to embrace the reforms of Vatican II, some Catholics overreacted. They felt that since the Church was not immune to criticism and reform, every Catholic doctrine and practice could properly be called into question. They so emphasized what was new and different in Vatican II that they neglected its support and reaffirmation of the great body of Catholic tradition.

This postconciliar ferment was very damaging to apologetics. The old manuals were abruptly cast aside, without anything to take their place. Catholics suddenly shied away from the defense of the faith, which had seemed to come so naturally to them. Father Redford in his answer to Question 51 puts the matter well: "In recent years, the catechesis of Catholic young people has not taken them through Hard Questions such as are posed in this book, as they grow to maturity. 'Apologetics' has to a large extent gone out of the Catholic school curriculum, and young priests themselves have perhaps been affected by this gap in Catholic upbringing."

To clear up some of the current confusion, the Holy See published in 1992 the *Catechism of the Catholic Church,* a work calculated to show the continuity of Vatican II with the previous teaching of popes and councils, as well as with Holy Scripture and the liturgy. In no way polemical, this catechism is a confident and attractive synthesis of Catholic doctrine. Although it admirably fulfills its designated purpose, the new *Catechism* does not engage in the task of apologetics, which remains to be done so that Catholics may be able to fulfill the precept to "always have your answer ready for people who ask you the reason for the hope that you have" (1 Peter 3:15).

As a defense of the faith, apologetics must proceed from a realization of what faith is. In accordance with recent councils, Father Redford shows that faith is a firm assent to the word of God motivated by reverent trust in the God who reveals. The act of faith, as a free and voluntary submission to God's word, presupposes an attraction of the will: We assent because we perceive that it is good for us to believe. Great apologists have never neglected what Blaise Pascal called the "reasons of the heart." The tedium of a pointless existence, frittered away in the endless search for wealth and security, or for amusement and distractions, arouses a craving to be informed about the real purpose of our lives. Why are we here on earth? What is the true measure of success and failure? In the depth of our hearts, we are all eager to find a truth and a goodness to which we can dedicate our full capacities to give and to serve. When we find a treasure that it is worthy of our full devotion, we experience a joy that is not of this world. It is precisely this treasure, this truth and goodness, that God has revealed to us by his word in Jesus Christ.

The problem of God, therefore, is not a mere exercise in logic; it is not like a game of chess or a mathematical problem. It is an existential search for what concerns us ultimately. For many of us, God would be a shadowy ideal except for the splendid reflection of the Father that we find shining in the face of Jesus Christ, who manifests God's love and faithfulness by all that he teaches and does, but especially by his redeeming death on the cross and his glorious resurrection. Christ himself might seem to be a remote figure of ancient history except that he perpetuates his living presence in the Church, which he founded and then enlivened by his Spirit. The Christian therefore encounters God through Jesus Christ, who continues to be active in the ministry and sacraments of the Church.

The Christian message, with its three main elements of God, Christ, and Church, is beautiful and consoling. But is it true? The question of truth, which no responsible inquirer can ignore, is the special concern of apologetics. In his *What Is Catholicism? Hard Questions — Straight Answers*, Father Redford does not shrink from giving solid reasons for holding that God is real, that Jesus is indeed the Son of God, and that he remains present in his Church, which subsists in the Roman Catholic communion.

A distinctive characteristic of Catholic Christianity is the realization that the faith is conveyed to believers of each generation by a living tradition, sustained by the Holy Spirit, and authoritatively interpreted by the *magisterium*, through popes and councils. Catholics believe that Christ provided for this mediation, and that without it divine revelation could not survive in its purity and fullness. The fragmentation and doctrinal disarray of some Protestant churches seems to confirm the necessity of a Church that can teach with authority. As Cardinal Newman recognized a century and a half ago, it is hardly possible to believe in divine revelation without also believing in a power that keeps the revelation from being corrupted by human error. It is in this context that the Catholic doctrine of infallibility must be understood.

All of this is said without detriment to the Bible, which God has inspired for our instruction and correction. Precious though the Bible is, it was never intended to be self-sufficient, self-authenticating, and self-interpreting. Experience proves the need for a Church to give force and clarity to God's word in Scripture.

These truths of faith, I repeat, are not just theoretical. For anyone who takes them seriously, they are spiritual dynamite. When grasped with firm assurance, God's revelation in Christ bursts open the limits of a purely selfish or worldly existence; it radically changes our whole scale of values, and calls us to new life in Christ. We begin to understand how Paul could say of himself: "I have been crucified with Christ, and yet I am alive; yet it is no longer I, but Christ living in me. The life that I am now living, subject to the limitation of human nature, I am living in faith, faith in the Son of God who loved me and gave himself for me" (Galatians 2:20).

Catholic Christians are incorporated into the body of Christ by baptism. They experience his forgiveness in the sacrament of penance and are nourished by his flesh and blood in the Eucharist. The incredible intimacy of these sacramental encounters should be a sufficient answer to anyone who complains that Catholics cannot experience a personal relationship to Jesus in the Church.

Father Redford does not content himself with treating these fundamental questions concerning God, Christ, and the Church. He also answers a multitude of typical objections that continue to be urged by persons who do not share the Catholic faith. Some of these objections will evoke echoes in the Catholic reader's own struggle of faith. Others will be perceived as needing to be answered so that sincere inquirers may be helped on their journey to faith. A study of these issues can better equip Catholics to take part in the Church's mission to spread the good news, to make disciples of all nations, and to evangelize every cultural sector of the world. The process of bearing witness to Christ is never done; it needs to be undertaken anew for every generation.

This work is notable because the author has thoroughly assimilated the spirit of Vatican II. Father Redford is respectful of other Christian traditions. His tone is patient and courteous. He does not feel a compulsion to profess complete certitude about matters that are still open to discussion within the Catholic communion. He is remarkably well informed about the state of current scholarship in many different fields. He is familiar with contemporary exegesis and historiography; he is a prudent and experienced pastoral guide; and he has an excellent grasp of the philosophical perspectives from which old and new questions have been raised. He alerts his readers to the harm done by a purely mechanistic conception of the universe associated with Isaac Newton and the deism of the Enlightenment. He also puts them on guard against the false materialistic understanding of evolution that we have come to connect with Charles Darwin. Even when dealing with profound and complex questions, Father Redford writes with a disarming simplicity of style.

For these and many other reasons, this book can be helpful to a broad range of persons, from the interested inquirer to the priest or theologian. I myself have learned many things from these pages, and my path to Catholic Christianity would no doubt have been shorter and smoother if I had had access to a work such as this some sixty years ago.

AVERY DULLES, S.J.

Introduction

The Church has always faced hard questions throughout its almost two-thousand-year history. This century is nothing new in that respect; although it has thrown up a few questions of its own.

This book is written in the belief that the Catholic Church can give satisfactory answers to the following Hard Questions, in fact to some of the most important questions about God, about life and its meaning. The Church can give those answers because Christ himself founded it to be the "pillar and support of truth" (1 Timothy 3:15b). This does not mean that a Roman Catholic claims to know all the answers to every question under the sun. A Catholic professor of philosophy began his course of lectures by showing his students a large blackboard with nothing written on it. "The blackboard represents what we do not know," he explained. Then he placed a white dot on the blackboard with his chalk. "The white represents what we do know," he said. "What we know is precious little; but what we know is precious." The present book, in its answers, will focus on the white chalkmark rather than on the mass of black representing what we do not know. What we know is precious, through the revelation of Jesus Christ given to his Church. This certainty links up with our quotation (at the beginning of this book) from Archbishop Thomas Becket to English Christians past and present, to the effect that "the Church of Rome is the head of all the churches, the source of all Catholic teaching." The source of all Catholic teaching is of course Christ himself; but we believe that the Bishop of Rome, as the successor of the Apostle Peter the "Rock," provides us with the ultimate reference point and authority here on earth, together with the bishops worldwide in communion with him, for Christian faith and practice.

Although written as a Roman Catholic reply to a book written by an Anglican scholar, the following Hard Questions raised are particularly relevant to any dialogue between Roman Catholics and Christians of the Protestant and Reformed tradition; and perhaps even more, are relevant to all those asking questions today concerning the authority and basis of Christian faith and practice.

The occasion of writing this book has been provided by some serious criticisms of the Roman Catholic Church in *What Is Catholicism?*[1] The author, the distinguished scholar Dr. David Edwards, asked for a reply to those criticisms, both in that book itself, and in a subsequent article in the Catholic weekly newspaper *The Tablet*[2] where he stated that "I should love to read a considered Roman Catholic reply." This reply has been written in that same ecumenical spirit.

This is all very different from a very famous and unpleasant encounter of the nineteenth century between Cardinal John Henry Newman and the Anglican clergyman and author of *The Water Babies*, Charles Kingsley. That was unquestionably polemical. Kingsley, who comes over as the worst type of Victorian macho parson, accused the sensitive Newman of Jesuitical dishonesty. "Truth for its own sake," he said trenchantly, "had never been a virtue with the Roman clergy."[3] It was a personal insult as well as a criticism of Catholicism, evoking Newman's celebrated reply *Apologia Pro Vita Sua* ("In Defense of His Life"). The atmosphere between Newman and Kingsley was one of utter hostility. It was not a dialogue. It was a contest. At that time, it was expected that Catholics and Protestants would always engage in polemics, scoring points against one another. The aim was not better mutual understanding, but a knockout blow to prove to the cheering onlookers that my side was better than your side.

Since then, we have enjoyed the fresh air of the movement for church unity, the ecumenical movement. The Church of England is now in constant and official dialogue with the Roman Catholic Church to try to find ways of coming closer together to that full visible communion of faith and life that is clearly the will of Christ for all Christians. This book is written in that new context, hoping to make a contribution to that ongoing dialogue.

Many speak of a loss of impetus in the ecumenical movement. Did we expect too much too soon? It is clear that many serious differences still remain, which cannot be swept under the carpet. They are Hard Questions, and must be honestly faced. Many, including David Edwards, consider that the intransigence of the Vatican — particularly that of Pope John Paul II and his right-hand adviser Cardinal Joseph Ratzinger (the Prefect of the Congregation of the Doctrine of the Faith) — is perhaps the main factor in the present apparent slowing down of the impetus of the ecumenical movement. In particular, the publication of the *Catechism of the Catholic Church* has, for Edwards, reinforced this process of conservative reaction:

> Vatican II was somewhat ambiguous. It opened windows to other churches, to the modern world and to the future; it resulted in

many changes in church life and some new emphases in official teaching; it seemed to acknowledge, and even to bless, some pluralism in the Church's life; it raised many hopes or fears of more radical changes, leading to a period of considerable uncertainty. Yet (not surprisingly) it was often conservative and it took care to be loyal to the papacy and to previous councils. It is this conservative side that the new catechism proclaims. . . .[4]

I shall try continually to argue in this book that underlying the above statement is a most basic misunderstanding of the way in which the Roman Catholic Church develops in its teaching and life. The Catholic Church, in progressing forward to a new understanding of its faith as happened in the Second Vatican Council, does not abandon the doctrines of the past; still less does the Church abandon its claims to authority. Rather, it reaffirms its fundamental teaching in a new and renewed context. Thus, to a reader who does not understand this process of development within the Catholic Church, it will, when operating well, appear to be both "conservative" and "progressive" at the same time; conservative, because the essential faith and practice of its tradition cannot be abandoned, and progressive, because there is always the need to reinterpret its faith and life in new situations.

The general judgment is that the new *Catechism of the Catholic Church* has tilted toward the side of conservatism. But this is only because the element of reaffirmation and reassurance at a time of uncertainty does need some emphasis at the present time. Yet there is within the whole idea and in the reality of the new *Catechism* a thrust toward renewal, and not just a defense of past positions. Above all, the new *Catechism* is intended to be an instrument of creative catechesis throughout the world, to be adapted and inculturated in each country in its own way.

The reader will quickly discover that there are perhaps fewer quotations than expected from the *Catechism of the Catholic Church.* This is by no means because I do not like the new *Catechism.* On the contrary, my own work in taking part in the worldwide consultation on the new Universal Catechism, and even more in later coediting a new edition of a popular adult catechetical work[5] using the *Catechism of the Catholic Church,* has given me not only respect for it, but a genuine love for the inspired vision of the Catholic faith that the new *Catechism* gives, despite the deficiencies that any catechetical work will manifest when put under a theological microscope.

Rather, the limited number of quotations from the *Catechism* arises from the consideration that, in a book of this nature, it is more important to quote the sources used by the *Catechism*, in particular Scripture and the general council documents, both Vatican II and earlier councils, together with some appropriate papal encyclicals. This will hopefully serve to focus the reader's mind rather on the doctrine itself than on a consideration of whether it has been expressed well or not so well in the new *Catechism*.

I would even go further to say that very often the differences that give rise to these Hard Questions have in fact little to do with the *Catechism of the Catholic Church*, except insofar as it expresses these specifically Catholic doctrines in a more or less satisfactory way according to the critical judgment of any given theologian. They are Catholic doctrines that were part of the Church's teaching authority long before the *Catechism* was published, and expressed usually quite explicitly in the documents of the Second Vatican Council and in earlier councils. Above all, they are doctrines that are given with the authority claimed by the Roman Catholic Church and express that authority in matters of faith and morals. The new *Catechism* has only brought these issues more sharply to mind, and has given all of us an invaluable resource for now and the years to come.

Regarding my own qualifications to write this book, I hope that it does not sound too arrogant to say that I am as well qualified as anybody. In fact, that is a statement of self-deprecation rather than of pride, since the subject matter is so wide, covering the whole theological field of history, philosophy, Scripture, fundamental theology, and dogmatic and moral theology, that no theologian today, in this era of increasing specialization, could cover all the following questions as an expert on each.

This means firstly that I have been very careful to defer to acknowledged experts in their own field, where that is possible, unless I have very serious reasons for disagreeing with them. There is a strong tradition in Roman Catholic scholarship to follow usually the "common opinion" of theologians (which will of course include equally historians and biblical scholars; it is less easy, in fact usually impossible, to find a "common opinion" among philosophers!). Where I have disagreed with a given opinion, it is either because my own reflection and research lead me strongly to a different conclusion (using the author's privilege) or — and this causes me much regret — because I cannot see how a given opinion expressed can be compatible with the clear teaching of the *magisterium* of the Catholic Church. In the latter case, I would have to disagree with a theologian however eminent, and however much I might respect that theologian and his or her achievements. Of course, if I could be persuaded that I have misunderstood the views of that particular theologian, and such a view turns out not to be contrary to the teaching of the *magisterium*, no one would be happier than I.

The wide nature of the subject matter of this book makes me even more grateful for the help of colleagues and friends in the theological community for patiently reading various sections of the work in preparation, and giving their expert opinion. I give my special thanks to Father Garry Lysaght, Lecturer in History at St. John's Seminary, Wonersh; Dr. George Woodall, Nottingham; Father Ephrem Conway, O.F.M., Canterbury; and Father Michael Jackson, Secretary to the Ecumenical Commission of the Bishops' Conference of England and Wales. While my gratitude is deep for undoubtedly having improved the following text enormously, I must also take care to absolve them from all responsibility for its final contents, which ultimate responsibility is mine and mine alone.

I would also like to thank Patricia Gibson, who patiently helped me with the critical reading of the text. I am especially indebted to the editorial staff at Geoffrey Chapman/Cassell, always helpful, making particular mention of Ruth McCurry, who initially encouraged me to begin this book, Kathie Walsh, who was my editor, and whose advice was always so wise and professional, and Fiona McKenzie, the house editor. I would like to thank the parishioners of St. Dunstan's, my long-suffering "little flock," who have put up with months of distractions while their pastor was writing this book. Finally, I would like to thank Bishop John Jukes, O.F.M., Conv., my own area bishop, for his support and encouragement.

The broad scope of the Hard Questions answered has also meant that the Bibliography and list of sources used under Abbreviations are likewise incomplete, limited only to those books to which I make reference in this work. A substantial bibliography covering the subject areas involved, let alone a complete bibliography, would be much longer than this whole book. However, if the reader consults the books and articles listed, more complete bibliographies will be discovered.

One source book is worth mentioning right at the beginning. Since 1990, we are singularly fortunate in having available in English translation on each right-hand page, with (on the left-hand page) the original text (usually in Latin) edited by Norman Tanner, S.J., the *Decrees of the Ecumenical Councils,* a translation of the edition by the Istituto per le scienze religiose, Bologna, of all the ecumenical councils from Nicaea (325) to Vatican II (1962-1965). This must become an essential scholarly tool along with the Scriptures and other theological sources.

The version of the Scriptures used throughout is the *New Jerusalem Bible* (Darton, Longman & Todd).

This work, *What Is Catholicism? Hard Questions — Straight Answers,* is a bold, even a rash, project, because the areas covered by it within theology and related subjects are so varied; although I also hope that the reader will see that some of the Hard Questions are better answered precisely because they are set within a wider context of interconnecting and interrelated Hard Questions. What has driven me to rush in where others, whether angels or not, fear to tread, is the need to give a reply, an *apologia,* not only to David Edwards, whom I thank for his courteous challenge, but to so many today at all levels of theological reflection who need some kind of answer to the following Hard Questions.

Endnotes

1. David L. Edwards, *What Is Catholicism? An Anglican Responds to the Official Teaching of the Roman Catholic Church* (London: Mowbray, 1994).

2. David L. Edwards, "Prejudice unmasked, no. 6: Roman Catholics as others see them," *The Tablet* (April 8, 1995), pp. 452-453.

3. J. H. Newman, *Apologia Pro Vita Sua, Being a History of his Religious Opinions* (London: Longmans, Green and Co., 1908), p. viii.

4. Edwards, *What Is Catholicism?* p. viii.

5. Rowanne Pasco and John Redford (eds.), *Faith Alive: New Catechism Edition* (London: Hodder and Stoughton, 1994).

The Hard Questions

Chapter 1 / Catholicism: Exclusive and Inclusive

1: How can apologetics (the defense of one's own faith) be reconciled with ecumenism (the search for visible unity among all Christians)? Is not apologetics by its very nature divisive, tending toward fixed positions?

2: How can a convert to Roman Catholicism be a genuine ecumenist? Is not in this case "ecumenism" simply "you-come-in-ism"? Instead of dialogue, does not a convert simply wish to convert Anglicans to the "one true faith"?

3: Has not the Roman Catholic Church taken many steps backward toward a more defensive form of its faith under Pope John Paul II, after the promising days of the Second Vatican Council?

4: Is not a prime example of this stepping back precisely the publication of the new *Catechism of the Catholic Church*?

5: Does not the use of the phrase "The Catholic Church" to describe Roman Catholics emphasize the arrogant claims of the Roman Catholic Church to be the True Church of Christ? How can this be reconciled with a truly open ecumenical spirit?

Chapter 2 / The Truth About the Bible

6: Has not the Roman Catholic Church discouraged Christian laypeople from studying the Bible because of the threat this might pose regarding its official doctrine?

7: Does not the *Catechism of the Catholic Church* fall back into fundamentalism, despite the widespread use of the critical method of studying Scripture among its leading scholars?

8: How can the *Catechism of the Catholic Church* sustain the traditional doctrine of Original Sin in the light of modern theories of evolution?

9: Even more, are we committed to the story of the fall of the angels, and to the literal existence of angels as is the *Catechism of the Catholic Church*?

10: How can the Constitution on Divine Revelation, *Dei Verbum,* "unhesitatingly affirm" the historicity of the four Gospels in the light of modern New Testament criticism?

11: One doctrine that still divides other Christians from Roman

Catholicism is the Catholic belief that, besides Scripture, some doctrines are contained within "Tradition." Surely, such a doctrine must reduce the importance of Scripture as the rule of faith?

12: Even more controversial than the concept of Tradition is that the *magisterium* of the Church is the ultimate criterion of what is contained in Scripture and Tradition. What hope for unity is there when this teaching still remains part of the claims of the Catholic Church?

13: Has not the Roman Catholic Church, in its doctrines of the Virgin Mary, confused doctrine and Tradition with legend?

14: Are we still committed to belief in hell and purgatory in the terms stated in the *Catechism of the Catholic Church*?

15: Also, granted that, according to the Catholic Church's teaching, the blessed enjoy the vision of God immediately upon death, what is there to wait for with the resurrection of the body?

Chapter 3 / Infallibility, Primacy, and Episcopacy

16: The Roman Catholic Church claims infallibility for the statements of faith of its bishops as successors of the apostles in union with the Pope, the Bishop of Rome, the successor of Peter. But do the actions and personalities of the possessors of this gift of infallibility justify these enormous claims?

17: What evidence is there in the primitive Church that the apostles were convinced of their infallibility in questions of faith or morals?

18: Is not the Catholic Church's claim to infallibility in fact a blank check to make every Christian believe whatever is proposed for faith by the *magisterium*, and a denial of legitimate freedom of dissent in the Church?

19: Is not the definition of the infallibility of the Pope at the First Vatican Council (1870) a source of continual embarrassment to the Catholic Church as we enter the twenty-first century?

20: Matthew 16:13-20 is cited by the Roman Catholic Church as the Scripture text where Jesus gave Peter primacy and infallibility. But scholars dispute that this is the meaning of the text. How then can Roman Catholics justify using it to promote papal claims?

21: Granted that Peter was the leader of the apostles during the first days of the Christian Church in Jerusalem, surely the New Testament shows us that other Christian leaders, for example James and Paul, had equal claim to "universal primacy" as Peter after the Gentile mission began?

22: The power of the papacy unquestionably developed during the first four centuries of the Christian era. But was not this development the result of political expediency and theological opportunism on the part of the popes, rather than being a movement of the Holy Spirit?

23: Has not the papacy a poor historical record in terms of its tendency to political corruption, power struggles, and displays of arrogant power? Was not this in itself adequate reason for the Protestant Reformation?

24: Although the papacy in modern times has a better record in terms of moral example and of leadership qualities than during the Middle Ages, has the papacy not been rather a force for repression of new ideas in recent centuries?

25: Does not the new *Catechism,* in limiting the idea of *magisterium,* or teaching authority, to the bishops in union with the Pope, present an unbalanced view of *magisterium,* which originally referred to theologians and teachers also?

26: It is clear from historical studies that there is no evidence of the universal practice of "monarchical episcopacy" (i.e., one bishop over each local church) before the middle of the second century. How, then, can the Roman Catholic Church claim that the bishops are, as a college, the successors of the apostles?

27: Are the Anglican formulations, and indeed more recently the writings of Hans Küng, not more correct in stating that general councils of the Church can and have erred, and that a better word for the Church's consistency of proclamation of the Gospel is "indefectibility" rather than "infallibility"?

28: Is it not an even greater source of injustice when the faithful are compelled to give "religious assent" to doctrines proposed by the Pope and the bishops in communion with him even when those doctrines are not infallibly proposed? Does not this remove the possibility of theological dissent?

29: The Anglican/Roman Catholic International Commission (ARCIC) attained important agreements on "authority"; but the official response of the Vatican Congregation for the Doctrine of the Faith maintained the traditional position regarding the primacy and infallibility of the papacy. What is the future for such dialogues if the Vatican always overtrumps their agreements?

Chapter 4 / Faith and Reason

30: How far is a Christian committed to orthodox doctrine, and how much can our perception of the ancient Christian truths as expressed in our creeds be changed? Does not life itself demand that we change with changing times and perceptions?

31: How can the First Vatican Council maintain that "God, the first principle and last end of all things, can be known with certainty from the created order by the natural light of human reason"? Does not this go far beyond what the human mind can attain, especially in the light of modern scientific theories of the origins of the universe?

32: How can the *Catechism* tell us that faith "is more certain than all human knowledge, because it is founded upon the very word of God who cannot lie" (CCC 157)? Surely, faith leads not to certain knowledge but to stable trust?

33: How can God's "absolute sovereignty" as expressed in the *Catechism* be consistent with terrible evils that God apparently permits? Is there not some limitation of God's power resulting from his creation of a universe with its own laws? Does not the fact that God's own Son, Jesus, suffered on the cross and said "My God, my God, why have you forsaken me?" emphasize the weakness of God rather than his "absolute sovereignty"?

34: Is not the idea that God is "three Persons in One God" too bound up with past thought patterns to be sustained today?

35: Surely we do not have to accept the full teaching of the ancient councils of the Church, that Jesus is truly "of one substance" with the Father? Can we not be satisfied with calling Jesus the "Son of God," without calling him actually God?

36: Is the miraculous in the life of Jesus, his miracles, his virginal conception, his bodily resurrection, really important for our faith in him? How can we accept all this and truly believe in the humanity of Jesus for us?

37: If we are to have a religion "for all nations," must we not be more open to different approaches to Christ than appear simply in a narrow orthodoxy?

Chapter 5 / A Realistic Look at Sexuality

38: The Roman Catholic Church surely cannot sustain its rigid line in sexual ethics in the face of so much criticism both inside and outside of its ranks?

39: The changes in the Roman Catholic Church's attitude to war, Vatican II for the first time in Church documents giving positive support to those who are pacifists, are clear evidence that moral teaching can change. Cannot these changes signal similar changes in other areas of morality?

40: Why does the Catholic Church still insist that sexual activities that exclude procreation and are outside of the marriage situation, namely "two in one flesh," are against the "natural law"? Cannot only situations determine what is right and wrong, and not absolutes?

41: People today cannot accept the Church's prohibition of masturbation, homosexual acts, fornication, contraception, and adultery. Is it not time for a change in the Church's teaching in this respect?

42: Why are celibate clergy able to dictate to married or unmarried people what to do or not to do in bed?

43: Jesus himself did not leave a legalistic set of commandments. Why has the Church made Christ's morality seem so restrictive?

44: Another major problem is the Catholic Church's refusal to allow divorced people to remarry while the previous partner is still alive. Is this not totally unrealistic and insensitive in this day and age?

Chapter 6 / Realism About Unity

45: Has not the change in leadership in the Roman Catholic Church set back the cause of unity in the past ten years? Does not the condemnation of some theologians highlight this intolerance and put back unity still further?

46: Cannot there be some flexibility in the question as to what doctrines need to be believed in a future united Church? Is this not taking seriously the "hierarchy of truths"?

47: If baptism is the sacramental source of unity among Christians, then why does the Roman Catholic Church still continue to refuse to give Holy Communion to, and refuse to receive Holy Communion from, those it considers "separated Christians"?

48: Why does the Roman Catholic Church still insist upon the doctrine of transubstantiation, which seems to be a formula from a dead scholasticism? Why does not the Catholic Church accept the agreements of ARCIC in this respect?

49: Why does the Vatican still insist upon refusing to recognize the validity of Anglican orders?

50: Does not the future unity of the Church mean also a legitimate diversity?

51: For how much longer will the Roman Catholic Church insist upon its priests being celibate?

52: For how long will the Roman Catholic Church persist in its refusal to ordain women to the priesthood?

53: In a future united Church, there must surely be more democratic structures operating within Roman Catholic hierarchical institutions?

Catholicism: Exclusive and Inclusive

1: How can apologetics (the defense of one's own faith) be reconciled with ecumenism (the search for visible unity among all Christians)? Is not apologetics by its very nature divisive, tending toward fixed positions?

In the Introduction, I hinted at a distinction between polemics and apologetics. Polemics is of necessity a hostile encounter between two adversaries. Polemics is clearly incompatible with ecumenism, which is of its essence irenical ("peaceful"), within a peaceful environment and a peaceful agenda, to bring Christians together, not to drive them further apart.

Apologetics is more generally a defense of one's own position, for whatever reason. Such a defense may stem from a neurotic fear of any change whatsoever. On the other hand, its motivation may even be just good sport, as with the University Debating Society. Life would be quite boring if we all meekly gave way to each other's views, particularly when we ourselves were not sure of that other person's opinion as being acceptable. We would be even more dishonest if we pretended to accept another opinion when we were passionately convinced that our view was right. Honesty demands that we defend our position, especially when we are dealing with our deepest convictions.

In this sense, the word "apologetics" (Greek *apologia*) is used in the New Testament quite a few times (e.g., Acts 25:16; 2 Corinthians 7:11;

Philippians 1:7, 16). The apostles were convinced that Jesus had risen from the dead, and would die for that truth if necessary:

> Simply proclaim the Lord Christ holy in your hearts, and always have your answer ready for people who ask you the reason (apologia) for the hope that you have. But give it with courtesy and respect and with a clear conscience, so that those who slander your good behavior in Christ may be ashamed of their accusations. And if it is the will of God that you should suffer, it is better to suffer for doing right than for doing wrong. (1 Peter 3:15-17)

This text, from the early Christian community, gives us a model for apologetics. This text gives no justification for polemics. Tragically, in Christian history, as for instance in the Crusades, we have not been content just to "suffer for doing right." We have had to defend our position by force of arms, even by torturing those who differ from us. That applies to both Catholics and Protestants. At the time when this First Letter of Peter was written, Christians were being persecuted for their faith. In "speaking up" for it (and the Greek *apologia* has here something of that meaning[1]), Christians would have to be prepared to die for the truth; and not to slander their enemies, but to pray for them.

In this context, ecumenism not only permits apologetics, it demands it. In ecumenical dialogue that is in any way genuine and not sheer play-acting, Christians must be able to share with one another their deepest convictions, particularly where they disagree profoundly with one another. If they are limited to platitudes, or feel that they must water down their convictions when speaking with one another, then genuine ecumenism has not even begun. A marriage cannot grow to maturity unless the couple are able to share their differences as well as their agreements. Anything else is sham.

Also, it is quite mistaken to consider that to defend one's own position vigorously is to be closed to all future change. Roman Catholics in Britain were forced to attend the services of the Church of England during and after the reign of Elizabeth I. Many died rather than attend those services, attending the Catholic Mass, for which the penalty if discovered was death for treason. Catholics justified their position on the quite correct defense, *apologia*, that it was quite unjust to be compelled to attend a service the religious beliefs of which they were at variance with. They paid a crippling financial penalty, and often were caught and put to a torturous death for attending the illegal Roman Mass rather than go to the Anglican service.

In a new ecumenical situation, where Christians are now coming together to attempt to resolve their differences, Catholics are very happy to attend the liturgies of other Christian bodies, and regularly now do so, particularly on special ecumenical occasions. This does not mean that their previous refusal, in a situation of religious persecution, was wrong. On the contrary, in that past situation, to refuse to attend the Anglican service was not only right, but was in practical terms the only way of maintaining their own Catholic faith in integrity. It was a necessary bid for religious freedom.

Regarding dogmas of faith, and some elements of clearly affirmed moral teaching, there is no prospect that the essential truth of the statement can change. We will have to discuss this matter of the nature of Christian dogma in a later chapter. The very term "dogma" means something fixed, permanent. Doctrines such as the Trinity, the divinity and humanity of Christ, and for Catholics the infallibility of the Church, will always be affirmed as true. In such a case, apologetics has a most important function: that of indicating areas where a Christian can only stand ground, and may not retreat. Failure to stand ground where necessary is not good ecumenism, but infidelity to the truth as we see it.

But even in this instance, while the essential core of the dogma may not change, our understanding of a dogma will develop in changing circumstances. One clear example of such a change of perspective is the Catholic understanding of the ministerial priesthood. The Council of Trent, in 1545, was called to restore the Church after the ravages of what to it were the disasters of the Protestant Reformation. Trent insisted that there was a genuine "new, visible and external priesthood into which the old has been changed,"[2] not just the priesthood of all believers as Protestants affirmed, and that the priest offered a genuine sacrifice, the sacrifice of the Mass "to remit or retain sins." This was not to deny the unique once-for-all nature of the sacrifice of Christ on the cross, but to represent that offering as a sacrament and liturgical act, making that Presence once more real for us. Now, in an ecumenical age, the Catholic Church has not abandoned its Tridentine doctrine of the priesthood and of the Mass, but on the contrary developed that aspect in the new *Catechism* (CCC 1532-1559). However, there is later a new emphasis upon the *shepherding* role of all those in orders: bishops, priests, and deacons (CCC 1554-1571).

In any case, whether ecumenical dialogue concerns those matters that can change or those that seemingly cannot, apologetics need not freeze debate, but will rather enrich it. Naturally, this is always provided that a vigorous defense of one's own position is combined with a genuine desire for unity and a genuine openness to change where change is possible.

2: How can a convert to Roman Catholicism be a genuine ecumenist? Is not in this case "ecumenism" simply "you-come-in-ism"? Instead of dialogue, does not a convert simply wish to convert Anglicans to the "one true faith"?

We may freely admit that converts have a tendency to fanaticism. Hitler, the Nazi leader, was born not in Germany itself, but in Austria. Stalin, the equally murderous leader of Communist Russia, came not from Russia but from Georgia. Napoleon, the hero of France but the villain of Tolstoy's *War and Peace*, came from Corsica. Originating from outside of a community may lead to a greater commitment to that society on the part of the outsider, since that outsider may have a greater appreciation of what makes that community distinctive. The convert has freely chosen that community's values rather than simply accepted them as a hereditary right. A convert could therefore have a natural antipathy toward the ecumenical movement. In seeking common ground between Christians of different denominations, the convert will have a natural fear that the differences, some of which might have been the specific cause of his or her conversion, will be blurred in an uncritical desire for visible unity. The convert will wonder whether there is here a case of "unity at any price," making the painful journey that he or she originally made from one Christian communion to another quite superfluous, even mistaken.

Converts could be also guilty of an unbalanced perspective as reasons for conversion. Doctrinal beliefs could be mixed up with many other nondogmatic, even subconscious, factors, as motivations for the transfer from one ecclesial community to another. One good lady told me that the main reason why she became a Roman Catholic in the late 1950s was the beauty of the Latin Mass. When, ten years later, the Second Vatican Council allowed the introduction of the Mass in the vernacular, the poor lady was totally at sea.

Converts do not necessarily make the best ecumenists. But some converts, and not a few, have become leaders in the ecumenical movement. An Anglican convert, Father Paul Watson, founded a religious order, the Franciscan Friars of the Atonement, precisely for the purpose of praying and working for visible unity. The most notable figure in Catholic ecumenism in Britain since the Second Vatican Council was the late Bishop B. C. Butler. Butler was a convert from the Anglo-Catholic wing of the Church of England. After his conversion to the Roman Catholic Church, Butler became a monk of Downside Abbey, and was abbot of that monastery before being made bishop. As a newly ordained member of the episcopate, he attended the Second Vatican Council, and made a most significant contribution to its debates. It is said that it was his intervention which ensured that the Council's theological study of Mary the Mother of Jesus was placed not in a separate document, but at the end of the document on the Church, *Lumen Gentium*. This emphasized particularly to Protestant observers at the Council that the Church was seeing Mary in her role as spiritual mother within the Church and the plan of salvation, not as an isolated part of Catholic doctrine. Later, in the 1970s, Butler was co-Chairman of ARCIC (the Anglican/Roman Catholic International Commission), and played a leading role in that body's famous Agreed Statement on the Eucharist, ministry, and authority.

Converts can also have a more positive attitude to their past. I hope that, despite leaving the Church of England for the Roman Catholic Church thirty years ago, I retain a great love for the Church of England. I learned about Christ and his Church from the Anglican communion. I love the Morning and Evening Prayer of the Anglican Church, and for this reason have taken quickly to the Roman Catholic Breviary, which is likewise based upon the Psalms. Even more, the convert is more likely to stay at the ecumenical task when it becomes difficult and discouraging. That same divine call that was seen in the convert's conversion is also seen in Christ's call for us all to be visibly one. The convert realizes perhaps as well as anyone that ecumenism will not come only by theological discussion or summit meetings. It will finally come only by the action of the Holy Spirit, by mutual conversion of heart.

Finally it is very important to realize that there is no conflict between the conversion of an individual from one ecclesial community to another, which will always be a valid move if sincerely followed, and the coming together of communities of faith, which is the aim of ecumenism.

The history of the Church gives examples where whole communities became Christians, rather than individuals, the whole nation under its ruler being baptized. The ecumenical movement envisages unity between communities already divided. That is the aim, the vision, even if it seems at present a miracle that would make the miracle of the loaves and fishes pale into insignificance.

3: Has not the Roman Catholic Church taken many steps backward toward a more defensive form of its faith under Pope John Paul II, after the promising days of the Second Vatican Council?

The Second Vatican Council, as Pope John XXIII stated, threw open the windows of the Roman Catholic Church and let in some fresh air of freedom and renewal. But there were a few bugs and alien creatures that flew in at the same time.

The history of every society contains movements forward and backward, checks and balances. No one could deny that the pontificate of the present Pope has contained some strong moves to defend the traditions of the Church both doctrinal and moral. But, to quote Newman, an essential element of any genuine development is "conservative action upon the past."[3] Necessary action to conserve does not prevent development. It makes development possible. A society that abandons its essential traditions loses the very sources of its life. Making a general defense of the "conservative" or "restoration" policies of the present Pope does not necessarily commit us to accept every action or policy of Pope John Paul II as right. But I personally would in general agree with the present Pope, that some "restoration" and "conservatism" was necessary both to correct extreme positions both on the right and on the left that had developed since Vatican II; and, even more, to make some courageous reaffirmation of doctrines unpopular in some quarters, both regarding the *magisterium* of the Church and regarding morality.

I say positions "both on the right and on the left." It needs to be remembered that the first opposition to the teachings of the Second Vatican Council came not from the radical left, but from the extreme right wing, led by Archbishop Lefebvre. Lefebvre not only attacked the vernacular liturgy, but claimed that the Pope had no right to change the form of the Mass set since the Council of Trent. He was also most unhappy with the Dogmatic Constitution on Divine Revelation, *Dei Verbum,* which he saw as a concession to the Liberal Protestant approach to

Scripture. He was also violently opposed to the ecumenical approach of Vatican II, and to its Declaration on Religious Liberty. It is said that extreme right-wing French groups, in favor of the *ancien régime*, gave the Lefebvre movement financial support. A conservative seminary was founded at Écône, Switzerland, to train priests in the pre-Vatican II ways, to save them from "modernist corruption." Members of these right-wing groups vary in the basis for their opposition, from general unease with the situation in the Catholic Church today, to an extreme belief that the post-Vatican II Church has actually fallen into heresy.

The present Pope and his principal theological consultant, Cardinal Ratzinger, were both enthusiastic supporters of the Second Vatican Council and its decrees. They had no truck whatsoever with Lefebvre and his right-wing opposition. The Pope was present at the Council as one of the Polish bishops; and Ratzinger was one of the theological luminaries of the 1960s. The Pope, since his election by the College of Cardinals to be Bishop of Rome, has not ceased in his efforts to bring back the extreme right-wing groups to the mainstream of the Church, and has had some considerable success. No doubt some would say that it is precisely his "conservatism" that has attracted the Lefebvrites back to the fold.

But again it must be remembered that the Pope has never wavered in his demands that the right wing should accept all the decrees of the Second Vatican Council. Whereas concessions have been granted for the pre-Vatican II liturgy to be celebrated with the local bishop's permission, those who celebrate it must not declare that the new liturgy is heretical. And the Pope has insisted that Vatican II's theology on ecumenism, on religious liberty, and on divine revelation must also be accepted by all Catholics. John Paul II has himself raised right-wing eyebrows by meeting leading members of all the world faiths at Assisi, and conducting a religious service with them.

How, then, has the Pope acquired this "conservative" reputation? First and foremost, by his strong opposition to those who attack the teachings of the Second Vatican Council from the other side, from the left.

A major crisis arose when Hans Küng, a major influence in the Vatican II era, attacked the doctrine of the infallibility of the Church.[4] Küng claimed that the issuing of the encyclical *Humanae Vitae* in 1968 by Pope Paul VI, which condemned all forms of contraception, destroyed the credibility of the Church's teaching. No Church, claimed Küng, which condemned married couples using any forms of artificial birth control as committing a seriously sinful act, could sustain the claim as a Church to be infallible. Many Catholics, as is common knowledge, questioned the teaching of *Humanae Vitae.* But Küng went much further than the usual protest against an unpopular moral prohibition. He questioned the definition of the First Vatican Council that the Pope, in declaring matters to be believed, rejoiced in that infallibility with which Christ wished his Church to be gifted. The Second Vatican Council itself repeated and expanded the definition by Vatican I of the infallibility of the Church's teaching authority, headed by the Pope in union with the College of Bishops worldwide. For Vatican II's Dogmatic Constitution on the Church, *Lumen Gentium,* the Pope has as an individual that power of defining doctrine infallibly that the Church possesses collectively:

> This infallibility, however, with which the divine redeemer willed his church to be endowed in defining doctrine concerning faith or morals, extends just as far as the deposit of divine revelation that is to be guarded as sacred and faithfully expounded. The Roman pontiff, head of the college of bishops, by virtue of his office, enjoys this infallibility when, as supreme shepherd and teacher of all Christ's faithful, who confirms his brethren in the faith (see Lk 2, 32), he proclaims in a definitive act a doctrine on faith or morals. (LG 25)[5]

Thus Pope John Paul II, supported by his favored assistant Cardinal Joseph Ratzinger, made only the same demands on Hans Küng as were made to the Lefebvre right wing: that he accept the teachings of the Second Vatican Council.

The eventual declaration that Küng could not be accepted as a Catholic theologian was only the culmination of a long and inevitable process. No Christian body, and indeed no society, can tolerate a major thinker to represent its interests who explicitly denies a central tenet of its teaching, as Küng had done. As a Methodist said to me at the time, no Methodist scholar would be able to teach at a Methodist theological college who denied an essential teaching of Methodism, as Küng had done regarding the Catholic doctrine of the infallibility of the Church. It would be similar to a Methodist lecturer in doctrine announcing to his amazed students that he now accepted the doctrine of papal infallibility.

There were many other issues dealt with by the present Pope during his pontificate, on which he may be judged to have acted wisely or otherwise. But nothing is closer to the foundations of Catholicism than the authority of its doctrine. Something had to be done if the Catholic Church was to maintain its own beliefs. Some defensive action had to be taken in this area if in no other.

The Church, like any other organization, will have to defend its central beliefs when attacked. But defense is ineffective if it is not accompanied by a positive affirmation and effective proclamation of faith. This is where the publication of the *Catechism of the Catholic Church* finds its place within the main achievements of the present pontificate.

4: Is not a prime example of this stepping back precisely the publication of the new* Catechism of the Catholic Church*?

From the beginning, the project of compiling a catechism presenting the teaching of the Second Vatican Council was controversial. On the one hand, there was a strong precedent for such a catechism, since the Council of Trent had produced its own catechism of some six hundred pages (*Catechismus ex Decreto Concilii Tridentini*), especially for pastors, in 1566. This was a substantial tome, not in the "penny catechism" mold, but a summary statement of doctrine for teachers of the faith. It is a very fine piece of work from a literary and a theological viewpoint; but, like all such large tomes, it tended to be replaced by smaller and more accessible works.

Those who wished the Second Vatican Council to have its catechism parallel to the Tridentine catechism were opposed from many angles. Catechists felt that it would drag teachers back to learning doctrines by rote as had so often happened using short catechisms prior to Vatican II. Theologians were of the opinion that a catechism would restrict the expression of the faith to that of a particular kind of theology. No doubt also many in Rome would have been apprehensive at the idea, since the difficulties connected with producing a text acceptable to the whole Church would seem insurmountable.

In any event, the *Catechism of the Catholic Church* was produced, as the end of a process beginning with the decision of the Bishops' Synod on Catechesis for there to be a "catechism or compendium of all Catholic doctrine regarding both faith and morals. . . , that it might be, as it were, a point of reference for the catechisms or compendiums that are prepared in various regions."[6] All recognized the dangers of producing such a catechism; but there appeared to be a greater danger, which would hopefully be averted by the proposed catechism. The bishops saw the need to have produced a clear statement of the Church's doctrine and morality, to be used by all those involved in teaching the Catholic faith. The danger was that the teaching of the Second Vatican Council would be obscured in the confusion of theological debate. There is a legitimate theological pluralism within the Church, as I shall argue later in this book; but such pluralism has limits, the limits of what is believed authoritatively by the Church. The greater need was seen to present that teaching clearly and universally.

The *Catechism* has had its fierce critics, both inside and outside of the visible boundaries of the Catholic Church. Some of those criticisms may well be justified, as some of those expressed in a critical commentary on the new *Catechism*[7] published soon after the publication of the English version of the *Catechism of the Catholic Church*. I agree with some of those criticisms, and disagree with others. Care needs to be exercised in criticizing the *Catechism*, as to whether those criticisms are of the *Catechism* itself, which is of necessity a human and imperfect document, or of the Church's teaching. Sometimes, what is criticized may be a particular form of expression of the new *Catechism*. Sometimes, what is at stake is the teaching of the Catholic Church itself, which preceded the publication of the *Catechism of the Catholic Church* by many centuries. The questions relating to infallibility, Scripture and Tradition, Mary in the Catholic Church, sexual ethics, transubstantiation — all these issues preceded the Second Vatican Council and the *Catechism of the Catholic Church*. The new *Catechism* at the very most has only reopened these questions. It has not introduced them. What it is saying is that these questions cannot be just quietly dropped because they may be unpalatable in this day and age. These doctrines should not only be discussed by theologians. They should be taught to all the people. That is the whole essence of what a catechism is, a teaching document.

There is another danger where excessive analytical criticism of the *Catechism* is concerned. It is to be read as a whole, as a "symphonic" document. The faith and morals of the Church are rooted in divine revelation, and form a unity, the unity of God's plan of salvation in Christ. This unity is quite inspiring when it is grasped. One who reads the whole *Catechism* is above all struck by the coherence of the Catholic faith and its inner dynamism, drawing all to the center of unity in Christ. Whatever criticisms may be valid for individual texts of the *Catechism*, or individual sections of it, the inspiring quality of this vision of unity is manifest to all those who are open to that vision. That vision must never be lost, however valid criticisms of individual texts of the new *Catechism* might be.

The publication of the new *Catechism* was in no way a merely defensive move. A catechism can only be effective if it positively affirms teaching with good reasons. That is what the authors of the *Catechism of the Catholic Church* were attempting to do, whether or not they may be judged to have succeeded. I hope to demonstrate this positive aspect of the *Catechism*'s teaching time after time in what follows.

5: Does not the use of the phrase "The Catholic Church" to describe Roman Catholics emphasize the arrogant claims of the Roman Catholic Church to be the True Church of Christ? How can this be reconciled with a truly open ecumenical spirit?

The word "Catholic" comes from a combination of two Greek words *kath holou*, "according to the totality" or "in keeping with the whole," for short "universal." It is a fairly stupendous claim for one Christian body to describe itself as "The Universal Church."

The titles that Christian churches give themselves often reflect their specific claims. The *Baptist Church* reflects the claim that that body of Christians believes that baptism should only be conferred on those adult enough to make an act of faith in Christ themselves, not on infants who cannot make such a personal act of faith. The *Church of England* reflects the claim of that Christian body to be the national established Church of that country. The *Orthodox Church* reflects the claim of those Eastern Christians to teach the Orthodox faith of Christ, as opposed to those who taught one or other of the Christological heresies such as Monophysitism or Nestorianism. The *Pentecostal Churches* reflect the claim by those churches to have received a special gift of the Holy Spirit as the apostles received at that first Day of Pentecost.

Generally speaking, most of us would be prepared to call the church of any Christian by the name which that Christian gives to his or her church. Thus we are quite happy to call Baptists "Baptists," even though we believe that our form of baptism is perfectly valid. We would be happy to refer to the "Church of *England*," even though those of us who are English Christians and who are not members of the established "Church of England" are quite convinced that we are members of the *Ecclesia Anglicana,* the communion of English Christians. We would be happy to refer to the "Orthodox Church" even though we are convinced of our own orthodoxy. We would be happy to refer to the "Pentecostal Churches," even though we would like to think that we also have received the Holy Spirit. Thus, many Christians are prepared to call us by our most common name, "The Catholic Church," even if it is the claim of Anglicans, as indeed of other Christian churches too, to be part of that Universal Church. But many Christians are sensitive to the use of the term "The Catholic Church," as a result of which it has become generally accepted for us to be called "Roman Catholics," particularly in ecumenical dialogue.

The use of the term "Roman Catholic" is itself ambiguous. In the Middle East, where there are Catholic Christians in full communion with Rome, but who are not part of the Latin or Western discipline (or rite), the term "Roman Catholic" refers to Catholics of the Latin rite, while "Greek Catholic" refers to Catholics of the Eastern or Greek rite. Worldwide, the term "The Catholic Church" persists as a description of our Church, and will fairly certainly remain such in the foreseeable future.

Humpty Dumpty in *Through the Looking Glass* said, "When I use a word, it means just what I choose it to mean." It is important to understand that the meaning of the word "Catholic" is itself complex, and has a developing history.[8] It surely must mean much more than just "universal." After all, many associations are universal, including the Union of Stamp Collectors. Many Christian churches are universal in their membership.

By the fourth century, "Catholic" referred to those Christians who accepted the universal faith of the Church, as opposed to those who accepted only part of it. The word "heretic" referred to one who selects for himself or herself only part of the Christian faith, the word "heretic" coming from the Greek word *hairesis* (which means option, choice, or inclination). During the Christological controversies, the term "Catholic" referred especially to those who accepted the orthodox doctrine of Christ, and "heretics" to those who "chose" Arianism or one of the other heresies.[9]

St. Vincent of Lérins in the fifth century gave us the most famous historic definition of the meaning of "the Catholic faith": *Quod ubique, quod semper, quod ab omnibus creditum est* ("That which is believed everywhere, always and by everyone").[10] This definition is by no means watertight. We could argue that the Catholic faith is not believed everywhere, since everywhere will be found people who do not accept it. We could argue that the Catholic faith has not always been believed, since there has been development in its own expression of faith. But Vincent introduces us to a vital dimension of Catholicity; the universality of its doctrine, which binds Catholics together "as a whole."

As the centuries went by, and the power of the papacy increased (which increase of power we will have to discuss much more later on), the criterion of unity with the Bishop of Rome, the successor of Peter, became more and more a touchstone of Catholicity. If the Pope is the universal bishop, who has ordinary jurisdiction over all the bishops of the world, as Vatican I defined,[11] then one is a "Catholic" who accepts the wholeness of the Christian faith as expressed in that fullness of communion with the See of Rome. With this development of meaning, the ecumenical term "Roman Catholic" becomes identical with the term "Catholic," since a "Roman Catholic" is now one who sees communion with Rome as an essential part of Catholicity.

Being a Catholic means accepting the *whole* of the means of salvation offered by Christ. The Dogmatic Constitution on the Church of the Second Vatican Council uses the word "integral," which is close to the words *kath holou*, "according to the whole," the unity of a whole in its parts:

> They are fully incorporated into the society of the church who, possessing the Spirit of Christ, accept its whole structure (*integram eius ordinationem*) and all the means of salvation that have been established within it, and within its visible framework are united with Christ, who governs it through the supreme pontiff and the bishops, by the bonds of profession of faith, the sacraments, ecclesiastical government and communion. (LG 14)[12]

Only a "Roman Catholic" is a "Catholic" in the sense described above in *Lumen Gentium* (no. 14). In this sense, the word "Catholic" is an exclusive claim. But does not this claim to Catholicity on our part mean that those who are not members of our Church are not in any sense "Catholic"? We used to say so in our polemics with Protestants. But this is where perhaps the most important development of all took place during the Second Vatican Council, and found expression in the Decree on Ecumenism, *Unitatis Redintegratio*.

The Decree on Ecumenism stated that those who are baptized Christians, but who are separated from full communion, are in partial yet real communion with the Catholic Church. That means that they are in some sense members of the Catholic Church. "For those who believe in Christ and have been truly baptized are in some kind of communion with the catholic church (*in quadam cum ecclesia catholica communione*), even though this communion is imperfect (UR 3)."[13]

Perhaps the phrase "in some kind of communion" could sound a little patronizing. But the Latin original *in quadam cum ecclesia catholica communione* is by no means in any way deprecating. It means that all those truly baptized, whatever their "denomination," are in a *certain unspecified kind* of communion with the Catholic Church. That is the precise meaning of the Latin. In what way they are actually in communion, the further definition of *quadam*, "a certain kind" of communion, depends upon what elements of Catholic faith and life are enjoyed by those Christians.

Again, the Decree on Ecumenism specifies many elements of faith and Christian life that can be and in fact are present outside the full visible unity of the Catholic Church:

> Moreover some, and even most, of the significant elements and endowments which together go to build up and give life to the church itself, can exist outside the visible boundaries of the catholic church; the written word of God; the life of grace; faith, hope and charity, with the other interior gifts of the holy Spirit, and visible elements too. All of these, coming from Christ and leading back to Christ, properly belong to the one church of Christ. (UR 3)[14]

Clearly, therefore, those churches such as the Anglican Church, which are strongly linked historically with the ancient form of Christian faith, have very close links with the Catholic Church. The Anglican confession of faith in the "Quadrilateral" (creeds, Scripture, ministry, worship), stated by the Lambeth Conference of 1888, shows clearly, in terms of the Vatican Council definition above, that the Anglican Church has "most of the significant elements and endowments which together go to build up and give life to the church itself." This means that members of the Church of England are already in a most significant form of communion with us in the Roman Catholic Church. This communion exists despite the fact that we are not yet in full intercommunion with one another; and it exists despite the apparent setbacks of the past few years in the ecumenical movement, such as the discouraging response to the issue of Anglican orders from the Congregation for the Doctrine of the Faith, and the decision of the Church of England General Synod of 1992 to ordain women to the ministerial priesthood, both of which issues we will look at later.

What comes, then, of the Roman Catholic Church's claim to be the "True Church" to which all must conform? The key is in the quotation from the Dogmatic Constitution on the Church; that in the Catholic Church (and by that is meant in context "The Roman Catholic Church") is the fullness of the means of salvation:

> For it is only through Christ's catholic church, which is the all-embracing means of salvation, that the fullness of the means of salvation can be attained. We believe that our Lord entrusted all the blessings of the new covenant to the one apostolic college of which Peter is the head, in order to establish the one body of Christ on earth into which all should be fully incorporated who belong in any way to the people of God. (LG 3)[15]

Is it not a case of the old claims still being there, only now in a more irenic way of expression? We must be honest and respond to that question: "In a way, yes." The claims of the Roman Catholic Church are just as exclusive as ever. It is only in our communion, we believe, that the fullness of grace and life are to be found, as handed on from Christ to the apostles and their successors. The inclusiveness of Vatican II lies not in a reduction of the claims of the Roman Catholic Church, but rather in the explicit and full acceptance that elements of ecclesial faith and life that are genuinely part of the Catholic Church are to be found in communions other than our own.

We could still say "outside the Church is no salvation" (*extra ecclesia nulla salus*); that is, outside of the "Roman Catholic Church," meaning the Catholic Church in its fullness of visible faith and life, containing the fullness of the means of salvation, there is no salvation. But after Vatican II our developed theology would say that Anglicans, Baptists, Lutherans, and others are not "outside the Church" but "inside the Church" in the sense of that partial yet real communion of which we spoke above.

Partial yet real communion is also the clue to the meaning of the controversial phrase of the Second Vatican Council, "subsists in": "This church, set up and organized in this world as a society, subsists in the catholic church, governed by the successor of Peter and the bishops in communion with him, although outside its structure many elements of sanctification and truth are to be found which, as proper gifts to the church of Christ, impel toward catholic unity (LG 8)."[16]

The word *subsistit* has caused much discussion among interpreters of the documents of Vatican II. The Council Fathers here seem to abandon a simple identification of the Catholic Church with the Church of Christ. If they had wished to say that the Catholic Church *is* the Church of Christ, why did they use the Latin *subsistit in* ("subsists in"), rather than the simple *est* ("is") the Church of Christ?

Once we understand the Vatican II concept of partial communion, the use of *subsistit* becomes obvious. The Council Fathers could not deny that the Church of Christ exists in those Christian bodies, such as the Anglican, Orthodox, and Free Churches, where it had already admitted partial communion with the Catholic Church. The Church of Christ must be in some sense or other "in" those churches that rejoice in such partial communion with the Catholic Church. The phrase *subsistit in* preserves the concept that only in the visible Catholic Church is to be found the fullness of the means of grace handed on by Christ; the word of God, the sacramental life, and the visible communion with the Pope, the successor of Peter. It also preserves the idea that those partial elements of faith and life to be found outside the visible membership of the Roman Catholic Church have in themselves a dynamism toward visible "catholic" unity. The ecumenical movement must have an essentially Rome-ward direction.

We must admit that these claims are still uncompromising, indeed blasphemous, if they cannot be justified. The old apologetic for Jesus Christ used to argue that he was either bad, mad, or God. He could not just have been a decent chap. Likewise, the claims of the Roman Catholic Church as outlined above to contain all the elements of ecclesial faith and life given by Christ are either right, or those of us Catholics who make those claims for our Church must be either arrogant, blasphemous, or at the very least desperately misguided.

Endnotes

1. In Classical Greek, the verb *apologeomai* has a legal connotation, making a defense in court. Cf. J. Hope and G. Milligan, *The Vocabulary of*

the Greek Testament, Illustrated from the Papyri and Other Non-Literary Sources (Grand Rapids, MI: Eerdmans, 1930), p. 66, col. 2.

2. Tanner, II, p. 742, lines 7-8.

3. J. H. Newman, *Essay on the Development of Christian Doctrine* (seventh edition) (London: Longmans, Green and Co., 1890), p. 199.

4. Hans Küng, *Infallible? An Enquiry,* trans. Eric Mosbacher (London: Collins, 1971). Cf. Hard Question 27 on infallibility.

5. Tanner, II, p. 869, lines 30-36.

6. *Final Report* of the Extraordinary Synod of Bishops, December 7, 1985. Quoted in CCC Introduction, p. 3.

7. Michael J. Walsh (ed.), *Commentary on the Catechism of the Catholic Church* (or CCCC) (London: Geoffrey Chapman, 1994).

8. Avery Dulles, *The Catholicity of the Church* (Oxford: Clarendon Press, 1985).

9. Cf. J. H. Newman, *The Arians of the Fourth Century* (sixth edition) (London: Longmans, Green and Co., 1890), pp. 463-464. Newman quotes St. Hilary to Constantius: "Surely, your clemency should listen to the voice of those who cry out so loudly, 'I am a Catholic, I have no wish to be a heretic.' "

10. ODCC, p. 1443.

11. Tanner, I, p. 812, lines 37-41.

12. Tanner, II, p. 860, lines 20-25.

13. Ibid., p. 910, lines 7-9.

14. Ibid., lines 17-22.

15. Ibid., p. 910, line 37 — p. 911, line 4.

16. Ibid., p. 854, lines 26-30.

The Truth About the Bible

Christian faith is based upon Christian revelation; upon the fact that "God has spoken to our ancestors through the prophets, but in our time, the final days, he has spoken to us in the person of his Son" (Hebrews 1:1-2a). The First Vatican Council asserted (and in this, I am sure, it has the agreement of all Christian denominations) that Scripture *contains revelation,*[1] namely that God has spoken to us through his written word in Scripture. Thus, in discussing Christian faith, discussion of what Scripture is, its authority in matters of doctrine, and its interpretation, precisely as containing revelation, is a most suitable starting point for any theological dialogue.

The question of the Bible and its interpretation is closely linked with the whole question of revelation, how God communicates his word to us, above all in Jesus Christ, who is the Word made flesh. This branch of theology is called the "theology of revelation"; or, as Karl Barth, the greatest Protestant theologian this century, named it, "the theology of the Word of God."[2] Only in this way can we set the Bible in its proper context as God's word in human language — as the Second Vatican Council did in *Dei Verbum* ("God's Word"), the Council's Dogmatic Constitution on Divine Revelation.

Dei Verbum at Vatican II was considered by Protestant observers to be the most important document issued by that Council, for the precise reason that it dealt with so many issues related to Scripture and to the foundations of our Christian faith, which have divided Protestant and Catholic Christians since the sixteenth century. While, in terms of our discussion, we are now dealing with the treatment of Scripture in the *Catechism of the Catholic Church*, the central text that I will use as the basis of my answers to the following Hard Questions will be the text used by the *Catechism of the Catholic Church* itself, namely *Dei Verbum*, which from its promulgation in 1965 has to be viewed as the main ecclesiastical source of Catholic doctrine on Scripture and revelation.

While the Catholic Church has always taught that the Bible is the word of God, it has also taught that Tradition, the handing on of the deposit of faith in non-written form, "preserves the word of God as it was entrusted to the apostles by Christ our lord and the holy Spirit."[3] It also claims that the Church's teaching authority, its *magisterium*, is the final arbiter as to the interpretation of Scripture.[4] This is where the nub of the controversy still remains.

6: Has not the Roman Catholic Church discouraged Christian laypeople from studying the Bible because of the threat this might pose regarding its official doctrine?

Regarding the question of individual Bible reading, the Roman Catholic Church has not been as encouraging as it should have been. But we must immediately state that strenuous efforts, particularly since the Second Vatican Council, have been made to put this right, even though much more could still be done.

This neglect of Scripture among Catholic laypeople has arisen partly from historical reasons. During the Middle Ages, few people could read, and books, which were handwritten, were quite prohibitively expensive, limited to books for public reading in monasteries, churches, and universities or by the wealthy. Furthermore, Latin was the official language of clerks and students; hence those who could read could usually also read Latin, the language of the liturgy, and the official language of Catholic Europe. Thus books, and particularly sacred books, were seldom written in the local vernacular language.

The catechetical instruction of the people, as far as can be gathered, was given through parish sermons, and in particular through paintings and stained-glass windows in churches. The sense of symbol and of story was very strong, as Chaucer's *Canterbury Tales* illustrates. As the latter work of literary genius also illustrates, religion was part of everyone's life, and was by no means combined with prudery. If the average medieval Christian was illiterate and had no proper schooling, he or she knew a great deal more about the Christian faith from cultural contact with a society soaked in Christian symbolism than the modern secular European.

Contrary to what many realize, there were considerable catechetical movements within the Catholic Church at the time of the invention of printing. Duffy insists that "the fifteenth and early sixteenth centuries witnessed a period of massive catechetical enterprise."[5] However, Philip Hughes points out that unfortunately there was no evidence of an English translation of the Bible before the Reformation.[6] If in fact this were the case, that would be a major defect in catechesis that we must admit.

The Protestant Reformers used the new printing presses precisely to propagate their ideas, especially by printing vernacular translations of the Bible and short catechisms for popular consumption. By the time the Council of Trent was summoned by a beleaguered Pope in 1545, the damage had already been done. The new Protestant Bibles were the basis of the new preaching; and even where the translation itself did not favor the Reformation theology, the new vernacular Bibles were becoming the basis of anti-Roman invective.

Trent could only perform a salvage operation after the decisive communications battle of the dawn of the modern world had already been lost. First, the Council defined the Canon of Scripture, the list of sacred books, consisting of all the Old and New Testament books listed in the Greek Canon used by the early Fathers of the Church, which included certain books (e.g., 1 and 2 Maccabees, Tobit) that the Protestant Reformers rejected as "apocryphal."[7] Second, Trent gave an impetus to the printing of vernacular translations of the Bible, with doctrinal explanations designed to counter what were seen as the false interpretations of the Reformers. These vernacular translations (notably the Douay translation of the Bible for use among English Catholics) had to be translations not only from the Hebrew and Greek texts of the Bible (now appearing in new critical editions), but also *through the Vulgate*[8] *Latin version,*[9] which version of the Bible into Latin originated with the great St. Jerome, back in the fourth century.[10]

This restriction of translations of the Bible to renderings of the Vulgate Latin version was a means of doctrinal control, again to prevent translations appearing with Protestant dogmatic presuppositions. By the twentieth century, the compulsory use of the Vulgate was increasingly seen by Catholic scholars as stifling scholarship, and no longer necessary in a more ecumenical climate. The French *Bible de Jérusalem,* originating from the Dominican École Biblique in Jerusalem, was the first to translate directly from the original Hebrew and Greek, bypassing the Vulgate. From then on, Bibles published with Catholic authority have ceased to be translated through the Vulgate sieve.

Trent also promoted Bible reading among Catholics; but we would have to admit that the general feeling among Catholics from the Reformation onward was that reading the Bible was a dangerous activity. Look at what happened to Martin Luther after he read the Bible! Laypeople tended to rely on the transmission of the Tradition for their faith. After all, the Mass and the Divine Office contain mostly Scripture, as do the prayers of the Church such as the Our Father, the Hail, Mary, and the Glory be to the Father.

It is again the Second Vatican Council that has at last unambiguously encouraged all faithful Christians to read the Bible, and for the highest of theological motives: "The Church has always held the divine scriptures in reverence no less than it accords to the Lord's body itself, never ceasing — especially in the sacred liturgy — to receive the bread of life from the one table of God's word and Christ's body, and to offer it to the faithful."[11] *Dei Verbum* directs a whole chapter, Chapter VI, to "Holy Scripture in the Life of the Church." The Council Fathers wanted the "force and power in the Word of God"[12] to become available to the Christian faithful. No one, after reading this chapter of *Dei Verbum,* could possibly say that the Roman Catholic Church discourages its members from reading Scripture. If an individual priest or catechist might, that is clearly against the mind of the Church.

One final note here: There are many ways in which Scripture can come alive to people. The traditional way in the Reformation tradition is by means of the "daily portion," whereby an individual reads a text of Scripture daily and meditates upon it. This goes back in essence to the *lectio divina* (the "divine reading") used by the monks in their daily prayer. But there are many ways in which the riches of the Scriptures could become available to Christians: group Bible study, particularly of an ecumenical nature; the Divine Office of Readings, which gives a rich selection of readings from Scripture and from the Tradition of the Church; reading the daily readings at the Eucharist; a more systematic reading of the books of Scripture together with notes provided by a specialist. There are many approaches to Bible reading, and the Church should be open to all possibilities of growth in understanding of God's word, and of meditation upon it.

7: Does not the* Catechism of the Catholic Church *fall back into fundamentalism, despite the widespread use of the critical method of studying Scripture among its leading scholars?

Many scholars are critical of the biblical approach of the new *Catechism.* The first article in the *Commentary* on the new *Catechism* — which has many distinguished Catholic theologians contributing to it — is that of Robert Murray, S.J.[13] Murray is a Catholic theologian and biblical and patristic scholar, who accepts all the principles of Catholic biblical hermeneutics, but is of the opinion that the *Catechism of the Catholic Church* is seriously inadequate and even unbalanced in its presentation of the Catholic doctrine of Scripture and of revelation. Murray considers that the new *Catechism* is defective in failing to present the riches of a biblical approach, and of giving the impression of fundamentalism. But he is much too cautious, and too careful a reader of the text of the new *Catechism,* to accuse its authors of actual fundamentalism, because it clearly is not fundamentalist if its doctrine of revelation is viewed as a whole.

What *is* fundamentalism? It is much easier to accuse one's opponent of fundamentalism (and, regarding fundamentalism, it nearly always is one's opponent who is called such) than it is to say precisely what is meant by the term. The media in calling a person or group "fundamentalist" often refer to religious groups, particularly within Islam, who are prepared to commit acts of terrorism to further their aims. The media also reserve the title "fundamentalist" for religious sects whose religious practices (e.g., in extreme cases such as mass suicide) act contrary to the acceptable mores of society.

Historically, fundamentalism arose in revivalist USA of the turn of this century. Fundamentalists reacted against the modernism of their day, which rejected the miraculous in Scripture such as the miracle stories about Jesus and above all the physical resurrection and the bodily return of Christ at the end of time. Fundamentalism first hit the news when J. T. Scopes, a schoolteacher of Dayton, Tennessee, was convicted on the charge of violating the state law by teaching the doctrine of biological evolution.[14]

The essence of fundamentalism is the *essential historicization* of every story in the Bible, from the seven days of creation to the angel blowing his trumpet at the beginning of the series of seven woes in the last book of the Bible, Revelation (Revelation 8:6). For the fundamentalist, to say that the Bible is *true* means essentially that it must all be *factual* and *historical.* It cannot accept the fact that God, in speaking to us as human beings, might speak to us in parable or story form.

Every fundamentalist, of course, will accept that there are parables and nonfactual stories in the Bible, for example the parables of Jesus such as the story he told of the Good Samaritan (Luke 10:29-37). But these are instances where the context makes it plain that a story is being told (Jesus "told them many things in parables," Matthew 13:3). The fundamentalist cannot accept the possibility that an account might *appear* to be factual (e.g., the story of Job in the book of that name) while in reality it is a fictional poem or story with a moral. Nor could the fundamentalist accept that the numbers of the book of Revelation do not enable us to predict with certainty the actual date of the Second Coming of Jesus; but that those numbers are symbolic, and do not give us any knowledge of the "when" of future events, but only prepare us for the coming of Christ whenever that will be.

Behind the fundamentalist view of Scripture, therefore, is what we might call a *univocal* approach to the interpretation of the Bible. The fundamentalist cannot accept the possibility that some passages of Scripture are historical, and others not; and that it is not always easy to tell the difference. For example, did the writer of Genesis intend us to accept the six days of creation *literally*? Or could it be that he was only writing symbolically, and that the scientific view that the world took millions of years to create is not incompatible with a Christian view of creation?

Throughout the nineteenth century, Catholic biblical scholars tended toward a fundamentalist approach in the sense defined above; although great scholars such as M.-J. Lagrange, the rector of L'École Biblique in Jerusalem, were already developing a more nuanced approach to the interpretation of Scripture. Catholic authorities were concerned that the early "critics" of the Bible were denying essential Catholic doctrines such as the possibility of God working in the world beyond the laws of nature, so denying God's omnipotence and his ability to communicate with us through "supernatural" acts in the created order. Pope Pius X at the turn of the present century reinforced this quasi-fundamentalism through what amounted to a reign of terror in the seminaries and Catholic universities, purging academic staffs of those who tended toward "modernism."

But Catholicism could never remain essentially fundamentalist, because its interpretation of Scripture has never been, like the fundamentalist, univocal, but is on the contrary *multivocal*. The Catholic Church has always taught that the Church itself is the final interpreter of the Bible. The early Fathers (the bishops and great writers of the first centuries of the Church) always taught that Scripture has different meanings, discernible only by the Spirit of God in the Church, in particular Old Testament events such as the exodus from Egypt having the deeper meaning of referring to the final exodus, the death and resurrection of Christ, his "passing over." Once these deeper meanings are recognized, and once the Church as final interpreter of Scripture is recognized, the death-blow of fundamentalism with its univocal view of Scripture is already dealt.

It is not surprising that Martin Luther, in his doctrine of Scripture, rejected entirely the "spiritual meaning" of Scripture as a relic of Romanism, because the acceptance of the deeper or "spiritual meaning" would undermine completely his doctrine of *sola scriptura*. For Luther, if the Bible and the Bible alone is to be the source of our faith without the authority of the Church, then the meaning of the Bible must be contained within itself, in the letter, and in the sense delivered by the historical context. Otherwise, Luther argued, we would once more be under the yoke of ecclesiastical interpretation.[15] The advantage of this approach was that Luther gave an enormous impetus to the new movement, linked with the Renaissance, of the historical study of the Bible, in order to discover its plain meaning. The disadvantage of this approach was that Scripture studies became more and more linked to advancing historical science, and meanings that could not be immediately historically justified were increasingly seen as obsolete.

When this essential hermeneutical point is understood, then the new *Catechism* could never be seen as fundamentalist, at least in essence. The *Catechism* accepts the deeper meaning of scripture (CCC 115-118), and of the Church as interpreter of Scripture (CCC 119). It states clearly that Christianity is not the religion of a book (CCC 108), but of a person, Jesus Christ, who is himself the Word of God made flesh. The object of faith, what is believed, is not what texts of Scripture can be salvaged by the individual believer. Rather, the object of faith is Christ himself, and the doctrines of faith are presented in the Creeds and in the Church formulations, that is, the true Tradition of faith handed on from the apostles. The Anglican theological adage is apt at this point: "The Church to teach, the Bible to prove." With such an approach to faith on the part of the *Catechism of the Catholic Church,* there is no place whatever for a univocal approach to Scripture. It can be read as a rich and varied document, testifying in many different ways to the Tradition of faith handed on from Christ and the apostles.

What also contradicts any possible fundamentalism in the new *Catechism* is its affirmation from *Dei Verbum* of the fact that, in Catholic faith, not only is God the author of Scripture, but the human writers are themselves true authors also (CCC 106). Once the human authorship of Scripture is admitted, then the existence of different literary forms springing from the cultural and historical context of the human authors becomes immediately possible.

What sometimes gives the *impression* of fundamentalism in the *Catechism of the Catholic Church* is that figures particularly of the Old Testament are described *as if* their historical existence was itself a matter of faith. We shall see this particularly regarding Adam and Eve in the next Hard Question. But the *Catechism* never teaches: "Noah and Abraham actually existed" (cf. CCC 56-59). It simply tells their story, relating it to the history of salvation before Christ. Some have argued that the new *Catechism* should have brought in modern biblical scholarship at this point, mentioning the difficulties of proving the historicity of these ancient biblical figures. This could be argued, and no doubt those who compiled the new *Catechism* agonized over this problem, as to how much modern biblical scholarship to bring into discussion. Certainly, to have mentioned even briefly some of the critical problems of historical biblical scholarship would have enormously complicated the new *Catechism.* In any case, the writers of the *Catechism of the Catholic Church* themselves see the need clearly to "inculturate" the teaching of the *Catechism* in the local scene. This is the task of those involved in biblical catechesis, to "inculturate" the new *Catechism* by making modern Christians aware of the complexities and the fascination of modern biblical studies.

We shall see later that the new *Catechism* is equally clear when it wishes to assert *unambiguously* the historicity of certain events, for example the virginal conception of Jesus (CCC 498), and his bodily resurrection (CCC 643). The very assertion of the historicity of these events again underlines the non-fundamentalism of the new *Catechism*. If the whole of the Bible was seen as univocally factual and historical, then there would be no need to assert the historicity of the miraculous events in Jesus' life. But, on the contrary, the *Catechism of the Catholic Church* wishes to make clear the historicity of certain events related to our salvation, whose factuality is questioned in modern theology and exegesis, while leaving freedom of research concerning the discussion regarding the historicity of other stories in the Bible.

8: How can the* Catechism of the Catholic Church *sustain the traditional doctrine of Original Sin in the light of modern theories of evolution?

The Catholic Church is committed to the doctrine of Original Sin as a dogma of faith; as also, I understand, is the Church of England, bound as it is to the orthodoxy of the first six centuries of the Christian era. The problem is to define exactly what the doctrine of Original Sin is. This is debated among Roman Catholic theologians, as among theologians of all denominations.

The doctrine of Original Sin was first put at the top of the theological agenda by St. Augustine of Hippo, who opposed the views of the British monk Pelagius.[16] Pelagius was of the opinion that human beings were born, not in a state of sin, but fundamentally good. God's activity, his grace, was required only to aid us to become better human beings, rather than to save us from sin and damnation. Pelagius was not too far removed from your average decent British chap, who thinks that we humans are not too bad, provided we have a good chance in life and a little help from our friends. Augustine argued that, on the contrary, human beings, as sons and daughters of Adam and Eve, participated in the first act of disobedience of that unfortunate couple whose fall is recounted in Genesis 2 and 3. For Augustine, we are actually born into the sin of Adam and Eve, and are bound by the chains of that sin until we are set free in Christian baptism. Augustine's views were accepted as orthodox by the Church; but that did not mean that it became entirely clear as to how it meant to say that we as human beings are all bound in solidarity with the sin of Adam and Eve. What Augustine was strenuously arguing for was our fundamental need as human beings for the grace of God given in the redemption of Jesus Christ and communicated to us in our baptism. This by no means answered all the questions.

Since Augustine, the biggest theological problem seems to have been the question as to how the Original Sin of Adam and Eve is transmitted to each human being down the ages of the human chain. Some have tried to avoid the problem by stating that we simply *imitate* the sinful disobedience of Adam and Eve. But the Council of Trent in 1546 insisted that this view just will not do. Trent asserted as a dogma of faith that Original Sin has been transmitted down the centuries to the human race "not only by imitation."[17] But Trent did not define how it was actually transmitted.

In my opinion, the most coherent presentation of the doctrine of Original Sin is in the *Summa Theologiae* (or *Summa Theologica*) of St. Thomas Aquinas.[18] Aquinas sees the essence of Original Sin as the "defect of original justice," that right relationship between us and God, which was God's gift to us at the beginning. For Aquinas, therefore, Original Sin is first and foremost a defective disposition (*habitus*), the result of that first sin. With the loss of original justice, according to Aquinas, is given also a disorder within human nature called "concupiscence," uncontrolled desire, not only related to sexual matters, but covering the whole of human life, causing avarice, hatred, self-righteousness, orientation away from prayer, and all other moral disorders.

How was this state of Original Sin transmitted from one human being to another? According to Aquinas, by the transmission of nature. When a child is born, it is given a tendency toward sin that is based upon inheritance from its own father and mother. Without entering into speculation about genetic codes being transmitted, it is surely not difficult to see how a *defective relationship* could be communicated down the line of human evolution. Psychologists identify such relationship-transmission regarding families (relationships with parents). Why should there be an insuperable difficulty in accepting that this defective relationship between ourselves and God can be transmitted down the evolutionary chain?

The growth of theories of evolution in the nineteenth century further sharpened the debate concerning the transmission of Original Sin. Darwin's view that we are all descended from apes, and that we have no single proven ancestor, seemed to the Victorians to undermine the entire faith of the British people. Bishop Wilberforce's attempt to ridicule his Darwinian opponent Huxley by asking whether the question "If Mr. Huxley is descended from an ape, could he inform us whether the ape was on his father's or on his mother's side?" only succeeded in losing Christian orthodoxy's sympathy with the public.

Darwinism raises three main questions regarding Original Sin. First, is it necessary to take the story of Adam and Eve literally, to the extent that we are all descended from one original couple Adam and Eve (a position called *monogenism*)? If so, this seems to conflict with evolutionary theories, namely that we humans are descended from many original couples (the polygenist position). Second, if we are descended from apes, as Darwinism claims, then what comes of the biblical teaching that God created Adam directly "from the soil of the ground" (Genesis 2:7) and his wife Eve from Adam's rib? Third, evolution presents the natural history of the world as "red in tooth and claw" from the beginning. Evolution knows of no Paradise before the fall, no Paradise Lost as presented in Milton. How can this be reconciled with the account in Genesis, where Adam and Eve are put into a perfect garden by God, only to mess up the proceedings by their disobedience?

These issues came to the fore in Catholic theology after the encyclical on biblical studies issued by Pope Pius XII in 1943, *Divino Afflante Spiritu* ("By the Breath of the Spirit"). Biblical scholars call this the Magna Carta of Catholic biblical studies. *Divino Afflante Spiritu* acknowledged the presence of different literary forms in Scripture. By this the Church formally abandoned any suggestion of univocity in the interpretation of Scripture, and was from now on explicitly committed to the presence of different literary types, as well as the factual and historical, in Scripture.

Immediately, Catholic biblical scholars and theologians saw the deep implications of this radical document on Scripture from one who had the reputation of being a conservative-minded Pope. What if the story in Genesis 2 and 3, of the fall of Adam and Eve, was not historical entirely, but typological or symbolic? What if the story of Adam's creation by God's breath, and Eve's being taken from the rib of Adam, was likewise symbolic? Could not we have then actually descended from apes? What if even Adam and Eve were not themselves historically one couple, but were symbols of the past fall of the human race? In this way, polygenism, the origin of the human race from more than one couple, would not be anymore seen as incompatible with orthodox Catholicism.

Prior to the Second Vatican Council, which opened in 1962, these matters were seriously debated, and answers given by the teaching authority of the Pope in his encyclical *Humani Generis*,[19] promulgated in

1950. First, the Pope demanded "moderation and caution" regarding the question of the evolution of the human body from lower forms of life. Second, he discouraged polygenism, on the basis that he could not see how, if the human race were descended from more than one couple, the reality of Original Sin could be transmitted. However, if the Pope discouraged such novel opinions, it is clear that he did not condemn them as heretical — and theologians continued to teach both polygenism and the evolution of the human body from lower animals as a speculative viewpoint in universities and seminaries throughout the world. Third, the "Paradise" or "Golden Age" before the fall was increasingly seen as not necessarily a "time" of specific length before the fall. The state of original justice is an existential condition in the roots of our being. We were created in a state of a right relationship with God, but we have lost that state because of the sins of our first parents.[20]

The *Catechism of the Catholic Church*'s treatment of Original Sin is by no means its most inspiring; but I believe personally that the basics of the doctrine are most credible, and that the new *Catechism* has presented with accuracy the essence of Original Sin; a condition that I have never found any difficulty in recognizing in myself. While discouraging polygenism, the Church has not rejected as heretical the possibility that we were descended from more than one couple (although some scientists today are beginning to favor monogenism on scientific grounds). Note that nowhere does the *Catechism of the Catholic Church* explicitly insist upon monogenism, even though monogenism is the easiest interpretation of CCC 404. Nor does the new *Catechism* insist that it is necessary to believe as a dogma of faith that our bodies were directly created. We could have descended from lower creatures, provided that the truth is preserved that our soul was directly created by God.

What is retained is the essentials of the doctrine, namely that we human beings have an innate tendency toward sinning (concupiscence) that is the consequence of a historical fall. This has deprived our state of a right relationship with God, which relationship can only be restored by God's grace in baptism. The new *Catechism* explicitly acknowledges that the account of the fall in Genesis 2 and 3 uses figurative language (e.g., the "tree of the knowledge of good and evil, Genesis 2:17, symbolically evokes the insurmountable limits that man, being a creature, must freely recognize and respect with trust": CCC 396); but it isolates a core of doctrine that makes sense of the present human condition.

9: Even more, are we committed to the story of the fall of the angels, and to the literal existence of angels as is the* Catechism of the Catholic Church*?

We recite in the Creed that we believe in "all things visible and invisible," which presumably includes a world of spirits. My own firm belief in the actual existence of angels began as a teenage Anglican with my reading of C. S. Lewis's *The Screwtape Letters,* which was both amusing and deeply perceptive from the spiritual viewpoint. What actual difficulty is there in believing in such a world of beings beyond our sight? If we insist that everything be accessible to our senses, then that immediately disposes of belief in God. The Creed is here quite logical. If we believe in God, who is above all transcendent and unseen, then it becomes reasonable that we recognize that a world of spirits, related to God and dependent upon him, exists and is present to us throughout our lives.

One difficulty that has been presented regarding angels is that the language of Scripture is full of varied, even confusing, imagery regarding the visitation of angels to humans. In fact, we are sometimes not sure whether, particularly in the Old Testament, we are dealing with a visit from angels, or some kind of manifestation of God in human form (see, for instance, Genesis 18, the visit of the "three men" to Abraham). This is not surprising, since the biblical traditions handed down stories of heavenly visitations, which of their nature tend to be less than clearly defined. It is also true that the names of angels (Raphael, "God's healing"; Michael, "Who is like God?"; Gabriel, "God's strength") represent attributes of God. It is therefore tempting perhaps to think that these angels are not beings at all, but symbolic representations of some aspect of God. Combine this with the chubby cherubs of Renaissance art, and the existence of angels becomes highly questionable as to its street credibility.

Contrary to this is the clear pre-Christian tradition, continued from the apostolic age onward, that angels have a real existence, and that they help us in our human lives. The beautiful story of Tobias and his healing encounter with Raphael is testimony to the pre-Christian Jewish belief in angels. In the New Testament, angels have a key role as messengers of the good news: at the incarnation, helping Jesus during his Agony in the Garden (Luke 22:43), leading Peter from prison (Acts 12:7-11). Are we to reject all these manifestations of angels as symbolic representations only, without real existence on the part of the angels? I fail to see why we have to, particularly because it is clear that both in late Judaism and in early Christianity the belief was in real angels, that is, spiritual messengers (Greek *angeloi*). Again, if we reject angels on scientific grounds, what then becomes of God, that supreme spiritual being, who is even more unseen than the angels?

The relevance of angels lies in the spiritual help they give us on our journey through life. If we ask why the help of God is not enough without angels, then we would have to ask the same question regarding other human beings. God uses other human beings to help us; he also uses spiritual beings to help us. I would suggest that we need all the help we can get; and many Christians throughout the centuries have been conscious of the presence of these unseen beings especially at difficult times in their lives.

The same applies, from the opposite point of view, regarding evil spirits. The Pauline writings make the position quite clear as to the New Testament belief in the powers of darkness: "Put on the full armor of God so as to be able to resist the devil's tactics. For it is not against human enemies that we have to struggle, but against the principalities and the ruling forces who are masters of the darkness in this world, the spirits of evil in the heavens" (Ephesians 6:11-12).

We have also, of course, the story of Jesus' own temptation by the devil, in all three Synoptic Gospels. Also outside of Scripture there seems much psychic evidence of evil powers at work in the world. That great holy man — the Curé d'Ars, John Vianney, patron saint of parish priests — tells the story of regular visitations from the devil. They became so frequent that John Vianney almost treated the poor devil as a friend, calling him *le grappin* (the grappling-iron).

The *Catechism* teaches the "literal" fall of the angels (CCC 391-395). The context here does suggest a "historical" fall on the part of the devil, who according to Christian tradition was a high-ranking angel who fell from grace because of his pride. Scripture (specifically 2 Peter 2:4) talks of a sin of these angels. This is not inconsistent with the view of Scripture that we have explained above, as multivocal. Scripture is not univocally mythical, anymore than it is univocally historical. *In this particular instance* the Church teaches the actual fall of the bad angels, by their own will. This was stated unequivocally by the Fourth Council of the Lateran in 1215: "The devil and other demons were created by God naturally good, but they became evil by their own doing. Man, however, sinned at the prompting of the devil."[21]

There is no conflict between a scientific worldview and the acceptance of a world unseen, and of beings unseen, as there is a genuine conflict between the six days of creation and modern evolutionary theories of creation. A science that is truly humble will admit to realities beyond its ken. Even within the field of science itself, practitioners are more and more prepared to admit that elementary particles of the universe (atoms, neutrons) can only be described by means of models rather than by accurate definitions. A scientist who refuses to admit realities beyond the senses thereby ceases to be a scientist, and becomes a philosopher, making a metaphysical statement, and therefore crossing the bounds of his discipline. "Nothing exists beyond what I can see" cannot be verified scientifically.

The devil is very happy when we do not acknowledge his existence. Our understanding of the power of evil in the world is of necessity reduced when we do not realize that behind evil is the spiritual force of a created and disobedient angel. This does not explain the philosophical problem of evil, as we shall see later. The possibility of evil in the world is consequent upon creation itself. But the presence of the devil and of his angels makes the struggle with evil that much more urgent.

10: How can the Constitution on Divine Revelation, **Dei Verbum,** *"unhesitatingly affirm" the historicity of the four Gospels in the light of modern New Testament criticism?*

Church doctrines are forced to steer between Scylla and Charybdis, that is, between two extreme positions. Extreme positions to the right or to the left are always easy options, taking a doctrinal position to its logical conclusion but forgetting other apparently paradoxical truths that need to be accommodated in a rounded orthodox picture.

The Second Vatican Council in its Dogmatic Constitution on Divine Revelation, *Dei Verbum,* was attempting to steer between the Scylla of fundamentalism on the one hand, and the Charybdis of Bultmannian skepticism on the other. Rudolf Bultmann's name[22] is always linked with an approach that sees the Gospels as mainly if not entirely statements of faith of the early Christian community rather than accounts of events that objectively occurred. The Second Vatican Council wished to repudiate this extreme view as much as the fundamentalist position regarding the Gospels, that they are a blow-by-blow account of what actually happened two thousand years ago.

In the history of post-Enlightenment biblical studies, we find precisely that these two extreme positions are fundamentalism on the one hand and liberalism and modernism on the other. As we have already seen, it is very difficult accurately to define what we mean by fundamentalism, liberalism, or modernism. They tend to be slogans used like rotten apples to throw at our opponents, rather than sober definitions to be carefully debated. It is perhaps more fruitful briefly to look at what lies behind the movements concerned rather than initially to struggle for a definition. Behind the radical criticism of the nineteenth century and the early twentieth lay philosophical presuppositions that were often insufficiently noted by biblical scholars. Central to the post-Enlightenment issue was the question of *miracle*. With the post-Cartesian and post-Newtonian view of the world as a machine, miracles, representing the intervention of the Deity, seemed to be an insult to the original good order created by that Deity.

The "liberal" or "modernist" movement within biblical studies, therefore, tended not only to produce skeptical conclusions concerning biblical historicity, whether dealing with the ancient traditions in Genesis, or with the Gospels with their miracle stories. They tended to underpin their exegetical conclusions with philosophical views about God that were difficult if not impossible to reconcile with orthodox Christianity. Because an intervening God seemed a relic of prescientific superstition, God was either increasingly identified with the world (leading to pantheism), or became more and more remote from the world he had created already quite adequately, needing God's own intervention no more (deism).

The nervousness of the Catholic Church concerning biblical criticism from the beginning stemmed from its awareness of these radical philosophical presuppositions. Furthermore, it is naïve to consider that such presuppositions no longer are present in twentieth-century biblical scholarship. Rudolf Bultmann, the most influential New Testament scholar of the twentieth century, whose writings and influence span the two World Wars, shares all the presuppositions of Enlightenment theology: rejection of the supernatural in the world, refusal to speak of an objective incarnation so that we can call Jesus "God from God, light from light, true God from true God."[23]

The First Vatican Council was concerned, at the close of the nineteenth century, to stress both the possibility of the miraculous occurring and its usefulness in indicating the presence of the God revealing:

> Nevertheless (although faith is a supernatural gift), in order that the submission of our faith should be in accordance with reason, it was God's will that there should be linked to the internal assistance of the holy Spirit outward indications of his revelation, that is to say divine acts, and first and foremost miracles and prophecies, which, clearly demonstrating as they do the omnipotence and infinite knowledge of God, are the most certain signs of revelation and are suited to the understanding of all.[24]

The "conservative" wing of Catholic biblical scholarship saw in much modern criticism the rejection of the supernatural, which skepticism it saw as condemned by Vatican I. Those in charge of the early drafts of the Dogmatic Constitution on Divine Revelation saw the specter of modernist skepticism in any attempt to question the historicity of the four Gospels. The early drafts therefore condemned roundly any attempt whatsoever to undermine the historicity, the absolute historical veracity, of the four Gospels. Fortunately, these early drafts were radically changed after the intervention of none other than Pope John XXIII. Good Pope John — no doubt influenced by his theological adviser Cardinal Augustin Bea, who was formerly rector of the Pontifical Biblical Institute, which was to the fore in introducing the new critical ideas into Catholic scholarship — sacked the first theological commission and appointed another commission representing both "conservative" and "progressive" viewpoints.

Paragraph 19 of *Dei Verbum* represents both "right-wing" and "left-wing" positions concerning Gospel historicity in a superb synthesis. On the "right," the Council document insists that the Gospels have a "historical character," namely that they *do* speak of a real person, Jesus of Nazareth, who really existed, and who lived a human life that has been faithfully recorded. This is because the Gospels form the prime testimony for the center of our faith, concerning Jesus, who lived on earth as the Word made flesh. Jesus is no myth, but a man of flesh and blood, whose life itself was the sacrament of our salvation. The Council document gives no credence to Bultmannian skepticism, the view that the Gospels are mainly about the faith of the early Church. On the contrary, they are about "what Jesus, the Son of God, during his life among men and women, actually did and taught for their eternal salvation, until the day he was taken up (see Acts 1:1-2)."[25]

Furthermore, the history of Jesus is important for *faith*, as Latourelle demonstrates:

> The Christian Faith implies a continuity between the reality of Jesus and the primitive church's interpretation of him, because it was in the earthly life of Jesus that God manifested himself, and that life sanctions the Christian interpretation of it as the only authentic and true interpretation. If the apostles were able to confess Jesus as Christ and Lord, then Jesus must have performed certain actions and shown behavior, attitudes, and language that justify the Christian interpretation of the man Jesus in his earthly state.[26]

However, if skepticism is given short shrift in paragraph 19 of *Dei Verbum*, the fundamentalist can find little comfort to pursue an unnuanced approach to the historicity of the Gospels. The Council Fathers admit that the apostolic message was passed on in the Gospels "with the fuller insight which they now possessed" (i.e., after the resurrection). Paragraph 19 speaks of a process of "synthesis," "selection," and "explication" in the four Gospels.

The possibility is left open by the text of the conciliar document that, for instance, the Sermon on the Mount was not preached at a particular time, but was a "synthesis" of "selected" sermons of Jesus preached at various times, and put into an artificial contextual framework by the author of Matthew's Gospel, the whole presented as the "Sermon on the Mount." The ministry of Jesus is very differently presented in St. John's Gospel as compared with the Synoptic Gospels of Matthew, Mark, and Luke. John presents Jesus as going up three times to Jerusalem, the Synoptic Gospels as Jesus going up to Jerusalem only once. Scholars therefore consider that the framework of Jesus' ministry is artificially constructed for a literary and theological purpose.

Finally, we only rarely have the "very words" (the *ipsissima verba*) of Jesus in the Gospels, for example his words in Aramaic on the cross (from Matthew 27:46), *Eloi, Eloi, lama sabachtani?* ("My God, my God, why have you forsaken me?") Is it possible that on occasion, particularly in St. John's Gospel, which has long discourses of Jesus, the evangelist is expressing the words of the Lord *in his own language as the evangelist*?

This is the virtually unanimous view of Johannine scholars, and there would seem to be nothing incompatible with *Dei Verbum* (no. 19) in holding such an opinion.

We know that it is correct to interpret paragraph 19 of *Dei Verbum* in this nuanced way, both because of the fact that key "conservative" phrases about absolute historicity are left out of later drafts of the document; and because, at the same time as the text of *Dei Verbum* was being discussed, in 1964, the Pontifical Biblical Commission, many of whose members were acting as *periti* for the Constitution on Divine Revelation, were issuing a document precisely on the historical truth of the Gospel[27] that made just the points about historicity made in the above paragraph. This more moderate approach to historicity is confirmed by the view of most New Testament scholars that the four Gospels were written, not immediately after the life, death, and resurrection of Jesus, but from A.D. 60 to 90, in their final form. Thus the possibility, indeed the probability, arises that the Gospels have had a developed history from the initial traditions about Jesus to their final literary form, while, as *Dei Verbum* says, "preserving the honest truth about Jesus."

None of these nuanced notions of historicity undermines the essence of the doctrine of the incarnation, or the intervention of God in history supremely in the life, death, and resurrection of Jesus. They do not deny the historicity of the miracle stories, but rather clarify the process of their forming part of the four Gospels.

The views presented by *Dei Verbum* on the historicity of the four Gospels, which, as it says, "Holy mother church has firmly and constantly held, and continues to hold and unhesitatingly assert . . . ," are not fundamentalist, nor do they contradict modern New Testament scholarship. On the contrary, they are carefully framed to take account both of Christian incarnational faith and the conclusions of modern biblical scholarship. There is hardly a better example in all the documents of Vatican II of bishops and theologians wrestling with a complex issue so important for our understanding of the most important texts of our faith, the four Gospels.

11: One doctrine that still divides other Christians from Roman Catholicism is the Catholic belief that, besides Scripture, some doctrines are contained within "Tradition." Surely, such a doctrine must reduce the importance of Scripture as the rule of faith?

The Roman Catholic doctrine of Tradition is admittedly one of the most undeveloped of Catholic doctrines, in spite of the monumental work by Yves Congar, *Tradition and Traditions*,[28] and the fact that the whole concept of a living tradition of faith has been such a controversial issue from the Reformation onward. But the Catholic concept of Tradition, correctly understood, in no way undermines Scripture, but rather strengthens it with a parallel and unwritten source of the word of God.

First, we must make the necessary classical distinction between "Tradition" with a large "T," and "traditions." "Traditions" with a small "t" are those customs that the Church has handed on down the centuries (such as the use of incense in liturgy), and those "stories" by which a community lives. For instance, the tradition, handed on by Irenaeus of Lyons, is that the Apostle John, one of the sons of Zebedee, wrote the Fourth Gospel while at Ephesus in Asia Minor (present-day Turkey). Some scholars might support that tradition on critical grounds, although the majority of critics today do not accept the testimony of Irenaeus to this effect, and are agnostic regarding the literary origin of the Gospel of John, or at least are uncertain whether to accept Irenaeus or not.[29] In any case, this is a case of tradition with a small "t." The tradition that Zebedee's son John, one of the twelve apostles of Jesus, wrote the Fourth Gospel is not a matter of Catholic dogma, but an ecclesiastical tradition that may or not be historically verifiable.

No society, of course, can exist without its traditions, even if those traditions themselves taken one by one are not absolutely the lifeblood of that society. The Church encourages a solid critical attitude to traditions, in the light of changing knowledge and circumstances, while encouraging also a true respect for the past, since it is so much easier to destroy old and precious traditions than to create good ones in their place.

"Tradition," with a large "T," on the other hand, is the handing on of the essentials of apostolic faith and morals of the Church in *unwritten* form, as in the Tridentine formula:

> The Council clearly perceives that this truth and rule are contained in written books and in unwritten traditions (*contineri in libris scriptis et sine scripto traditionibus*) which were received by the apostles from the mouth of Christ himself, or else have come down to us, handed on as it were from the apostles themselves at the inspiration of the Holy Spirit.[30]

Let us return to our example of the Gospel of John. We saw above that the question of its authorship by the Apostle John, and its writing in Ephesus, is a matter of "tradition" with a small "t." But the teaching of the Church that the Gospel of John is inspired Scripture, that it is one of the four authentic Gospels, together with Matthew, Mark, and Luke, and that it is apostolic in origin, *that* is part of Tradition with a large "T." This is part of the rule of faith, not expressly in Scripture, but in the living tradition transmitted from the apostolic age down to us, equally the word of God with Scripture.

The statement as to what constitutes Scripture, the word of God, cannot be decided by Scripture itself. Karl Barth, the great twentieth-century Reformed theologian, admitted this point, what is called by theologians the "Problem of the Canon" (i.e., the "Canon" or "Rule" of what constitutes the list of books of Scripture). For Barth, the only answer is to say that ultimately we cannot be absolutely certain what constitutes Scripture; because, if we were, then we would be admitting an oral tradition with equal weight to Scripture, and an infallible Church.[31] We Roman Catholics solve Barth's problem by admitting what Barth denies, both an oral tradition equally the word of God with Scripture and an infallible Church.

The basis, therefore, of the Catholic doctrine of Tradition with a capital "T" is at root quite simple. It is that, from the beginning, there were unwritten Traditions (the sacramental life of the Church, its liturgy, its teachings) that were equally authoritative as Scripture, but were not written down. These were "handed on" (the word in Latin, *traditio,* comes from the verb *tradere,* to "hand on"). This again is obvious when we consider that the preaching of the apostles after the resurrection preceded the writing of the Gospels by decades. Was there no word of God for twenty or thirty years, simply because it was not written down, or not written down in what we call "Scripture"?

The more we consider the notion of the oral transmission of the word of God, the more obvious it becomes as a principle of revelation. The writing of the books of the prophets of the Old Testament is a good example. Eventually, the words of the prophets — Isaiah, Amos, Ezekiel, etc. — were written down, either by themselves or by their disciples. But it is clear from Scripture itself that the "word of God came" (cf. Jeremiah 34:1) to the prophet. Did not the word of God come to the prophet before that word was written down? And did not that prophet speak the word of God orally (*traditionibus sine scriptis*) before that oracle was preserved in writing?

This seems to me to be one of the easiest of doctrines to believe. It conforms so much also to the nature of the Christian revelation as the revelation of a person, Jesus Christ, which is communicated to us, "handed on" not by mere written words, but by interpersonal communication of a mystery. Note that the Council of Trent did not use the word "*oral* tradition" in its text. What is handed on is simply described as "written and unwritten." What is handed on in "unwritten" form may not necessarily be in oral form. It may be in the form of acted effective sign, as in the sacraments of the Church (Eucharist, baptism, marriage, etc.). These are, for us Catholics, truly the word of God communicated to us and effective for our sanctification and salvation, the very word of God in sign form (water for baptism, bread and wine for the Eucharist).

What has confused the whole question of Tradition (capital "T") is that it has become bound up with the controversy as to whether there are doctrines not contained *in any way* in Scripture. But that is not a necessary part of the Catholic doctrine of Tradition. Some of the Council Fathers at Trent wished to insert the adverb *partim . . . partim* into the phrase, so making the text, "The Council clearly perceives that this truth and rule are contained *partly* in written books and *partly* in unwritten traditions." This would have conveyed the meaning that Tradition contains some doctrines not in any way in Scripture. But the Tridentine Fathers did not vote for the insertion of *partim . . . partim.*

This becomes a live issue when we consider doctrines such as the Assumption of the Virgin Mary, which does not appear to be in Scripture. We will attempt to deal with that in a later Hard Question below. But, however we resolve that problem, it must not be allowed to obscure the fundamental point that essentially Tradition with a capital "T" is first and foremost the handing on of the word of God in Jesus Christ in an unwritten form, parallel rather than in addition to, the word of God in written form that we call Scripture.

Vatican II refused to settle the question as to whether there are doctrines contained in Tradition that in no way are in Scripture. It tries rather to enrich our understanding of the relationship between Scripture and Tradition in revelation:

> Hence sacred tradition and scripture are bound together in a close and reciprocal relationship. They both flow from the same divine wellspring, merge together to some extent, and are on course

toward the same end. Scripture is the utterance of God as it is set down in writing under the guidance of God's Spirit; tradition preserves the word of God as it was entrusted to the apostles by Christ our lord and the holy Spirit, and transmits it to their successors, so that these in their turn, enlightened by the Spirit of truth, may faithfully preserve, expound and disseminate the word by their preaching. Consequently, the church's certainty about all that is revealed is not drawn from holy scripture alone; both scripture and tradition are to be accepted and honored with like devotion and reverence.[32]

12: Even more controversial than the concept of Tradition is that the* magisterium *of the Church is the ultimate criterion of what is contained in Scripture and Tradition. What hope for unity is there when this teaching still remains part of the claims of the Catholic Church?

The real question, as far as I can see, is not whether or not a *magisterium*, a teaching authority, is or is not acceptable. The real question has to do with whether or not the Church could ever do without a teaching authority, as a final arbiter as to what or what not to believe.

If the Church's doctrine were based entirely upon human reason, then we could trust, hopefully, upon human wit to make sure that the truth was maintained within the Church. This is the case regarding the teachings of political parties, which do not base themselves upon divine revelation (excepting perhaps fundamentalist religious political parties), but upon at least ostensibly rationally based arguments both for their basic principles and for their practical agenda. Even in this case, as we know too well, there are enormous disagreements among the parties as to what are or might be the best policies.

But what happens when teachings are based, not upon rational argument, but upon what is seen as divine revelation? The First Vatican Council emphasized the supernatural character of the Christian revelation, against the rationalist movement that would subject all truth, including religious truth, to the bar of purely natural reasoning. The Council argued that, because of our "supernatural end" (i.e., the vision of God), revelation was absolutely necessary: "God directed human beings to a supernatural end, that is a sharing in the good things of God that utterly surpasses the understanding of the human mind; 'indeed eye has not seen, neither has ear heard, nor has it come into our hearts to conceive what things God has prepared for those who love him' (1 Corinthians 2:9)."[33]

Who then is to be the authority in such matters of religious truth? Reason is not adequate to decide, because the truths concerned are beyond reason. Either God gives each individual a private revelation, or God gives a revelation historically, to a community of people whom we call "The Church." In this latter case, it is the whole Church that decides what to believe, on the basis of revelation transmitted to it historically.

The first is traditionally the "Protestant" solution, where each individual decides what to believe, from reading the Bible, or from some kind of religious experience. This solution either resolves itself into chaos, where individuals disagree among themselves what that revelation is; or, and this is the most frequent result of such a belief, groups of Protestant Christians come together into churches, which churches themselves become some kind of authority as to what to believe. This latter comes very close to the "Catholic" solution. The Church of England is limited in its doctrine to those matters of faith defined during the councils of the first seven or eight centuries of the Church's history. This limitation follows logically from not having an infallible authority. As we shall see later, it is clear from history that those councils saw their teaching as infallibly presenting Christian truth. When that sense of an infallible authority is lost, then no longer is it possible to have binding dogmas of faith proclaimed by a church in a living and developing situation.

The "Catholic" solution is that what we believe is decided ultimately by the Church, because the Church is given the gift of the Spirit to discern what the revelation given historically to the apostles is. In this solution, the individual submits to the testimony of the Church, which is the "pillar and ground of truth." A Catholic believes that this is not a denial of freedom, but a legitimate use of freedom, where we submit to the body of Christ, the Church, to which Christ entrusted his revelation. This is the position that I will attempt to defend in this book; and constantly we will be returning to this central question of authority.

But do not all three elements (reason, religious experience, Church authority) play their part in the decision-making process? Yes, as *Dei Verbum* notes in an inspired paragraph on the whole concept of development of doctrine:

> This tradition which comes from the apostles progresses in the church under the assistance of the holy Spirit. There is growth in understanding of what is handed on, both the words and the reali-

> ties they signify. This comes about through contemplation and study by believers, who "ponder these things in their hearts" (see Luke 2:19 and 51); through the intimate understanding of spiritual things which they experience; and through the preaching of those who, on succeeding to the office of bishop, receive the sure charism of truth. Thus as the centuries advance, the church constantly holds its course toward the fullness of God's truth, until the day when the words of God reach their fulfillment in the church.[34]

It is in this context, of development of doctrine *within the whole Church,* that *Dei Verbum* sets the work of the *magisterium.* "The task of authentically interpreting the Word of God, whether in its written form or in that of Tradition, has been entrusted only to those charged with the Church's ongoing teaching function, whose authority is exercised in the name of Jesus Christ."[35] It is so important to recognize the fact that development of doctrine is the gift and task of the whole Church, not just of the *magisterium,* the Church's teaching authority. The *magisterium* has, according to *Dei Verbum,* the *charism of discernment* within an already developing process.

Robert Murray criticizes the *Catechism of the Catholic Church* for altering the perspective regarding the relationship between *magisterium* and the development of doctrine within the whole Church, as it appears in *Dei Verbum.* His criticisms are, I think, fair. A theologian could see the role of the *magisterium* in a completely Catholic way without beginning treatment of the subject with the *magisterium,* but rather, as does *Dei Verbum,* dealing with the role of the *magisterium* at the end of the chapter on the Transmission of Divine Revelation. Perhaps the approach of the *Catechism of the Catholic Church* could be justified in that the section heading is "The Interpretation of the Heritage of Faith" (CCC 84-100). Here, as the new *Catechism* states, the role of the *magisterium* is key, as *Dei Verbum* itself states. But Murray is quite right in insisting upon the need for a balance between the role of the *magisterium* and that of the role of theologians and indeed of nonprofessionals in the Church as a "shared ministry."[36]

It would help, I am sure, in an ecumenical context for this balance to be preserved; but nothing can avoid the fact that, at the end of the day, the new *Catechism* is right to insist that it is essential to the Catholic position that there is a final and indeed infallible authority where matters of doctrine and of morality are concerned. This is the only way ultimately that questions are settled, and finally settled; although it must also be added that final definitions of doctrine do not stifle further development. Having defined that "Jesus is God from God, light from light, true God from true God," the Church can never go back on such a definition; nor from the definition, equally important, that Jesus Christ is true man. But the very statement "Jesus Christ is God become man" is not the end of questioning, but only the beginning of the exploration of the mystery. We can never deny the mystery; but we can always plumb further its depths.

Far from being an obstacle to unity, I would see the Catholic *magisterium* as potentially perhaps the Roman Catholic Church's greatest contribution to a reunited Christendom. A key point throughout this book will be the necessity of such an authority within a developing and growing Christian community. This is not to say that such a *magisterium* is always exercised wisely. Even an authority that can in certain instances be infallible could exercise its role clumsily or with lack of insight. But the existence of such a *magisterium* I will argue is both necessary, for the reasons stated above, and can and should be seen as a positive gift for the development of the whole Church.

13: Has not the Roman Catholic Church, in its doctrines of the Virgin Mary, confused doctrine and Tradition with legend?

Without question, legends concerning the Virgin Mary, particularly in the Apocryphal Gospels, sprang up during the second century, without apostolic basis, but simply expanding the miraculous element of the life of Mary and her divine Son, Jesus. Stories about the infancy of Jesus in particular, about his miraculously causing clay pigeons to come to life and fly away, distort the sober account that we have of the life of Christ in the four Gospels and in the earliest traditions about Jesus.

But the central doctrine of Mary is testified in the New Testament, namely that she did not have intercourse with a man before Jesus was born of her. That is clear both from Matthew's and from Luke's account. There has been considerable debate within Roman Catholicism during the past twenty years concerning the historical basis for the tradition of the virginal conception. Was the story of the virginal conception in the four Gospels based upon historical evidence, handed on from Mary and her family? Or did the tradition spring up from theological development during the first two Christian generations?

Raymond Brown[37] is unconvinced by the arguments for what he calls the "family tradition," and takes up an agnostic position regarding the source of the story that Jesus was born of Mary without intercourse between her and any male. But Brown still accepts the doctrine of the virginal conception as a dogma of faith. That is quite an acceptable position for a Roman Catholic scholar, even though my own opinion is that Brown is overskeptical regarding the historical evidence for the virginal conception.[38] Brown accepts the dogma, even if he does not accept the historical reasons given for that dogma; just as many Christians accept that God exists, even if they cannot understand the proofs for God's existence, or even if they just cannot accept them as logical.

The doctrine of the virginal conception became the first linchpin of development of doctrine about Mary among the early Fathers. For the early Fathers, the virginal conception of Mary was the sign of a new beginning. Mary was the new Eve (CCC 494), and Jesus the new Adam, not contaminated by the seed of the first sinful couple. The early Christians strenuously defended the virginal conception against those who mocked it, indeed against some skeptics even claiming that Mary's Son, Jesus, was sired by a Roman soldier, who deceived Mary into thinking that he was an angel! First- and second-century Romans, Greeks, and Jews were by no means more credulous concerning virginal conceptions than twentieth-century scientists.

For the early Christians, it was important that the virginal conception was *not* a myth or legend, but that it actually happened. It remains that the only solid objection to the virginal conception is not the New Testament evidence (at the very least scholars have played to a draw concerning arguments for the historicity of the story), but the inability to accept the miraculous in the life of Jesus. For those first Christians, it was important that the Christian story began with a true miracle, the work of God, signifying the new beginning with the new Messiah, the Son of God, the Redeemer, with the act of faith of Mary, the new Eve.

The second major point of development in Mariology was the *theotokos* controversy[39] of the fifth century. Nestorius was a member of the theological school of Antioch, which emphasized the humanity of Jesus. For the Greek Alexandrian school, the emphasis was upon Jesus as the Word made flesh. Thus the starting point for Alexandrianism was the divine *logos* taking up a human nature into itself, thus raising the theological problem as to whether Jesus in so doing lost some aspect or other of his humanity (e.g., the Alexandrian heretic Apollinarius taught that the Logos took the place of the human soul in Jesus). For the Antiochenes, Jesus was a man upon whom the Spirit descended. Thus the tendency for the Antiochenes was toward Adoptionism (as with Paul of Samosata), that Jesus was a man who became the "adopted" Son of God.

Nestorius was not an Adoptionist; but he shared the Antiochene presupposition that Jesus was a complete man upon whom the Spirit descended for him to become God. This meant that, for Nestorius, Jesus had two kinds of action, "God-actions" (e.g., his miracles, his resurrection) and "man-actions" (e.g., dying on the cross). Nestorius could not accept that when the man Jesus died, God the Son died. Nestorius spoke of two "persons" in Jesus as well as two "natures," with two activities, godly and manly. Thus, for Nestorius, Mary was the mother of the man who was God, she was the mother of Christ; but she could not have been the mother of his divine nature. Thus he could call Mary *christotokos* ("Christ-bearer"), but not *theotokos* ("God-bearer").

The protagonist for orthodoxy was Cyril of Alexandria. Cyril, whose rough and authoritarian tactics earned him the nickname of "Pharaoh," insisted that when Jesus acted, he acted as one divine-human person, albeit with two natures, divine and human. Whether Christ performed miracles, or suffered our human condition, he was always acting as the "God-man," his activities being "theandric" (God-man activities). This meant that Mary was truly the Mother of God, *theotokos*.

Kelly, the prestigious Anglican scholar, sees clearly that it was these Christological debates that succeeded in enhancing the status of Mary:

> The Christological debates of the mid-fifth century, with the councils of Ephesus and Chalcedon in which they culminated, marked the climax of Mariological development in the classic patristic period. It was not their concern, of course, to do honor to the Blessed Virgin, but rather to clarify and define the union of divine and human in the incarnate Lord. But the generally agreed conclusion that this could only be achieved by recognizing that Mary was in a real sense *Theotokos*, mother of God, finally brought out the full significance of her role, and in doing so inevitably enhanced her status, integrating Mariology firmly with Christology.[40]

The basis, therefore, of Marian doctrine in the Roman Catholic Church is not legend, but a very definite theology fought for in the first five centuries of the Christian era, based upon an orthodox Christology, even if this was only the beginning of the development of Mariology. This development continued in the clarification of the doctrine of the perpetual virginity of Mary, emphasizing Mary's total commitment to Christ by having no more children. This same recognition of the divine presence in Mary led eventually to the definitions of the Immaculate Conception and of the Assumption; the Immaculate Conception because that title *theotokos* is incompatible with Mary's sinfulness; and the Assumption because that fullness of divine presence in her could only be fulfilled by her body as well as her soul being united with Christ immediately after her death. But these two doctrines we will be discussing more specifically later.

14: Are we still committed to belief in hell and purgatory in the terms stated in the* Catechism of the Catholic Church*?

The answer to this question is a plain "yes." Hell is an unpopular doctrine with most Christian preachers today; although a recent survey indicated that the majority of people, even those who do not attend church regularly, believe in hell, despite the fact that they have no actual fear of going there themselves.

It seems to me that the new *Catechism* puts the emphasis right where it should be: on the fact that "the affirmations of Scripture and the teachings of the Church on the subject of hell are a *call to the responsibility* incumbent upon man to make use of his freedom in view of his eternal destiny" (CCC 1036). Christian teaching about hell has always been related to the vital choice that all of us have to make. This life is important, and we are important, precisely because we can choose or not choose an eternal destiny of happiness with God. As with every kind of love, the love of God can be refused; otherwise it would not be a free act.

People can accept that some choices are radical in every area of life. The soccer manager will give his team a dressing-room *fervorino*, explaining how, if they win the coming match, they will go into the semifinal of the cup. He puts first the dream of honor, glory, and wealth before them. On the other hand, he warns, if they should lose, he as manager will probably get the sack, and they will be replaced by players bought in new transfer deals. These radical choices apply to every area of life. We realize to our cost that to make a wrong decision can be absolutely disastrous. So it is, argues the *Catechism*, regarding the most fundamental choice of all in life, as to whether or not to follow God's way that has been provided for us in his revelation through Jesus Christ.

How many people will go to hell? Will *anybody* go to hell? The Roman Catholic Church has defined that many saints have gone to heaven. But it has never defined that anyone, even Adolf Hitler or Eichmann, has gone to hell. Some theologians, including the great Church Father Origen, believed that in the end everyone would go to heaven, even the devil himself. This is generally called the doctrine of "universalism." Provided that a Catholic theologian at least admits the possibility that someone *could* be sent to hell, we could hold to the position that in the end everyone will repent, and no one will suffer eternal damnation.

Such optimism, according to Catholic theologians, would not be heresy. In this case, the severe threats in Scripture threatening us with fire and brimstone are only the sanctions of a teacher threatening the class with detention to keep everyone quiet, but knowing in fact that such a punishment will never be actually put into effect. But if such a view is not heresy, is it prudent? Can we take such a chance with our spiritual lives? We will always have to act *as if* hell is a real possibility, even if in the end no one goes there. The warnings of Scripture are too great, and we have to admit the real possibility of ultimate eternal frustration.

I see the biggest difficulty regarding hell as the following. If any of us were presented with the love of God as it really is, we would never refuse it. We would be totally enraptured with God's love. We only refuse it on this earth because what we can see, the attractions of sin, appears more pleasurable than God's love. Is God therefore giving us a fair choice, giving us such a frail body with such attractive worldly choices? Is he loading the dice fairly in our favor? But only God's freedom is totally compelling. God loves God in the Trinity, and cannot do otherwise. This is the only example of love that is totally compelling. Even the angels are able to choose freely, and can choose against God, as we have seen earlier.

But the glory of being human, as also sometimes its shame, is being able to make choices one way or the other. It is to exist on this earth for a short while, with a body whose major material content is water, with a choice clearly presented for or against God. The Church has always taught that these choices are clear enough, and we have enough material to make the right choice, especially as we are promised God's grace continually to help us. God will only accept our rejection of him if that rejection is based upon *adequate* knowledge on our part.

The Catholic doctrine of purgatory is first and foremost based upon the fact that this choice is continuous, after baptism as well as before it. Purgatory as a doctrine reminds us that after baptism we are dedicated to a process of change, of *sanctification,* which continues on this earth, and can be completed in heaven if it is incomplete here. The new *Catechism* puts it most positively: "All who die in God's grace and friendship, but still imperfectly purified, are indeed assured of their eternal salvation; but after death they undergo purification, so as to achieve the holiness necessary to enter the joy of heaven" (CCC 1030).

For the traditional Reformation Christian, when a Christian is "saved," then that Christian is justified and will go straight to heaven with or without good works. The Catholic doctrine of justification teaches that baptism effects a real change in the person but that salvation can be lost after baptism. God gives a person his Holy Spirit for daily responsible living. I was brought up as an Evangelical Anglican, with the doctrine of "assurance of salvation," "once saved, always saved." One of the factors that led me toward Catholicism is that I could never make sense of this doctrine, particularly when viewed in the light of Paul's teaching in 1 Corinthians 10:

> I want you to be quite certain, brothers, that our ancestors all had the cloud over them and all passed through the sea. In the cloud and in the sea they were all baptized into Moses; all ate the same spiritual food; and all drank the same spiritual drink, since they drank from the spiritual rock which followed them, and that rock was Christ. In spite of this, God was not pleased with most of them, and their corpses were scattered over the desert. Now these happenings were examples, for our benefit, so that we should never set our hearts, as they did, on evil things; . . . Now all these things happened to them by way of example, and they were described in writing to be a lesson for us, to whom it has fallen to live in the last days of the ages. Everyone, no matter how firmly he thinks he is standing, must be careful he does not fall. (1 Corinthians 10:1-6, 11-12)

Paul's teaching here could not be clearer. He uses the journey through the desert as an analogy (a "type") for the present Christian life.

Just as the Israelites fell in the desert because of their sin, so can we Christians fall in the "desert" of this life, even after being baptized as were the Israelites of old. We are never to think that we are sure of salvation, but rather to take care that we drive safely on the road of life, not to fall into sin.

Paul is here speaking about what traditional Catholic moral theology calls "mortal sin" after baptism: those serious sins that destroy the relationship with God established anew by baptism. These are deliberate choices against God that divorce us from him, just as a couple can be divorced by conduct totally inimical to their marriage. For the Church, to die in this state is to be eternally "divorced" from God, that is, in that permanent state of separation we call "hell." We must hasten to add that for a sin to be truly "mortal" in Catholic theology, there has to be "full deliberation and consent" on the part of the sinner. Often, acts of hatred and anger, sexual sins, even deliberate stealing of large sums of money by a person desperately poor, might not be carried out with that "full deliberation and consent," and so will not be a mortal sin (cf. CCC 1854-1864). For mortal sin, of course, there is always recourse to the sacrament of reconciliation (or confession), a sign of true conversion from post-baptismal sin, and the beginning of a renewed life of following Christ.

A sin that is not mortal is called a "venial" sin in Catholic theology, that is, "lighter"; among such sins are losing one's temper, using careless language, and becoming mildly drunk. These are sins that do not destroy our relationship with God as does mortal sin, but still harm that relationship. If we die in a state of venial sin, we are in what traditional theology calls a "state of grace"; but we are not in a perfect relationship with God. There is a need for purification, if you like, within the portals of heaven itself. The person in purgatory is straining at the leash to break that final thread between oneself and the vision of God. Purgatory, I repeat, is heaven, or at least its antechamber. This is totally different from the person who dies in a state of mortal sin, which means final separation from God, and from which may God spare us all.

One final note here. In recent centuries, the Church, in wrestling with the problem of the eternal destiny of infants who die without baptism, proposed the possibility of "limbo," a place between heaven and hell where they remain in a state of "natural happiness," but denied the final vision of God that is the destiny of the blessed. This view arose partly also from the theory among theologians that the human person could have an eternal destiny that was purely natural; but this view has now become unpopular, even obsolete. All of us as human beings are made for final blessedness, and there is no "halfway house" of natural happiness. But what happens to babies who die unbaptized? The Church is torn between emphasizing the necessity of baptism on the one hand, and an insistence that no one will go to hell apart from that person's own fault, a fault that infants who die could not possibly have.

> As regards *children who have died without Baptism*, the Church can only entrust them to the mercy of God, as she does in her funeral rites for them. Indeed, the great mercy of God who desires that all men should be saved, and Jesus' tenderness toward children which caused him to say: "Let the children come to me, do not hinder them" (Mark 10:14), allow us to hope that there is a way of salvation for children who have died without Baptism. All the more urgent is the Church's call not to prevent little children coming to Christ through the gift of holy Baptism. (CCC 1261)

15: Also, granted that, according to the Catholic Church's teaching, the blessed enjoy the vision of God immediately upon death, what is there to wait for with the resurrection of the body?

This is a question that has exercised Catholic theologians for many centuries. Perhaps it is only in recent years, with a renewed understanding of the unity of body and soul in the one human person, that we can begin to understand better the importance of the doctrine of the resurrection of the body. Catholic teaching is clear that, immediately upon death, our soul has the vision of God, the "beatific vision" (i.e., the blessed vision of God). For that vision, we do not have to wait for the general resurrection, which takes place at the end of time when Christ returns again in glory.[41]

But the problem is a real one for us today. It touches upon the whole question of the relationship between soul and body in Christian thought. Particularly since the time of Descartes, the sixteenth-century French philosopher, we have tended to think of the soul as totally distinct from the body, almost like a jack-in-the-box. At the other extreme, more skeptical modern philosophers have tended to reject the soul as a medieval superstition, and have seen the human person as mere matter, a more sophisticated machine, but a machine nevertheless.

Before the Renaissance and Reformation, Christian thinking was dominated by a middle position concerning the relationship between soul and body, influenced by the philosophy of Aristotle. The Islamic philosophers Averroës and Avicenna were the first to see the potential for religious philosophy in the works of Aristotle, newly discovered in the eleventh century, and then avidly studied by the Christian scholastics in the new universities such as Oxford, Cambridge, and Paris. Aristotle, the Greek philosopher who had lived in the fourth century B.C., had rebelled against his master Plato concerning the real existence of universal ideas (e.g., manness, infinity). For Plato, these universal ideas had a real existence. In fact, they were the only reality, the world of matter being only of shadows cast by the ideas. Aristotle contradicted Plato, and claimed that universal ideas did not have a separate existence from matter, but existed only *in* matter as its "form" or "substance."

Up to the time of Albert the Great and Thomas Aquinas in the twelfth century, Christian thinking had been dominated by Plato. Augustine in particular was deeply influenced by Platonism. For Christian Platonists, there is no difficulty whatsoever concerning the immortality of the soul. If the soul's ideas exist apart from matter, as they do in Plato's schema, then clearly after death the soul relates to its true object, the eternal ideas that exist independently of the material world, from which the soul has just escaped. The only problem then remains as to what possible purpose the resurrection of the body can have in such a schema. If the soul is perfectly happy with its eternal ideas, what need has it anymore for the body?

With the new scientific, philosophical, and theological revolution in the eleventh, twelfth, and thirteenth centuries, the philosophy of Aristotle with its greater realism became very attractive to Christian theologians. In Aristotle's philosophy, the soul is related to the body only as its *principle of life,* not as something existing independently of it. That is what Aristotle called its "form"; the soul is simply the "act" of the body. From the great synthesis of the greatest of the scholastics Thomas Aquinas onward, the Church used Aristotelian categories to describe the relationship between soul and body. The soul was not, as in Plato, an independent entity, but was truly the "form" of the body, its principle of life, its *anima.* The general council of Vienne in 1311 in fact defined that the soul was the "form of the body."[42] Thus, from this time onward, the jack-in-the-box imagery of the soul-body relationship was no longer in favor with Christian thought.

But, with this new insight of the interrelationship between soul and body provided by Aristotelianism, there arose a new problem. If, as in Aristotle's thought, the soul is simply the form, the act, of the body, then what happens to this "soul" after death? Where an animal is concerned, when the animal dies, then the "form" simply ceases to exist as does the body. Should not the same happen regarding the human soul? Should it not, as the form of the body, cease to exist when the body dies?

The same Council that defined that the soul was the "form of the body" also reassured the faithful that the soul had a substantive existence after death precisely *as* the form of the body. This is because, as Aquinas argued, the human form (or soul), with its abstract ideas, could have a substantive existence without the body, unlike the animals who only have a "sensitive soul" that could never have any existence without the body.[43] But this doctrine of the natural immortality of the soul, when viewed through Aristotelian glasses, did not rest easily within Christian scholasticism. Duns Scotus, for instance, was not convinced by Aquinas's arguments for the immortality of the soul, and argued that only by divine revelation could we be sure of immortality, not by purely philosophical reasoning.

This state of unease regarding the relationship between soul and body has not gone away from Christian theological reflection. It is only in recent years, with the insights of post-Enlightenment philosophy, that theologians have begun again to reflect on the soul-body relationship perhaps with fresh insights. Karl Rahner and Herbert Vorgrimler, for instance, pursue the idea of the essential relationship between soul and body. Even after death, and even with the beatific vision granted to the soul, the soul still lacks the body and is deprived without it. It is still the "form of the body" (which itself still exists, waiting for the resurrection), and will not be fully fulfilled without its body.[44] Perhaps we could use an analogy of sexual love. A man and a woman may love each other, and their love may be perfect, without blemish. But their love will not, in this instance, be complete until they are married, and they become two in one flesh in sexual union. So the soul, even if it has the vision of God, will still yearn to be united with its body to achieve that completeness of being in the resurrection of the body.

To the forefront of the new thinking about the essential relationship between soul and body is Vatican II's Pastoral Constitution on the Church in the Modern World, *Gaudium et Spes*. The importance of this document is that, as many have noted, it weans Christian thought away from both Catholic and Protestant pessimism regarding the world, "which Christians believe has been established and kept in being by its creator's love, has fallen into the bondage of sin but has been liberated by Christ, who was crucified and has risen to shatter the power of the evil one, so that it could be transformed according to God's purpose and come to its fulfillment."[45] From being a "sin-laden" theology, and an individualist piety, it summons Christian thinking to focus on the creation of a new heaven and a new earth, which begins on this earth, and is only fulfilled in the resurrection of the body.

Endnotes

1. Tanner, II, p. 806. Vatican I in its decree on revelation states that the books of Scripture "contain revelation without error" (*revelationem sine errore continent*): ibid., lines 33-34.

2. K. Barth, *Church Dogmatics,* vol. I.2, *The Doctrine of the Word of God: Prolegomena to Church Dogmatics* (Edinburgh: T. and T. Clark, 1956).

3. Tanner, II, p. 975, lines 2-3.

4. Ibid., lines 8-13.

5. E. Duffy, *The Stripping of the Altars,* p. 3.

6. P. Hughes, *The Reformation in England,* vol. I, p. 100.

7. Tanner, II, p. 663.

8. "Vulgate" is from the Latin *vulgata,* "common." Jerome translated the Bible into the common language of his day, which was Latin, in the declining Roman Empire.

9. Tanner, II, p. 664, lines 12-19.

10. Cf. ODCC, p. 731.

11. Tanner, II, p. 979, lines 14-17.

12. Ibid., line 23.

13. CCCC, pp. 6-28.

14. ODCC, p. 542.

15. Hans-Joachim Kraus, *Geschichte der Historisch-Kritischen Erforschung des Alten Testaments* (Neukirchener Verlag, 1956, 1959), p. 10.

16. ODCC, p. 1058.

17. Tanner, II, p. 666.

18. ST, I-II, q. 81.

19. ND, pp. 125-126.

20. Gabriel Daly gives a radical critique of the *Catechism of the Catholic Church* in its treatment of Original Sin in CCCC, pp. 97-111. I fully appreciate Daly's concern to escape from the negativity of the post-Reformation theology of the fall in line with Vatican II's *Gaudium et Spes* without falling into the opposite error of the New Age and its rejection of Original Sin. However, I do think that we can make full sense of the traditional doctrine as I have expounded above.

21. Tanner, I, p. 230, lines 13-15.

22. DFT, pp. 88-91.

23. "In short, Bultmann's creed amounts to the following articles: Jesus is only a man; he is the last on the list of OT prophets. There is such a hiatus between kerygma and history that we know practically nothing of the life and personality of Jesus. The primitive church gave him the titles Son of God and Savior, for 'marketing' reasons — i.e., in order to allow him to compete with the Greek gods. When the NT speaks of miracles and of the resurrection of Jesus, it uses a mythic language, under the influence of Hellenism, Gnosticism and Jewish apocalyptic, but the modern mind cannot accept the notion of a miracle or the resurrection of the dead. Finally, Jesus is in no way savior of humanity, redeemer of men and women, in the sense adumbrated by the present-day Catholic Church, but merely the historical locus chosen by God in order to tell human beings about their salvation by faith" (DFT, p. 91).

24. Tanner, II, p. 807, lines 10-15.

25. Ibid., p. 978, lines 27-31.

26. DFT, p. 377.

27. *Instruction of Pontifical Biblical Commission Concerning the Historical Truth of the Gospels* (April 21, 1964) in J. J. Megivern (ed.), *Official Catholic Teachings: Bible Interpretation* (Wilmington, DE: McGrath Publications, 1978), pp. 391-398.

28. Y. Congar, *Tradition and Traditions: An Historical Essay and a Theological Essay* (Wheathampstead, Hertfordshire: Anthony Clarke Books, 1966).

29. R. Brown, *The Gospel According to John,* vol. I *(I-XII)* (The Anchor Bible; London: Geoffrey Chapman, 1971), p. xcii: "Thus it is fair to say that the only ancient tradition about the authorship of the Fourth Gospel for which any considerable body of evidence can be adduced is that it is the work of John, son of Zebedee. There are some valid points in

the objections raised to this tradition, but Irenaeus's statement is far from having been disproved."

30. Tanner, II, p. 663, lines 22-25.

31. K. Barth, *Church Dogmatics*, p. 476: "The answer (to the question of the Canon of Scripture) is itself a divine and therefore an infallible and definitive answer. But the human hearing of this answer, whether that of the Church or our own to-day, is a human hearing, and therefore not outside the possibility of error, or incapable of being improved." But how can the "human hearing" be fallible, in Barth's view, without the act of faith itself in the truth of what constitutes Scripture being fallible in consequence, thus undermining our faith in Scripture as the word of God?

32. Tanner, II, p. 974, line 37 — p. 975, line 7.

33. Ibid., p. 806, lines 19-24.

34. Ibid., p. 974, no. 8, lines 20-27.

35. Ibid., p. 975, no. 10, lines 14-16.

36. CCCC, p. 19.

37. R. E. Brown, *Responses to 101 Questions on the Bible* (London: Geoffrey Chapman, 1990), pp. 90-91.

38. For a more positive assessment of the historicity of the New Testament narratives of the virginal conception of Jesus, cf. J. McHugh, *The Mother of Jesus in the New Testament* (London: Darton, Longman and Todd, 1975), pp. 157-347.

39. J. N. D. Kelly, *Early Christian Doctrines* (fifth edition) (London: Adam and Charles Black, 1977), pp. 310-330.

40. Ibid., p. 498.

41. CTD, pp. 50-51.

42. ND, p. 120, §405, no. 902.

43. ODCC, p. 1292.

44. CDT, pp. 408-409.

45. Tanner, II, p. 1070, lines 1-3.

Infallibility, Primacy, and Episcopacy

It is in a way a great pity to focus so much on the question of infallibility, even if it was necessary for us to do in answering objections to Roman Catholicism. To understand the riches of the Church, to have a rounded picture, it is necessary to begin away from controversial issues such as the infallibility of the Church, to see what really makes the Church tick. Thus the Dogmatic Constitution on the Church, *Lumen Gentium*, spends its first chapter on the "Mystery of the Church,"[1] and its second chapter on the "People of God,"[2] fourteen pages of closely typed print, before its third chapter on "the hierarchical constitution of the Church and in particular the episcopate."[3]

The Roman Catholic concept of infallibility cannot be understood except in the context of a whole ecclesiology, an integrated theology of the Church. Vatican II was itself concerned to present this whole ecclesiology, precisely because it was the heir of Vatican I, which for historical reasons focused on a one-sided presentation of the Church because of the issue of the infallibility of the Pope so threatening to divide the Church at the end of the nineteenth century. Vatican II's *Lumen Gentium* was a superb latter-day act of theological healing, to set all the controversies of the post-Reformation era into a unified picture of the Church, using all the depth of biblical and patristic imagery.

The Church is more than the Pope and bishops. It is the whole people of God, itself a priestly people. It is even more than an organization that can produce divine criteria for its truths. However, Catholic theologians have always argued that if we understand infallibility correctly in its proper context, it will be seen as a necessary charism within the Church to preserve its truth, and perhaps even more important, to provide for future development. A church that is not infallible in its teaching can never present its doctrine, necessarily in a continually changing situation, as truly Christ's word to his people the Church.

Newman also argued that the Church, developing throughout history in different situations, has always been aware of this infallibility, and always acted *as if* infallibility was its charism, many centuries before the Pope's infallible charism was defined.

This recognition of infallibility was particularly true during the Christological controversies of the first six centuries. By excommunicating those who disagreed and calling them heretics and schismatics, the bishops of the councils (under the increasing influence of the Bishop of Rome, as we shall see later) were exercising a practical infallibility. They were not merely *certain* that they were right, and that Paul of Samosata, Arius, Nestorius, and Eutychius were wrong in their views about Jesus Christ, they were themselves convinced that the Catholic Church, meeting in general council, *could not be wrong* when it defined matters of faith and morals.[4]

B. C. Butler, in his superbly argued *The Church and Infallibility*, quotes Newman's *Grammar of Assent* in distinguishing between certainty and infallibility. Understanding of this distinction between certainty and infallibility answers the old Protestant objection of Salmon's *Infallibility*, namely that if I accept an infallible Church, then I am making myself infallible. Not so, argued Newman. I may be certain that the Catholic Church is infallible, but I may be wrong in many other kinds of judgment (e.g., that my soccer team will win the cup):

> A certitude is directed to this or that particular proposition, it is not a faculty or gift, but a disposition of mind relative to a definite case which is before me. Infallibility, on the contrary, is just that which certitude is not; it *is* a faculty or gift, and relates, not to some one truth in particular, but to all possible propositions in a given subject-matter.[5]

This charism of infallibility is given for a purpose, in order to preserve the faith in its integrity for the whole people of God. The new *Cat-*

echism of the Catholic Church puts it well: "In order to preserve the Church in the purity of the faith handed on by the apostles, Christ who is the Truth willed to confer on her a share in his own infallibility. By 'a supernatural sense of faith' the People of God, under the guidance of the Church's living Magisterium, 'unfailingly adheres to this faith' " (CCC 889).

Note that, for Vatican II, quoted by the new *Catechism,* infallibility is a gift of the whole Church. It arises from the fulfillment of the promise of Jesus Christ to send a Paraclete, the Spirit of Truth, "Who will lead you to the complete truth" (John 16:13). In order that the truth of revelation may be preserved, Christ promised that his Church, by the charism of the Holy Spirit of Truth, could not err when teaching faith and morals.

However, although the gift of infallibility belongs to the whole Church, both for Vatican II and for the new *Catechism,* the *exercise* of this gift of infallibility seems to be only through the *magisterium,* the teaching authority of the Church. Regarding the whole Church, *Lumen Gentium* says that "it adheres indefectibly to the faith which was once for all delivered to the saints. . . ."[6] The word "indefectible" rather than "infallible" is used of the body of the faithful in general.

There may be room for further discussion and development of thinking here. Newman, in his essay *On Consulting the Faithful in Matters of Doctrine,* seems to go further than this, when he says "because the body of the faithful is one of the witnesses to the fact of the tradition of revealed doctrine, and because their *consensus* through Christendom is the voice of the Infallible Church."[7] Is it possible that the whole body of the faithful by their consensus are infallible, even more than indefectible? Possibly, it would seem to me, as an exercise of the ordinary *magisterium.* But Vatican II and the *Catechism of the Catholic Church* emphasize that the gift of infallibility is formally exercised through the teaching authority of the Pope and bishops, with whom in any case the body of the faithful would have to submit its judgment in the case of an infallible pronouncement from that *magisterium,* and with which *magisterium* the body of the faithful must agree.

Infallibility then in its usual exercise by the *magisterium,* is a *charism,* a gift within the Church, necessary for the whole Church to remain indefectibly faithful to Christ's revelation, but a ministry given to some, not all, within the Church. This links up with Vatican II's approach, which sees hierarchy itself as a gift: "For the nourishment and continual growth of the people of God, Christ the Lord instituted a variety of ministries which are directed toward the good of the whole body."[8]

It is in this context, that of a charism within the Church, serving the whole Church in preserving the truth of revelation within the Church, that Vatican II wishes us to see the gift of infallibility. As Paul himself says, "There are many different gifts, but it is always the same Spirit" (1 Corinthians 12:4). The charismata are for all the Church, but are not possessed by every member of the Church. As we shall now see, the charisma of infallibility is very much the gift of those in apostolic succession to Peter and the first apostles.

16: The Roman Catholic Church claims infallibility for the statements of faith of its bishops as successors of the apostles in union with the Pope, the Bishop of Rome, the successor of Peter. But do the actions and personalities of the possessors of this gift of infallibility justify these enormous claims?

To put the question the other way, is not the greatness of the Holy Spirit's power predicated on the premise that the infallible truth of God's revelation can be preserved in the Church in spite of the sinfulness and weakness of those chosen to preserve that truth?

As a charism, the Holy Spirit of Truth is given in the Church to those who are unworthy of it, namely the bishops in union with the Bishop of Rome. Peter, the first leader of the Church, denied his Master Jesus three times through cowardice at Jesus' trial (Matthew 26:69-75). Paul, although no doubt morally impeccable, was a difficult person to live with, and split up from Barnabas, the early Church's nice guy, because they had a "flaming row" (not a bad translation of the Greek of Acts 15:39, translated by NJB as Paul and Barnabas having a "sharp disagreement"!). They had to go their separate ways, and although both Paul and Barnabas were eventually canonized, while on earth they lived in a state of permanent divorce as missionaries.

When I was first considering becoming a Catholic, my Anglican archdeacon said, "I cannot submit my mind to a crowd of Italian bachelors," taking a gentle swipe at the Roman Curia. My reply was unusually smart for one who seldom seems to produce the memorable riposte: "Two thousand years ago, I would have had to submit my judgment to Galilean fishermen. What is the difference?" As Paul tells us: "We hold this treasure in pots of earthenware" (2 Corinthians 4:7). The amazing miracle of the Christian faith is that the revelation of God was entrusted to people who were by no means special in human terms, but who proved themselves in the end worthy of that trust, in spite of their human failings on the way.

17: What evidence is there in the primitive Church that the apostles were convinced of their infallibility in questions of faith or morals?

The other amazing fact as I read the New Testament is this: David Edwards says that "there is no evidence in the New Testament that Peter exercised the kind of authority which was to be claimed, step by step, in the history of the papacy."[9] I find completely opposite evidence in the New Testament, of the most blatant authoritarianism. First, Peter seems to be very much in charge of the Jerusalem church, even seeing to the death of two deceivers, Ananias and Sapphira, who lied about the amount of money that they had given to the church community (Acts 5:1-11). But still more remarkable is the case of Paul. Where Peter is concerned, we do not have clear evidence of his writing. The two epistles bearing his name (1 and 2 Peter) are disputed as to authorship by critical scholars. But we have ample evidence of Paul's mind through his writings. A good proportion of Paul's letters are judged authentic by even the most skeptical of New Testament scholars.

One such is Paul's letter to the Galatians, accepted by all as indubitably genuine. Paul is writing this letter to a group of Christians somewhere in present-day Turkey (the geographical location of the "Galatia" to which Paul wrote is a long-running dispute among scholars).[10] He is writing in a state of white heat. He is desperately concerned that these new convert Christians are being led back into Judaism by a Judaizing party who wished to take over the fledgling Church. The issue was whether Gentile Christian males had to go through the initiatory rite of circumcision. According to Acts 15, the Council of Jerusalem decided that Gentile Christians would not have to be circumcised. There are historical problems regarding the date and indeed the whole agenda and decrees of this "council" in Acts 15. Was it after or before Paul wrote to the Galatians? But in any case, with or without any council to back him, Paul was convinced in his own mind. If a man is circumcised, Paul argued, that man is obliged to keep the whole Law. And those Galatian Christians who persist in teaching that Gentile Christians must be circumcised are, according to Paul, to be excommunicated (*anathema sit:* Galatians 1:8, 10).[11] To us, it might seem a small matter, and a theological quibble among Jewish Christians. But to Paul, and in reality to us if we consider carefully the matter, the issue was crucial for the infant Church. If Gentile Christians were to be circumcised, and so to keep the Law, then all the decrees of the Torah (the Sabbath, the dietary regulations, the legal code) would have to be kept by them. And Paul argued that these decrees were superseded by the resurrection of Christ. The Christian, according to Paul, goes back to the faith of Abraham, who preceded the Law of Moses by centuries.

What I find so convincing about Galatians in connection with the whole question of infallibility is the total certainty of Paul, indeed his consciousness that he cannot be wrong in this matter. First of all, he bases his authority on the risen Lord, whom he has seen. He was given his divine mandate. Not even "an angel from heaven" (Galatians 1:8) can change this Gospel he was given originally at his conversion. Furthermore, not only does Paul have certainty concerning his revelation from Christ, he is totally certain about its implications in terms of Christian action. It is highly unlikely that the risen Christ said to Paul: "Gentile Christians must not be circumcised." Rather, Paul believes that he has the authority, and the right judgment from the Spirit given to him, to make the right decisions for the churches for which he has responsibility.

In other words, it seems Paul has the consciousness of the gift of infallibility in matters relating to revelation. Only this could justify his anathematizing (i.e., excommunicating) those who disagreed with him; unless we care to explain away this otherwise extraordinary arrogance on his part. Again, neither is this authoritarianism simply a private religious experience on Paul's part. He is convinced that he has here the right interpretation of the revelation of Christ, binding not only on himself but on all the other apostles. They, including Peter, must agree also.

Galatians has often been used as an argument against Petrine authority. I wish to use it here as an argument for infallibility in exercise, not of Peter, but of Paul the apostle. The Catholic Church's tradition is that not only the Pope possesses the charism of infallibility, but the whole body of bishops united with the Pope. Similarly, regarding the New Testament era, not only was Peter an apostle, but Paul also. According to commonly held Catholic theology, each of the apostles possessed this gift of infallibility. Paul certainly thought he did, if we read Galatians in a plain manner.

As we shall discuss in more detail later, no Scripture argument is totally watertight. The authority Paul wields in Galatians could be interpreted in a different manner by different scholars (but only, in my opinion, by stretching its meaning). What I would submit here is that the New Testament presents us at least with one example of a supremely confident apostle (and there are many other examples that could be quoted, both of Paul's letters, and the letters of other apostles); a confidence that at least looks likely to be based upon his own conviction of his own infallible judgment regarding revelation, due of course not to his own powers, but to the Spirit that has been given to him. Could Paul's "infallibility" be in his case an instance only of "certainty"? Paul does not say, "I am infallible here," only "I am right." The problem here is that Paul might be certain that he was right, but how could he anathematize those who disagreed with him unless he (and ultimately they also) believed that in matters of revelation he was infallibly right, at least in the kind of limited instances that Catholic theology has worked out for its own *magisterium*? Certainty does not give authority for and neither does it justify anathematization; only the infallible exercise of authority justifies such apparently arrogant, even blasphemous, behavior.

This confidence, this infallibility, I would submit was necessary for the miracle of the growth of the early Church. Its powerful growth in numbers and in different places in the Roman Empire was based upon the deep conviction of Christians of the truth of their faith, and the deep conviction that those who led them, the apostles, were right in their interpretation of the words and deeds of the risen Lord. This rightness of judgment was ongoing, the simplest explanation of which was that the early Christians considered that the apostles were so guided by the Holy Spirit as to be infallible as to the truth of the revelation of Christ and its practical outworkings in Christian morality.

No matter how holy Paul was, this gift of infallibility would have to be supernatural. That is why the Hard Question above proceeds from a false premise. No human personality could in itself justify the claim to infallibility. The only justification for claims to infallibility lies in no way in the personality of the one who might be infallible, but in the promised gift of the Holy Spirit in the Church as a charism to certain people. The gift must depend upon God alone, and its credentials can only be found in revelation itself. Paul himself was insistent upon the divine gift of revelation: "Now I want to make it quite clear to you, brothers, about the gospel that was preached by me, that it was no human message. It was not from any human being that I received it, and I was not taught it, but it came to me through a revelation of Jesus Christ" (Galatians 1:11-12). Paul has quite as much conviction as had the prophets of the Old Testament, that what he was dispensing was the very word of God itself, now fulfilled in Jesus.

What is finally most remarkable is that Paul claims to know, not only the revelation from Jesus Christ, but its implications in terms of the Church's sacramental discipline; that is, allowing Gentile Christians to be initiated in the Church without Jewish circumcision. This appears to be an ongoing and developmental exercise of infallibility. This implication we will examine further in answer to a later Hard Question.

18: Is not the Catholic Church's claim to infallibility in fact a blank check to make every Christian believe whatever is proposed for faith by the* magisterium*, and a denial of legitimate freedom of dissent in the Church?

One fact is clear from the history of the Church: that there never has been a "liberal church," at least before the eighteenth century of the Christian era. In no era before the Enlightenment is there evidence that any church, Catholic, Orthodox, or Protestant, allowed any dissent from what was considered by that Christian body to be the faith of the Church. In this sense, the Christian Church has always denied any freedom of dissent to what has been considered to be revelation by that Church. Freedom of dissent to official doctrine has entered into Christian and Jewish denominations since the eighteenth century precisely because the Enlightenment critics insisted that all doctrines be submitted to the bar of reason. Enlightenment philosophy insisted that we could not be absolutely certain of a given revelation by supernatural means, by the Holy Spirit. The only certainty that we could gain would be by rational thought. But Vatican I insisted that the certainty of faith was not through intrinsic reasoning, but through the Holy Spirit within the individual believer:

> This faith, which is the beginning of human salvation, the catholic church professes to be a supernatural virtue, by means of which, by the grace of God inspiring and assisting us, we believe to

> be true what he has revealed, not because we perceive its intrinsic truth by the natural light of reason, but because of the authority of God himself, who makes the revelation and can neither deceive nor be deceived. *Faith,* declares the Apostle, *is the assurance of things hoped for, the conviction of things not seen.* (Hebrews 11:1)[12]

If therefore we follow Vatican I's view of revelation, that it is a supernatural gift, then we have only two alternatives. Either the individual believer is left with his or her own gift of the Holy Spirit, and we all believe what the Holy Spirit is saying to us individually (the extreme Protestant solution, with thousands of different denominations). Or we believe that Jesus Christ has left the Church with his Spirit, the Spirit of Truth, and the Church proposes to us infallibly what that revelation is. Through the assistance of the Holy Spirit, we then make the act of faith on the authority of God himself who reveals.

We have already seen Paul proposing to his Galatian fellow-Christians what they were to believe. For Paul, the individual is not able to make that judgment himself or herself, but only from one, Paul himself, who is a genuine apostle of Christ, who has received Christ's revelation. Our very act of faith becomes therefore an act of *communion,* of *koinonia.* In believing in Christ's revelation, we unite ourselves with the community of faith, united in its infallible certainty of the truth of that revelation, namely the community of the apostolic faith. Why this is so goes back to our link between revelation and infallibility; that if a revelation is to be preserved that goes beyond reason, that revelation can only be preserved and developed within the Church by means of an infallible teaching authority. We saw in the question above how Paul was totally convinced that he was the recipient of a revelation, which gave him the authority to decide within the early Church how it should behave regarding the initiation of believers. The Catholic position is simply that the mode of revelation which applied to the first days of the Church (that of an infallible authority, conscious of the Spirit preventing error) was continued after the death of the first apostles to their successors. As then, so now . . .

A simple hypothesis may be presented here. Everyone would agree that *if* we were sure that a given proposition X is the truth of God, we would not be able to dissent from it. We could only dissent from it if we were at least a little unsure as to its truth. The Catholic position is that we *can* be totally sure, through the Spirit given to the Church. We can be just as sure as Paul was in writing to the Galatians. In such an instance, there is no room for dissent within the Church, at least regarding dogmas of faith, because the Church testifies, through the Spirit of Truth, to the infallible truth of revelation.

The impossibility of dissent from what the infallible Church proposes as a revelation from God is linked with the statement of the Creed, which reads: "I believe one, holy, catholic, and apostolic Church." Much has been made of the fact that the Creed states: "We believe *in* God," but "We believe [without *in*] one, holy, catholic, and apostolic Church." I am still not quite sure what we are to make of that distinction. But what is clear is that, even if the Church itself is not an object of faith, as is God, Jesus Christ, and the Holy Spirit, it still remains that our faith is related to the Church. We believe that the Holy Spirit will preserve the Church from error in its defined and ordinary teaching. This faith is exercised despite the defects of the members of the Church; and that is precisely where the act of faith comes into the picture.

19: Is not the definition of the infallibility of the Pope at the First Vatican Council (1870) a source of continual embarrassment to the Catholic Church as we enter the twenty-first century?

The definition of the infallibility of the Pope was most certainly a controversial issue, both among Catholics and among non-Catholics at the time when it was defined in 1870. But two points must be made clear here. First, the infallibility of the *Church* was not an issue at that time. Newman himself had become a Catholic twenty-five years previously because he saw the need for an infallible Church. Second, the vast majority of Catholic theologians actually supported the infallibility of the Pope, at least as a commonly held theological opinion. The opposition to the definition of the infallibility of the Pope at the First Vatican Council was not concerned with whether or not it was a true doctrine, but whether or not the definition itself was opportune or inopportune.[13]

The Church teaches that it cannot err when it defines matters of faith or morals. But that does not mean that the act of definition itself is at the right time. The act of definition may be imprudent at a particular time in history. The "left wing" on this issue at the First Vatican Council considered that if the doctrine of papal infallibility was defined, it would lead to all kinds of misunderstandings. In particular, there was concern as to whether the statesmen of Europe would believe that the papacy was renewing its claims for political power. There was also a fear that it would lead to a much more centralized bureaucracy in Rome. Finally, there was a sense that the definition of papal infallibility was unnecessary. Dogmas should be defined because of the danger of heresy. What heresy was being propounded that papal infallibility was intended to counteract?

The fears of the "inopportunists," as they were called, had some justification, as subsequent history proved. The leaders of European states were indeed put into a panic when they heard that it was likely that the Pope would be declared infallible, because they felt that he would insist upon his old claims to the papal states, when the movement was then toward a united Italy. The political unease felt by the European leaders concerning the papacy was not resolved until the formation of the Vatican State, a sovereign territory belonging to the Pope only a mile square, which guaranteed the Pope's political independence while removing from him all effective political power in the world. It is also true that the definition of papal infallibility massively increased the power of the centralized Roman Curia, and set the pattern for the following century. It led to the antimodernist witch-hunt at the turn of the nineteenth century directed by Pope Pius X, which removed from seminaries and Catholic universities any professors or teachers suspect of modernism, often without any possibility of them defending themselves against the whispering campaign.

Some would still argue today that the definition of infallibility at Vatican I was "inopportune." We can certainly argue that the politicking that took place in order for the definition to take place, led by the right-wing ultramontanist (the extreme papalist party) Cardinal Manning of Westminster was unsavory.[14] ("Ultramontanist," incidentally, means "beyond the mountains," i.e., beyond the Alps, a reference to those whose views favored power being exercised south of Germany, Austria, and Switzerland, namely by Rome.[15])

But, I would submit, there are grounds for arguing that, however clumsy the definition was from a political viewpoint, and how unbalanced an ecclesiology it presented at the time (remembering that the First Vatican Council did not finish its work on the theology of the Church, but was brought prematurely to an end by the Franco-Prussian war), yet there are still grounds for believing that the definition of the infallibility of the Pope at that time was providential, and a working of the Holy Spirit.

The first good effect of the definition was that it silenced those in the extreme right wing, who wanted much more than the Pope's infallibility in matters of doctrine. It is said that W. G. Ward, the extreme ultramontanist, wanted to have an infallible papal pronouncement each morning on his breakfast table together with his correspondence and a copy of *The Times*. But, as we see from the definition itself, it gives the Pope very limited powers:

> We teach and define as a divinely revealed dogma that when the Roman pontiff speaks *ex cathedra*, that is, when, in the exercise of his office as shepherd and teacher of all Christians, in virtue of his supreme apostolic authority, he defines a doctrine concerning faith or morals to be held by the whole church, he possesses, by the divine assistance promised to him in blessed Peter, that infallibility which the divine Redeemer willed his church to enjoy in defining doctrine concerning faith or morals.[16]

The points here to note are, first, that it is only when the Pope is acting in virtue of his supreme apostolic authority that he can issue an infallible definition. He cannot be infallible when acting outside of his apostolic authority as a private individual. That is why a Pope could be even heretical in his private opinions. Second, he can only be infallible when treating of a matter concerning "faith or morals to be held by the whole church." Thus even when a Pope uses his apostolic authority, he is only infallible when he actually defines a doctrine to be held by the whole Church, usually with anathemas against those who oppose the doctrine. In general, papal statements on moral matters, while being authoritative, are not exercises of the Pope's infallible office of teaching, even if they are authoritative and infallible statements of the ordinary *magisterium* of the Church.

The third and perhaps most important point to be made here is that the Pope, in using his office of teaching infallibly, "possesses . . . that infallibility which the divine Redeemer willed his church to enjoy in defining doctrine concerning faith or morals." The Pope only shares in the *infallibility of the Church* in defining matters of faith or morals. It is in this respect, I believe, that the definition of papal infallibility has performed an essential function in preserving the faith of the Church in our age.

It is common knowledge that the Pope has only used his power of personally making infallible statements of faith or morals in very rare instances; in two, in fact, when he defined the Immaculate Conception of Mary in 1854,[17] and in defining the Assumption of the Virgin Mary in 1950.[18] If this was the only significance of the definition by Vatican I of papal infallibility, then we might argue that there is precious little to discuss.

But, I would submit, the most important aspect of the definition of papal infallibility is its *underpinning of the infallible teaching authority of the whole Church.* The history of the early councils points time and time again to the interventions of successive popes to assure orthodox definitions in the general councils. Very often indeed, without the Pope, there would not have been such a definition of doctrines of revelation. The popes in these first centuries of the Church, for instance Leo the Great at the Council of Ephesus,[19] acting through his "legates," or representatives, were not personally using the charism of infallibility, but were protecting the infallible *magisterium* of the whole Church.

In our own age, particularly in the stormy times succeeding the Second Vatican Council, it is the doctrine of the primacy and infallibility of the Pope that has steadied the Church. Without the definition of papal infallibility in Vatican I, there would not have been the necessity of the richer and more expanded exposition of the infallibility of the Church in Vatican II's *Lumen Gentium,* paragraph 25:

> Although individual bishops do not enjoy the prerogative of infallibility, nevertheless, even though dispersed throughout the world, but maintaining the bond of communion among themselves and with the successor of Peter, when in teaching authentically matters concerning faith or morals they agree about a judgement that has to be definitively held, they infallibly proclaim the teaching of Christ. This takes place even more clearly when they are gathered together in an ecumenical council and are the teachers and judges of faith and morals for the whole church. Their definitions must be adhered to with the obedience of faith.[20]

The influence of Vatican I's definition of papal infallibility is evident in this paragraph from *Lumen Gentium.* The same conditions noted about papal infallible definitions are laid out here concerning judgments of the college of bishops that are "to be definitively held," which definitions must, like papal infallible definitions, "be adhered to with the obedience of faith." The role of the Pope in these definitions, particularly those of the general councils of the Church, is not to make these definitions himself, but to act as the principle of "maintaining the bond of communion among themselves and with the successor of Peter. . . ." This, surely, is a much more important role, and a much more commonly exercised role, than that of exercising his own personal charism of infallibility. In acting with the bishops, in defining matters of dogma collegially as in a general council, the Pope is "confirming his brethren," the apostolic college of bishops.

But now, let us put the question the other way around. Could the college of bishops effectively exercise their charism of infallibility without the unifying authority of the successor of Peter, the Bishop of Rome? The Orthodox bishops of the Eastern Churches, separated from Rome at least practically speaking from the tenth century onward, have never exercised such a collegial act of infallibility. They have never had a general council in the days since the Great Schism. Is the fact that they are separated from the Bishop of Rome, the Patriarch of the West, whose primacy of honor they recognize, of no relevance here?

It is a fact of human life that human authority needs a single leader, who at one and the same time unites and effects the group and its decisions. This is true even in modern democracies. Which country throughout the world has not a single leader, even if that leader must go through the agonizing process of election? In England, we might have a symbolic leader in the Queen; but, executively, we have a single Prime Minister, who enables the day-to-day decisions of our Parliament to be effected. Likewise in the USA, in a country which above all prides itself on having a government "by the people and for the people," still an enormous amount of authority is vested in the elected President, unquestionably America's single leader for his term of office, even if his authority is hedged around by Congress and the Constitution.

If the Church is to have an infallible authority, then that infallible authority to be effective must be exercised through an individual, who is for us the Bishop of Rome, the successor of Peter. That is why the infallibility of the Pope is closely allied to his primacy. Because the Pope is the "bishop of bishops," able to exercise the same authority over the college of bishops as the bishop exercises in his own diocese, then it follows that an aspect of such primacy is the charism of infallibility. The Pope possesses individually what the bishops possess (primacy and infallibility) as a group, or "college."

This is precisely where, in my opinion, traditional Anglo-Catholicism founders. The nineteenth-century Oxford Movement produced great theologians, who called the Church of England back to its Catholic roots. Those who, unlike Newman and Faber, did not become Roman Catholics, but stayed in the Church of England (such as Keble and Pusey), maintained strongly the infallibility of the Church as exercised through the college of bishops worldwide. However, the nineteenth- and early twentieth-century Anglo-Catholic saw no need for an infallible Pope, but rather saw the infallibility of the Church as exercised through the bishop. But how could such a position be maintained when the Anglo-Catholic bishops were in schism from a church, the Roman Catholic Church, which claimed infallibility? The Anglo-Catholic bishops, by refusing to join the Roman Catholic Church, implicitly rejected the infallibility of that church in its ongoing decisions, which the Catholic Church had made in the ecumenical councils since Nicaea (325). The Protestant could justify schism and rejection of these councils by the belief that the Catholic Church had actually fallen into heresy. But the Anglo-Catholic was denied this escape route, precisely because the Anglo-Catholic proclaimed the infallibility of the Church. How could an infallible Church fall into heresy? It was this fundamental *cul-de-sac* in the Anglo-Catholic position that led me more and more to consider the claims of Rome back in the 1950s when I was already considering Anglican ordination.

In response to this difficulty, many Anglo-Catholics take refuge in the "branch" theory; namely that a divided Christendom, split into Orthodox, Roman, and Anglican, cannot make collegial infallible decisions because the Great Church of the first six centuries is now divided. But this leads us into no better a position than that of the Protestant. Is a church able visibly to divide any better than a church unable to make infallible pronouncements concerning its doctrine?

Bishop B. C. Butler, in his last book, *The Church and Unity,* spoke of one visible Church that was indivisible in history as a mark of the Church throughout the centuries. Butler argues that the Church throughout the centuries has been conscious of this gift of visible indivisible unity. Those who separated from this Church were in "heresy" precisely because they had separated from the visible Church. Butler argues, "Thus for Jerome, both ecclesiastical communion and doctrinal orthodoxy depend on Rome."[21] For Butler, that even applied to the Eastern Orthodox Christians, who are not divided by any specific doctrine, but simply do not accept the authority of Rome.

The doctrine of infallibility is closely allied to the doctrine of visible indivisible unity; indeed one depends upon the other. If the Church is not infallible in its doctrine, it is unable to preserve that visible unity because at some time or another, one part of the body will secede from the other. Who is to say authoritatively that it should not, if the Church is itself not infallible? Thus visible unity is seen to depend upon infallibility, as a precondition of permanent communion within the Church, which depends for its life upon doctrines proposed for belief that go beyond the power of reason, and so need an infallible authority to back up its credentials.

This again links up closely with what we have said previously concerning the essential visible unity of the Church in the chapter on catholicity, that the Church of Christ "subsists" in the Catholic Church. Christ promised that "the gates of hell would not prevail" against his Church, that gift for Catholics being that his Church will never lose its visible unity, of the people of God united in full visible communion with Pope and bishops. An essential element of and means of this visible unity is now seen to be the gift of infallibility, which binds the Church together in its profession of the one faith.

This, naturally, takes us back to the issue of the historical credentials for both the primacy and the infallibility of the Pope. This talk of infallibility and visible indivisible unity may sound fine in theory. But what evidence is there in Scripture for the stupendous claims of Roman Catholics regarding the Pope, the Bishop of Rome?

20: Matthew 16:13-20 is cited by the Roman Catholic Church as the Scripture text where Jesus gave Peter primacy and infallibility. But scholars dispute that this is the meaning of the text. How then can Roman Catholics justify using it to promote papal claims?

The interpretation of Gospel texts, as of any Scripture text, is complex, and there are few certainties. In particular, regarding the historicity of the Gospels, which we have treated earlier, even more complex issues are involved. Most scholars consider that the Gospels were written some two or three generations after the events recorded in the life and ministry of Jesus. Even if we could demonstrate with complete certainty that

Matthew 16:13-20 refers to the primacy of Peter as we understand it, then the question would still be: "How far is such a statement that of faith of the primitive community, and how much goes back to the historical Jesus?" As we said earlier, the affirmation in *Dei Verbum* (no. 19) concerning the historicity of the Gospels has to be qualified by the affirmation of that same paragraph that the four Gospels have undergone synthesis, selection, and explication in the process of their formation.

Very recently, a group of biblical scholars of different Christian persuasions produced an ecumenical study of the Petrine ministry, entitled *Peter in the New Testament.* Without all agreeing on the primacy and infallibility of the Pope as contained in the New Testament, they referred to "the developing impression of Peter as it was projected into the continuing life of the Christian community."[22] This they called "the developing Petrine trajectory" in the early Church.

Raymond Brown, the distinguished Roman Catholic New Testament scholar, interprets this trajectory in a Catholic way, which in no way does violence to the New Testament evidence. In a recent book, *Responses to 101 Questions on the Bible,* he answers Q. 100: "The most important question is: Would Christians of New Testament times have looked on Peter as the pope?" Brown replies:

> Perhaps the proper way of phrasing an answerable question pertinent to the 60s is not, "Would the Christians of that period have looked on Peter as the pope?" but "Would Christians of that period have looked on Peter as having roles that would contribute in an essential way to the development of the role of the papacy in the subsequent church?" I think the answer is yes, as I tried to explain in response to a previous question where I pointed out the roles that Peter had in his lifetime, and the symbolisms attached to him even after his death. To my mind, they contributed enormously to seeing the Bishop of Rome, the bishop of the city where Peter died, and where Paul witnessed to the truth of Christ, as the successor of Peter in care for the church universal.[23]

This is the kind of answer to the question about the Matthean text that would be totally in line with modern biblical scholarship, and would at the same time be totally in line with Catholic theology about the papacy. Vatican II's *Dei Verbum* tells us that the "tradition which comes from the apostles progresses in the church under the assistance of the holy Spirit."[24] "The church's certainty about all that is revealed is not drawn from holy scripture alone."[25] The Church did not understand everything about Jesus during his lifetime, nor even immediately after the resurrection. Development was required with the assistance of the Holy Spirit. This is where again the infallibility of the Church in its growth in the understanding of the faith is relevant.

This development, as understood in Catholic theology, also continued after the apostolic period, when the New Testament books were already written. Catholic theology sees the history of belief in the role of the papacy rooted in the historical Jesus, but only being understood progressively, to be expressed explicitly in Vatican I and Vatican II, twenty centuries after the Day of Pentecost. We must say this initially, because only in this context today can we understand the dogmatic statements about the papacy in Vatican I:

> We teach and declare that, according to the gospel evidence, a primacy of jurisdiction over the whole church of God was immediately and directly promised to the blessed apostle Peter and conferred on him by Christ the Lord. It was to Simon alone, to whom he had already said, *You shall be called Cephas,* that the Lord, after his confession, *You are the Christ, the son of the living God,* spoke these words: *Blessed are you, Simon Bar-Jona. For flesh and blood has not revealed this to you, but my Father who is in heaven. And I tell you, you are Peter, and on this rock I will build my church, and the gates of the underworld shall not prevail against it. I will give you the keys of the kingdom of heaven, and whatever you bind on earth shall be bound in heaven, and whatever you loose on earth shall be loosed in heaven.*[26]

Today, we would view the phrase "according to the gospel evidence" (*iuxta evangelii testimonia*) in a different perspective as compared to the viewpoint of the Council Fathers of Vatican I, although such a development would be quite legitimate in Catholic theology. A modern Catholic scholar would see Matthew 16 as testifying to the developing belief among the Christians of the Matthean community of the role of Peter, which would continue after his death, of caring pastorally for the whole Church. Such statements in Matthew from Jesus about Peter would be seen as rooted in the historical Jesus and in the historical Peter, but their expression would be the result of a tradition growing during the two generations until the Gospel of Matthew was written some time in the 80s and 90s of the first century, just when the apostles were dying off and there was a need for continuing apostolic ministry in the Church.

I do think that the Petrine text in Matthew here testifies to Jesus' conviction during his lifetime that his own work would continue in the creation of a community later called "the Church." I do not therefore accept the extreme "eschatological" view of Wrede and Schweitzer[27] that Jesus did not in any way intend to found a church, but was awaiting the final kingdom of God when he went up to Jerusalem for his final journey on earth. I do not think that the New Testament evidence in any way demands this, but rather the opposite more positive viewpoint about Jesus and his own self-understanding.

There are reasonable grounds for accepting historically that Jesus foresaw that he would eventually be vindicated by God after his death[28] (he would read that in Psalm 22, which he quoted on the cross), and therefore that he would have to make provision for a community that was to succeed him. How long it would be before the final kingdom could have been speculation in the mind of Jesus; but again, there is no positive evidence in the New Testament that Jesus was sure that his death would immediately be succeeded by the final kingdom of God, thus rendering the existence of a community continuing his work unnecessary. All the New Testament evidence (if we dissect it with a critical knife rather than with a chopper) testifies that Jesus saw the need to make provision after his death. Particularly is this true regarding his institution of the Eucharist, a memorial until he should come again.

The new *Catechism*, while not speculating on questions as to how much secular knowledge was enjoyed by Jesus the Son of God while on earth (e.g., did he know all of Einstein's mathematics?), insists that Jesus did understand the purpose for which he had come to earth in the plan of salvation willed by God his Father: "By its union to the divine wisdom in the person of the Word incarnate, Christ enjoyed in his human knowledge the fullness of understanding of the eternal plans he had come to reveal" (CCC 474).

If Jesus therefore intended after his death for there to be a community to continue with his work, then it is again most reasonable that he would choose *one leader* to whom he entrusted that church.[29] This makes entire sense of the Matthean text, as the developed understanding of the Matthean community of the mind of the historical Jesus. Jesus responds to Peter's act of faith in him, with a *title*, as setting out the text in parallelism demonstrates:

Matthew 16:16	*Matthew 16:18*
Then Simon Peter spoke up and said, "You are the Christ, the Son of the living God."	Jesus replied, ". . . So I now say to you: You are Peter and on this rock I will build my community."

Since Cullmann, more and more scholars are prepared to admit that Jesus' words to Peter are the conferring of a title (parallel with Messiah, itself a title) rather than that Jesus is simply referring to the faith of Peter. Jesus wishes Peter to continue his work of leadership in the Church after his death. The title *christos* (Messiah) is parallel with *petros* (rock), another title, not a name. This interpretation is even more strongly confirmed if we compare Matthew 16:18-19 with Isaiah 22:22, the handing on of the authority of Shebna to the new-favored Eliakim as Master of the House:

Matthew 16:18-20	*Isaiah 22:20b-23*
So now I say to you: You are Peter, and on this rock I will build my community. And the gates of the underworld can never overpower it. I will give you the keys of the kingdom of heaven: whatever you bind on earth will be bound in heaven; whatever you loose on earth will be loosed in heaven.	I shall summon my servant Eliakim son of Hilkiah. I shall dress him in your tunic, I shall put your sash round his waist, I shall invest him with your authority; and he will be a father to the inhabitants of Jerusalem and to the House of Judah. I shall place the key of David's palace on his shoulder; when he opens, no one will close, when he closes, no one will open. I shall drive him like a nail into a firm place; and he will become a throne of glory for his family.

The parallel with the Old Testament text is clear. Peter is, like Eliakim, going to be a firm and reliable leader of the community. He will be given the keys, the symbol of office, to make the ultimate decisions of leadership. The difference is that, in Peter's case, the community over which he is set in charge will be the "kingdom of heaven," the eschatological community. This text from Isaiah could well have been part of the reflection of the Matthean community in considering the role of Peter in terms of the Old Testament.

Again, I would repeat, the argument from Scripture is not watertight, in keeping with all arguments from Scripture. Catholic theology always relies upon developing Tradition as well as upon the foundation texts of the Christian faith in the New Testament. But I think I have demonstrated in the answer to this Hard Question that there are good grounds for a developing Petrine ministry in the Christian Church of the first centuries; and the movement toward the developed statements of Vatican I and Vatican II, leading to the modern Catholic theology of the papacy, is a legitimate development under the guidance of the Holy Spirit in the Church.

21: Granted that Peter was the leader of the apostles during the first days of the Christian Church in Jerusalem, surely the New Testament shows us that other Christian leaders, for example James and Paul, had equal claim to "universal primacy" as Peter after the Gentile mission began?

Terms such as "universal primacy" are the result of later theological sophistication. Also, we have to admit the possibility that even if Peter did have a mandate from the Lord to be the leader of the post-Resurrection Christian community, this may not have been understood by the first Christians, even very clearly by Peter himself. The New Testament picture regarding leadership in the early Church is blurred. We would expect this, since that is still in the age of the apostles, before any clearly defined apostolic succession of ministry. That was not to come, as we shall see in a moment, until the end of the first century and the beginning of the second.

Moreover, the material in the Acts of the Apostles and particularly in Paul's letter to the Galatians is quite as difficult to interpret as are the Gospels, issues concerning which we discussed in the last question. Trying to reconcile the chronology of Acts 11 through 15 as compared with Paul's visits to Jerusalem in Galatians 1 and 2 is one of the most complex problems in New Testament scholarship.[30] This raises further questions as to who really was in charge at that time. Was it Paul? He certainly gives the impression that he is making all the decisions. Or was it James, who seemed to make the most important practical decisions at the Council of Jerusalem in Acts 15? Or is it Peter, who is clearly the leader of the Christians in those first days after Pentecost in Jerusalem?

Nevertheless, although the literary and historical questions concerning leadership in the infant Church are myriad, one negative conclusion is quite certain. There is nothing in the early literature that contradicts and is incompatible with Peter's universal primacy in the early Church, even if his primacy cannot be proven by those early New Testament texts. James might have made the final decisions at the Council of Jerusalem, perhaps as its president or chairman, and not Peter. But James was no more than the leader of that particular council. There is no evidence from that fact that James had universal primacy, or that if Peter had such primacy, this was contradicted by the role of James. The greatest likelihood seems to be that James was highly venerated as a Jerusalem elder, because of which veneration he was given the chairmanship of the council.[31]

Pope Paul VI in 1965 was not the president of the Second Vatican Council. That was one of the senior bishops. Nor were the decisions of the council the Pope's decisions, but the decisions of the council itself, even if the Pope had a considerable influence on the final documents of the council. Peter himself had a fair influence on the proceedings of the Council of Jerusalem in his day, according to Acts 15:7b-12, where he persuaded the council to accept Gentiles as well as Jews into the Church without circumcision. Universal primacy does not mean making all the decisions. It sometimes means allowing others to make those decisions, seeing the Spirit in others.

Similarly, regarding Paul, we have two instances where there appears to be a problem, but these instances do not constitute a serious problem where Petrine primacy is concerned. We could easily argue that Peter exercised his universal primacy in the case of Paul by recognizing the Spirit of the risen Christ in Paul, that Paul had had a genuine revelation.

First, some have seen a denial of Petrine primacy in Galatians 2:7, when Paul claims that his mission is to the "uncircumcised" (the Gentiles), while Peter was given a message to the Jews, as is clear from Acts 2, on the Day of Pentecost. But it is not necessarily at all the case that Peter and Paul were thus equal partners in universal rule of the early Church. It is quite possible to argue that Peter, by exercising his leadership role in the early Jerusalem days, was not necessarily demonstrating his universal primacy, only the opening mission of the infant Church to the Jews. But this argument works both ways. Paul, in exercising by divine revelation his Gentile mission, on this argument was also not demonstrating either his own universal primacy, nor any implicit contradiction of Peter's universal primacy. Peter could still have been universal primate while having a mission limited to the Jews, and Paul to the Gentiles.

Second, Paul's contradiction of Peter in Galatians 2:11-14 in no way demands necessarily a denial of universal primacy.[32] Paul argues that Peter has gone back from a previous decision, to "eat with gentiles." But universal primacy does not imply courageously keeping to the right decisions, or immunity from being rebuked for such prevarication. Did not St. Catherine of Siena in the fourteenth century rebuke Pope Gregory XI, pleading with him to return to Rome from the fleshpots of Avignon? And did not the Pope obey her, a laywoman?[33] One charism of primacy is precisely to recognize charismata in others, even to accept a rebuke by them.

It was necessary to discuss at least briefly some arguments in more detail, because serious objections to Peter's primacy have been raised on the basis of Acts 15 and Galatians 1-2 in particular. Still, we would have to recognize that Peter's primacy in the New Testament must be argued on more positive grounds than merely in answering the above objections. We would have to admit that there are certainly no *positive* arguments for Peter's universal primacy in the texts we have examined, only that there are no significant reasons to be found against it in those texts.

For positive reasons indicating, even demonstrating, universal primacy, we have already looked at Matthew 16, and found good evidence there in Jesus' words to Peter. Even better, possibly, is John 21:15-19, where Jesus asks Peter three times, "Simon, do you love me?" and to Peter's affirmation, Jesus says three times, "Feed my sheep." There is much more here, according to the scholars, than a simple reinstatement of Peter after his threefold denial of Jesus at his Master's trial (Matthew 26:69-75). Rather, according to the *New Jerusalem Bible*: "To the triple profession of love by Peter Jesus replies with a triple investiture. He entrusts to Peter the care of ruling the flock in his name, cf. Mt 16:18; Lk 22:31 seq. It is possible that this triple repetition indicates a contract made in due form, according to semitic custom. cf. Gn 23:3-20."[34]

We might perhaps expect the Catholic *New Jerusalem Bible* to manifest some Roman bias in its interpretative notes. What is even more remarkable is that such a radical Lutheran scholar as Rudolf Bultmann agrees with this judgment, stating regarding this text in his classic commentary on John that "the theme of the first conversation, vv. 15-17, is the entrusting of Peter with his task as leader of the community."[35] Bultmann's approach to form criticism, whereby he sees the community tradition influencing the transmission of a text, leads him to see the community here acknowledging Peter as leader in succession to the Lord over all Christians. By "leader of the community" we have a meaning not too far removed from "universal primacy," even if not made precise. For Bultmann, this would be even more significant in that this is acknowledged by the Christian community that produced the Fourth Gospel (called by some the "Johannine community"), which would naturally have had a bias toward its own "beloved disciple" John rather than toward Peter.

Even if we ignore historical questions as to how John 21:15-19 relates to the "historical Jesus," what is clear from this text is that a Christian group not biased toward Peter yet acknowledges his leadership over the whole Christian Church of that time, just at the end of the apostolic age. This is a very significant argument for the first beginnings of the doctrine of the primacy of Peter, which provides an excellent foundation for the development of the papacy in the following early centuries of the Christian era.

What is significant also is that this Johannine community looks back to these dispensations from Jesus making Peter the leader of the community as going back to the Lord himself after the resurrection. This Petrine leadership, for the Gospel of John, is part of the foundation of the Church, not its own creation.

22: The power of the papacy unquestionably developed during the first four centuries of the Christian era. But was not this development the result of political expediency and theological opportunism on the part of the popes, rather than being a movement of the Holy Spirit?

No one would question that the papacy developed during the first four centuries, as indeed after it. It is not even the main issue as to whether political expediency and theological opportunism were involved, as doubtless they usually are in some way or other in the history of the Church.

The real question is whether such development of the papacy was an innovation, or whether it was a true growth from within, of something already there in seed; or whether it was a new mutation, an alien growth within the body.

C. F. D. Moule, the distinguished Cambridge scholar, speaking of New Testament Christology, makes a useful distinction: "But, if in my analogy, 'evolution' means the genesis of successive new species by mutations and natural selection along the way, 'development,' by contrast, will mean something more like the growth, from immaturity to maturity, of a single specimen from within itself."[36] I submit that the development of the papacy is, in Moule's terminology, a case of development rather than of evolution.

This is why it has been so important to deal with the New Testament evidence in the previous two questions. We do not find there in any sense a developed theology of the papacy; but, as we have seen, there is enough in the New Testament, in Matthew 16 and in John 21, to provide for us the seed from which legitimately would spring the full-grown doctrine of the papacy.

What drove the power of the papacy onward in the early centuries was not first and foremost politics, even if the favored place of the city of Rome no doubt helped the process, but above all the unity of the apostolic faith and practice. In a growing worldwide Church, with the apostles dead, it became a major concern even before Christianity was legalized to preserve the true tradition of the apostles. In this context, Christians more and more looked to the See of Rome, the place where both Peter and Paul were martyred.

Irenaeus of Lyons (130-200) gives us a famous early testimony to the importance of Rome. Irenaeus is asking, "How can we find out the true apostolic doctrine?" He answers:

> Rome is, on account of its civil greatness, a place to which every Christian must resort: that is to say, every Church does not come thither officially, but Christians cannot help coming to the city from Churches in every part of the world. We have no need, then, to examine the apostolic tradition of these Churches in their respective lands. We can learn it from their members to be found in Rome, who, being in communion with the Roman Church, must agree with it in doctrine; and thus the apostolic tradition preserved

in the capital has been preserved not by native Romans only, but by the faithful collected in the city from every part of the world.[37]

Butler notes the fact that, read casually, the above paragraph only seems to present Rome as a kind of clearinghouse for international Christianity, without special authority given to it. But Butler says that this is to neglect what Irenaeus has already said in the previous sentence:

> Since it is a lengthy matter, in a book like this of mine, to recount the [episcopal] successions of all the Churches, it is by pointing out, in the case of the very great and very ancient Church, known to all and founded and established at Rome by the two very glorious Apostles Peter and Paul, [by pointing out, I say] the tradition it has from the Apostles, and its faith proclaimed to men, coming down to us by successions of bishops, that we confound all those who . . . gather [for worship] otherwise than they ought.[38]

We are a long way from a developed doctrine of the papacy. But, as Harnack, the Liberal Protestant historian, noted, "the Roman church *had* to be named, since already its *votum* was the most respected and impressive in Christendom . . . the Roman church at that time counted as the special conserver of tradition and hence the churches naturally and *de facto* showed their orthodoxy in their agreement with this church."[39]

No doubt Rome's position at the center of an albeit already fading Empire was an advantage in its development. No doubt the prestige of both Peter and Paul as its founders also helped. But the central argument throughout is that Rome is safe where doctrine is concerned, because it most securely holds the succession of doctrine from the apostles. This was what focused Christian attention more and more upon Rome, and not its political position first and foremost.

As time went on, the need for such a firm anchor grew, particularly after the Edict of Milan in 313 made Christianity a legal religion. Now it was a social advantage to be a Christian, and more and more problems focused within the newly acceptable and politically powerful Church rather than pressures from outside of its membership. The Pope began to intervene more and more because of the necessity of providing a single doctrine throughout East and West, against the Christological heresies. No doubt also power was involved, and not always the best kind of its exercise. But more and more the Petrine text of Matthew was invoked in support of papal claims. The Pope was the successor of Peter who would provide the safe haven of doctrine, as the florid and somewhat cringing St. Jerome says, toward the end of the fourth century, in his address to the Pope of his day concerning heresies in his own adopted Antioch:

> Making none my leader save Christ I am united in communion to your Beatitude, that is to the see of Peter: on that rock I know the Church to have been built. He who eats the Paschal Lamb outside this abode is profane [sc. (i.e., namely) outside the shrine of true religion]. If a man is not in Noe's ark he will be submerged by the flood. . . . I beg you decide the matter, and I will without fear confess that there are three hypostases [sc. in the Godhead].[40]

From Jerome's time onward less and less emphasis was placed upon Paul's martyrdom in Rome; but again for the necessary reason that the Petrine ministry of the rock holding firm doctrine worldwide became more and more vital, rather than Paul's missionary spirit.

More and more also, this Petrine authority was being invoked against bishops of the East, not only within the Western patriarchate of the Pope. The most notable example, and perhaps the clearest example of a developed theology of the papacy, is contained in the condemnation of Dioscorus, Bishop of Alexandria, itself an apostolic see, by the Pope's legate at the Council of Chalcedon (451) named Paschasinus:

> The very holy and blessed Archbishop of the great and ancient Rome Leo, by us and by this very holy Council, along with the thrice blessed and glorious Apostle Peter, who is the rock and foundation of the Catholic Church, the foundation of the orthodox faith, has deprived [Dioscorus] of the episcopal dignity and of every episcopal function. Let the very holy and great Council pronounce in regard to the said Dioscorus what is conformable with the canons.[41]

By the fifth century, therefore, we have arrived at what is a richly developing doctrine of the worldwide primacy of the Bishop of Rome, in full exercise of its authority. Could we imagine that this authority could have been exercised as far away as in the Eastern Churches, often among hostile bishops and theologians, unless there was a real belief among

Christians of the time that the Bishop of Rome was the successor of Peter, and therefore did have a worldwide authority?

Of all the doctrines that were questioned, particularly doctrines concerning Christ as God become man, and concerning grace and predestination, no one seems to question the authority of the Pope to exercise his powers well outside of his own immediate episcopal area. I would submit that this was never challenged because the doctrine of universal primacy was accepted by Christians worldwide, even if it took time for such a belief to find its fuller expression.

23: Has not the papacy a poor historical record in terms of its tendency to political corruption, power struggles, and displays of arrogant power? Was not this in itself adequate reason for the Protestant Reformation?

To list all the corruptions, scandals, and self-seeking among those who have held the office of Pope down the centuries would fill many copies of a tabloid newspaper, and would sell millions of copies even without the pictures. A few years ago, the naughty doings of the Borgia popes provided good soap-opera entertainment on television, and, it is said, increased significantly the number of inquiries concerning the Catholic religion at the Catholic Enquiry Centre, London. Even the thought that religious leaders can manifest human weakness and sin can at least make people realize that such pillars of the Church are human.

But we would freely admit that such scandals during the late Middle Ages did cause the papacy to be seen in Europe as an institution ripe for reform. The "bad Popes"[42] in the centuries prior to the Reformation must have damaged its credibility. But such was not in any way adequate reason for the Protestant Reformation, anymore than a corrupt police chief means that there should be no more police chiefs. No doubt, the Reformation could be seen as tardy judgment upon an institution that refused to reform itself. The Lutheran Reformation, which tore Europe into schism, came in the end like a thief in the night, even though the papacy should have been prepared, but had become too self-assured:

> There was no particular reason why he (the Pope) should be worried about Luther. Over the past two centuries there had been an endless succession of misanthropes who objected to this or that aspect of papal power and the corruption that inescapably went with it.

> Dante, Huss, Petrarch, St. Catherine of Siena, Arnold of Brescia, Jerome of Prague, St. Bridget of Sweden — each generation brought its vociferous critics. Some had been burned, some canonized; none, it seemed, had had the slightest effect in diverting or slowing the momentum of the papacy.[43]

The papacy needed reform in the sixteenth century, and was reformed, together with all the institutions of the Roman Catholic Church, at the Council of Trent. The Church cleaned up its act from top to bottom, and did it so effectively that such scandals decreased more and more so as virtually to disappear from history.

However, it is easy to acquire a one-sided view of history, and particularly of the history of the papacy, especially during the Middle Ages. This is above all easy for an Anglo-Saxon, who has had four centuries of propaganda seeing the papacy as a corrupt foreign power. There is also a great deal of pure ignorance about the Middle Ages, even among the theologically literate. English theological history tends to end with the late Christological councils in the sixth and seventh centuries, and begin again at the Reformation in the sixteenth century. Thus a thousand years is written off as "The Dark Ages," and the popes as the political/religious rulers of a corrupt and backward Europe.

Like all half-truths, that is partly true. The Roman Empire did decline and fall, and there was a real danger in the last centuries of the first millennium that a Batman Gotham City anarchical situation would develop, with ravaging barbarians raping and pillaging at will. In this situation, popes such as Gregory the Great became of necessity political as well as religious rulers. Their very title *Pontifex Maximus* ("Supreme Pontiff")[44] was taken over from the Roman chief priest. They succeeded in taming the barbarians, and literally saving European civilization, by converting the barbarian tribes to Christianity. The monks, following the Rule of St. Benedict, provided cultural and economic centers all over Europe.

In the eighth and ninth centuries the popes encouraged the setting up of the "Holy Roman Empire" by anointing the rulers of Europe, and eventually Charles the Great (Charlemagne) became the sole Emperor.[45] Thus was initiated a centuries-long power struggle between Pope and Emperor, which was not as simple as a division between religious and secular authority. The Pope had large areas for which he was politically responsible. The Emperor saw himself as by no means only a secular ruler, but as the ruler of the "Christian Kingdom" of Europe, controlling the appointment of bishops and setting up monasteries and colleges of learning. The Pope saw the danger of losing his spiritual authority as the Emperor tried to acquire more and more Church business; while the Emperor saw the Pope as so often thwarting his own, the Emperor's, political ambitions.

In such clashes of power, successive popes needed to be worldly wise to survive. Inevitably, realizing the political nature of the task and its supreme prestige, some came to accept the papacy only because of its political power. Nevertheless, it is quite unjust to tar all the popes in the Middle Ages with the same dirty brush. Reading the superb *The Oxford Dictionary of the Popes* by the Anglican scholar J. N. D. Kelly[46] will quickly begin to put the record straight. Not only were there many saints and scholars among the popes at the end of the first millennium and during the first half of the second, but there were solid and innovative policies and achievements throughout the Church during that time, all promoted by the popes. Particularly, the popes all encouraged the setting up of the universities throughout Europe, during the heyday of the scholastic era from the eleventh to the fourteenth centuries. It could be argued that the scientific age began at this time rather than with the Renaissance.

Regarding "displays of arrogant power," the riches of the papacy did increase during this time; so much so that the story goes of a Pope sitting counting his money, while a simple monk came to see him. The Pope said, "Peter can no longer say, 'Silver and gold have I none,' " quoting the words of the Apostle Peter when asked by a beggar for alms at the Beautiful Gate of the Jerusalem temple. "But," replied the monk, referring to Peter's miracle on that occasion, "can Peter still say, 'In the name of Jesus Christ the Nazarene, *walk*!' (Acts 3:6)?"

But power displays were not always arrogant. Throughout Europe, the Pope was seen as the successor of Peter, not just as a distant ruler. That applied to England as to anywhere else in Europe. Unless this veneration for the papacy as the Apostolic See is realized, the power of the papacy in the Middle Ages cannot be understood. The Pope could exercise power, because he was the successor of the big fisherman Peter. In exercising such power, he was not being arrogant, but representing his predecessor, the Lord's disciple. That power could have been, and was, occasionally abused; but nothing could obscure the fact that the source of such power was seen in Jesus' mandate to Peter, and in nothing less. Not until the source of such power was rejected, and the authority of the successor of Peter itself challenged by the Reformation, was it really under threat, however corrupt it might have become.

24: Although the papacy in modern times has a better record in terms of moral example and of leadership qualities than during the Middle Ages, has the papacy not been rather a force for repression of new ideas in recent centuries?

It is relatively easy to provide a substantial list of what may be considered to be erroneous decisions and failures of policy by popes since the Reformation.[47] Everyone freely admits that the popes themselves have been free from the corruption of some of the medieval popes. But, in general, many consider that the popes of the past four hundred years have lacked the ability to be aware of modern developments, and too often have simply reacted by condemning new ideas rather than trying to understand them. It is not unfair to admit that that has sometimes, although not always, been true. We do not have to defend the policy decisions of the popes, anymore than we have necessarily to defend their personal morals if they are indefensible. The infallibility of the Pope in no way means that he will make the right decisions in the day-to-day governance of the Church, or that he will be an effective pastor for the universal body of Christ.

The condemnation of Galileo (which of course was not an infallible statement of faith or morals, but a fallible judgment on a particular scientific theory) was clearly wrong, and has been reversed by a recent Pope, specifically John Paul II. Another disastrous policy failure was the prohibition of Chinese rites in the eighteenth century. The Pope took the side of the missionaries who wished to retain the Latin Mass, and decided against the Jesuit missionaries, who wished to adapt the Catholic faith and liturgy to local culture and philosophy. Perhaps the conversion of China to Christianity was thereby irreparably set back.[48]

The papacy, as Edwards claims, has also had a bad record on tolerance. There was a general opinion that "evil has no rights," and therefore that a person who did not accept the Catholic faith was not free to propound his or her opinions in a society dominated by Catholicism (although we would hasten to add that Anglican and Protestant denominations have often been no better in the exercise of religious toleration).

The Decree on Religious Liberty, *Dignitatis Humanae*, of the Second Vatican Council was one of its most important documents:

> This Vatican synod declares that the human person has a right to religious freedom. Such freedom consists in this, that all should have immunity from coercion by individuals, or by groups, or by any human power, that no one should be forced to act against his conscience, whether in private or in public, whether alone or in association with others, within due limits.[49]

It is said that it was this decree which, more than the question of the Latin Mass, led the extreme right wing to condemn the Second Vatican Council, and to break away to form its own ultraorthodox movement within the Church. It was a far-reaching document, preparing the Church to live in a much more pluralistic society even than was already beginning to exist in the eighteenth and nineteenth centuries.

There is no point in a Catholic attempting to justify the erroneous policies of the past, where the exercise of the infallible *magisterium* was not involved. We simply have to change them. On the other hand, while we need to be honest about the failures of the past, we must also understand them, and also the positive achievements of our forebears. I am thinking in particular of the *Syllabus of Errors* of Pope Pius IX. Edwards quotes what seems to be an appallingly reactionary statement in that syllabus, to the effect that it was an error to think that "the Roman pontiff can, and ought to, reconcile himself to, and come to terms with, progress, liberalism, and modern civilisation."[50]

Taken in the context of today's understanding, one hundred fifty years later, such a statement looks impossibly reactionary. But we must understand that, at that time, liberalism was underpinned (as it sometimes is today) with a totally secular philosophy, as with the architects of the French Revolution. For the extreme liberal, God, if he existed at all, was a life force within a world process. The supernatural intervention of such a God was a medieval superstition. The people were free to make their own decisions about morality, religion, and everything else, because there was no revelation from God, and the human person was left to free rational decision. Faced with such apparently hostile forces, Pope Pius IX's reaction at least was understandable. Perhaps a leader of insight, even of genius, might have been able at that time to separate the wheat from the chaff in the new liberalism. Great thinkers in the Church such as Rosmini, Möhler, and Newman were able to see the good in the new movements. But even Newman's conversion to Catholicism was the end result of a long process of thinking on his part that began with a fundamental rejection of the liberal principle, contrary as it was as Newman saw it to the "dogmatic principle" accepting God's revelation with the full assent of faith.

Popes are often faced by such complex forces, and have to provide immediate solutions that effect a policy within the Church quickly and effectively; not legislating generally for geniuses or saints, but for the broad mass of people. Popes are also placed in agonies of decision, as was Pius XII regarding the condemnation of Hitler's mass extermination of the Jews. There was a genuine fear on the Pope's part that Hitler would only unleash further horrors on both Jews and Catholics if he condemned what was happening at Auschwitz and Buchenwald concentration camps. The Pope might have been wrong in his decision; but the sincerity of his decision must be acknowledged.

25: Does not the new* Catechism, *in limiting the idea of* magisterium, *or teaching authority, to the bishops in union with the Pope, present an unbalanced view of* magisterium, *which originally referred to theologians and teachers also?

I have already referred (under Questions 7 and 12) to Robert Murray's article in the Catechism Commentary. Murray criticizes the approach of the new *Catechism* to *magisterium* thus:

> The present writer believes firmly that the Catholic bishops in communion with the Pope have inherited apostolic authority and exercise this in teaching and interpretation. But historically they have done this, both in conciliar acts and in "ordinary" practice, with the help of theologians and relying on the whole structure of teaching in the Church. This is what *magisterium* has meant through most of the Church's history, a shared ministry; and the *singularis conspiratio,* the "unique harmony" in the Church, has shone out best when this understanding of the relationship has flourished.[51]

Historically, this may well be a fair criticism. It could be argued that "teaching authority" is a shared ministry, and that in the past century the

Roman Catholic Church has become too preoccupied with the final interpretative authority in the Church, located in the bishops in communion with the Bishop of Rome. This imbalance toward the teaching authority of Pope and bishops, Murray argues, is very much evident in the *Catechism of the Catholic Church.*

However, it needs to be reiterated particularly in this chapter, as the *Catechism of the Catholic Church* also felt necessary to reiterate, that Catholic faith locates the *infallible teaching authority* solely in the bishops in union with the Pope. As Francis Sullivan states:

> The [Second Vatican] council did not intend to deny that theologians and exegetes can interpret the word of God with such authority as their learning confers on them. What it asserts is that only the pastors of the church have inherited the mandate Christ gave to the apostles to teach in his name with such authority that he who hears them hears Christ, and he who rejects them rejects Christ and him who sent him (see Luke 10:16).[52]

The response of faith is always required from the faithful when, as Sullivan describes it, "The Extraordinary, Infallible Exercise of Magisterium" is in question. "Here we are speaking of the *solemn judgments* by which an ecumenical council or a pope defines a doctrine."[53]

This is made clear in the Dogmatic Constitution on the Church of the Second Vatican Council. After first reiterating Vatican I's teaching on the infallibility of the Pope, which as Vatican II says is exercised when he "is not delivering a judgment as a private person, but as the supreme teacher of the universal church in whom the church's own charism of infallibility individually exists,"[54] the Council then turns its attention to the infallible ministry of the college of bishops: "The infallibility promised to the church exists also in the body of bishops when, along with the successor of Peter, it exercises the supreme teaching office. The assent of the church, however, can never fail to be given to these definitions on account of the activity of the same holy Spirit, by which the whole flock of Christ is preserved in the unity of faith and makes progress."[55]

Theologians, experts of various kinds, and those exercising their teaching skills have a vital role within the Church, sometimes more important than popes or bishops. After all, who remembers the name of the Pope in Thomas Aquinas's day? I would have to look it up in J. N. D.

Kelly's *History of the Popes* to find out who were the popes in the thirteenth century, when the great Angelic Doctor was lecturing in the universities of Europe. We remember the name of that great theologian and teacher, St. Thomas Aquinas, much more than the name of the Pope, or indeed of any of the bishops of his day. In that sense, Thomas Aquinas's *magisterium* has been much more effective than the Pope and the bishops, in the works of theological genius that he produced, above all in the *Summa Theologiae,* which could almost be called the theology textbook of Europe.

But this is precisely where the *charism of infallibility* makes its contribution to the life of the Church. However much an expert theologian Aquinas was, however much the Spirit was in him contributing prestigiously to the teaching Church, he did not possess the charism of infallibility because he was not a bishop. If he went to a general council, he would no doubt be a vital *peritus* to the bishops. But their infallible doctrinal decrees would be theirs, the bishops in union with the Pope, and not his; because, at the end of the day (and the infallible *magisterium* is intended very much to be "at the end of the day," namely when the whole Church, especially theologians and teachers, have had their say) the Church is governed not by experts, however brilliant, but by those chosen and sacramentally ordained to preserve the apostolic tradition.

At that point, when the infallible teaching office of the college of bishops in union with the Pope makes its infallible judgments concerning matters of faith and morals, the theologian becomes *qua* theologian a member of the "simple faithful," bound to the definitions of faith proposed by the infallible teaching office; as the bishops, and indeed the Pope himself, also do, since they must make their affirmation of faith to those definitions proposed just as much as they have proposed them. Particularly in the early councils of the Church, there were problems with bishops who did not accept the doctrinal definitions of the whole body of bishops. In being required to make such an assent of faith, the bishops are no different from anyone else in the Church.

This reflects the very structure of the Church from the beginning. In the Old Testament, the word of God came to prophets, and they spoke that word authoritatively. They did not wait for democratic decisions. They knew what God was saying to his people, and they said it with or without the consent of the community as God's truth. When the Church was founded, a group of apostles (and this is clearly evidenced from the

New Testament itself) were given by Christ what we might call a *permanent prophetic word.* This word was entrusted to certain chosen apostles who themselves spoke with the authority of Christ through the power of the Spirit in them who gave them that particular charism.

Vatican II puts this unambiguously:

> Just as the office that was given individually by the Lord to Peter, the first of the apostles, is permanent and meant to be handed on to his successors, so the office of the apostles of nourishing the church is a permanent one that is to be carried out without interruption by the sacred order of bishops. Therefore the synod teaches that by divine institution the bishops have succeeded to the place of the apostles as shepherds of the church; and the one who hears them hears Christ but whoever rejects them rejects Christ and him who sent Christ (see Lk 10, 16).[56]

This leads us deeper into the question as to the historical origins of apostolic authority in the Church, represented as it is in Catholic theology by the college of bishops as successors of the apostles acting in union with the Bishop of Rome, the successor of Peter, proposing doctrine infallibly to be accepted by all Christians with the assent of faith.

26: It is clear from historical studies that there is no evidence of the universal practice of "monarchical episcopacy" (i.e., one bishop over each local church) before the middle of the second century. How, then, can the Roman Catholic Church claim that the bishops are, as a college, the successors of the apostles?

For the answer to this Hard Question, I am very much indebted to Raymond Brown's *Responses to 101 Questions on the Bible,* QQ. 89-92, which I think summarizes the evidence and its theological implications most adequately.

Brown argues that we cannot transpose ideas of a later developed Church into the earliest history of the Christian movement immediately after the resurrection and up to the end of the first century A.D. To begin with, the early Christians did not consider themselves a separate church from Israel, but a movement or community *within* Israel. This meant that the Twelve specially chosen by Jesus acted in a symbolic role as the embodiment of the renewed Israel. But they did not necessarily act as administrators or leaders at this early stage (although, as we saw, Peter did).[57]

The administration of the earliest churches is a very complex question. At this point, in any case, there was no question of bishops ruling as "successors of the apostles" because the apostles were still very much still alive. It seems that churches followed local traditions. Some have argued that there was a fundamental difference in the community structures of churches mainly of Jewish Christians (e.g., in Jerusalem and Antioch) and churches consisting mainly of Gentile converts (e.g., Corinth).

With the advent of St. Paul, the concept of "apostle" broadened from being simply one of the Twelve.[58] Paul never saw the historical Jesus during his life on earth, but claimed to be a genuine apostle equal with the Twelve because of his seeing the risen Christ. Perhaps there were others unnamed in the New Testament who had a similar role to Paul, specially anointed by the Holy Spirit to found churches and to proclaim the Gospel. This we do not know, except that Paul does mention "apostles" as one of the charismatic gifts of the Spirit. It may well be that originally the New Testament "apostle" was either one of the Twelve, or one of the "church founding" order, specially anointed by the Holy Spirit for the task.

How then, as this complex situation developed, can we say that later bishops were "successors of the apostles"? Brown explains thus:

> Someone had to take over the pastoral care of the communities brought into being by the apostolic mission. As I indicated, by the last third of the century and perhaps even slightly earlier, we find the name "bishops" for those who played a role of leadership in some communities. In the earlier stage there were plural bishops or overseers in an individual community; in the later stage there was the custom of having only one bishop per community. Therefore, one may very correctly say that bishops took over the pastoral care of communities founded by the apostolic evangelization and thus were the successors of the apostles.[59]

What lies behind Brown's flexible view of the early development of episcopacy is the acknowledgment that matters *could* have been different. Monarchical episcopacy became the norm in some areas at least by the time of Ignatius of Antioch, that is, by the end of the first century and the beginning of the second. How and why this became the norm, we cannot be sure. We can only be sure that it *did* so become.

But how does this view differ from the view among some Christian churches that the origin of ministry was determined, not by sacramental ordination from Christ, but by human decision among the churches? How does Brown's view square with the Catholic belief that Christ himself founded the sacrament of orders? If he did found the order of monarchical episcopacy as successors of the apostles, then why did this not become more obvious earlier in the history of the primitive Church?

Brown answers this question by taking up and expounding a theological opinion among Catholic scholars such as Rahner. Rahner considered that Christ founded the sacrament of *order*, but that it was later Church development that divided this order into bishop, priest, and deacon.[60] Christ's act of foundation was not necessarily explicit, but a charism permanently left to the Church by virtue of its constitution, in which the Spirit was left free post-Resurrection to develop more specific discipline. As Brown says again: "The doctrine of the Roman Catholic Church and of other churches that have a 'high' estimation of ordination involves tracing to Christ the sanctifying pastoral power exercised in the episcopate, presbyterate, and diaconate, but not all the aspects of the discipline that developed."[61]

My own suggestion is that the pattern of ministry was eventually decided most likely by the close of the first century, by analogy with the orders that developed in the Old Testament. These were the High Priest (*cohen harosh*, 2 Chronicles 24:11), Priests (*haccohen*, Leviticus 1:13), and Levites (*hallewiyyim*, 2 Chronicles 8:14, assigned "to their tasks of praise and of assisting the priests in accordance with day-to-day requirements"). These three Old Testament orders corresponded to the bishop, priests, and deacons of the Church respectively. Many, even within the Catholic theological community, have argued that, with the New Testament, there came an end of the cult of the Old Testament with its cultic orders. But the new *Catechism* argues that, on the contrary, the orders of the New Testament are a fulfillment of the orders of the Old Testament: "The liturgy of the Church, however, sees in the priesthood of Aaron and the service of the Levites, as in the institution of the seventy elders, a prefiguring of the ordained ministry of the New Covenant" (CCC 1541).

This view is most consistent with the New Testament evidence, in which 2 Peter 2:9 argues that Christians are "a kingdom of priests." But this in no way argues for the exclusive "priesthood of all believers." On the contrary, 2 Peter 2:9 contains a direct quotation from Exodus 19:5-6. The Old Testament people of God were indeed also a "kingdom of priests"; but this did not exclude that same Old Testament community from having divinely appointed ordained ministers acting with authority in that community.

Thus the Christians of the late first and early second centuries took the model of Old Testament orders, under the influence of the Holy Spirit. Their choice of orders was not arbitrary, but a true understanding of the New Testament as the fulfillment of the Old Law (cf. Matthew 5:17); and this was the will of Christ, his "institution" as forming a New Israel, whether that will of his was expressed verbally by him during his life on earth, or not.

We ought to add that, in Catholic theology, it is the Spirit who guided the early Church in these specific matters of discipline. The Church does not see itself as able to change matters determined in this early development regarding what is called the "matter and form" of the sacrament, the "matter" being the old scholastic word for the "sign" element of the sacrament (bread and wine for the Eucharist, water for baptism, a human male for the priesthood); and the "form" being the form of words used in conferring the sacrament: "I baptize you in the name of the Father and of the Son, and of the Holy Spirit. . . ." These elements are seen as the "foundation" from Christ which the Spirit has guided the Church to make essential in the structure of the sacraments. Naturally, there has always been a lively debate within Catholic theology as to how much actually is changeable regarding each sacrament. There has been a debate as to whether alcohol-free wine may be used for the Eucharist; and, most famously of all, recently the debate concerning the ordination of women to the priesthood has hit the media. We will discuss this question later.

With all the sacraments there will be gray areas, as to how much is clearly of apostolic origin, and how much is changeable. What is clear regarding the monarchical episcopacy is that the Church has established a single bishop over each local church, that single bishop (even if he might have auxiliaries) symbolizing the unity of the Church; and that that bishop represents the apostles, that is, he shares in the charism of apostolic leadership to preach the word, to guide and govern the Church under his episcopacy, and to share in the charism of infallibility given to the college of bishops together in union with the "bishop of bishops," the Bishop of Rome. But how necessary is this charism of infallibility?

27: Are the Anglican formulations, and indeed more recently the writings of Hans Küng, not more correct in stating that general councils of the Church can and have erred, and that a better word for the Church's consistency of proclamation of the Gospel is "indefectibility" rather than "infallibility"?

This, for me, is perhaps the hardest question to answer. This is not because I have any doubts about the infallibility of the Church; but that, in this instance, in order to defend it, I must radically disagree not only on an academic matter with a prestigious theologian, but on a matter of fundamental Catholic faith with that same theologian, when for so long I read avidly and with enormous enthusiasm everything that he wrote. For me, Hans Küng was *the* theologian of the Second Vatican Council. I was a student for the priesthood from 1961 to 1967, spanning the years of the Council. Küng's books made me and so many of the students studying with me excited about how the Second Vatican Council could renew the Church. I continued to read his books with great interest throughout the 1960s, although some problems were beginning to emerge in my mind from such reading.

The parting of the ways where I was concerned came with the publication in English of his book *Infallible? An Enquiry.*[62] This book followed hard upon the publication of the controversial encyclical letter of Pope Paul VI, *Humanae Vitae,* in 1968, which reiterated the teaching of the Catholic Church that all forms of artificial contraception were morally illicit. It is common knowledge that the encyclical caused a storm of protest, both within and without the membership of the Roman Catholic Church. The British media in particular lived off the controversy for the whole summer of 1968. Many Catholic theologians, while questioning the moral principles enunciated in the encyclical that forbade contraception, took refuge in the commonly expressed opinion that the encyclical was not infallible.

For Küng, however, this was not sufficient. In *Infallible? An Enquiry* he argues that this throws into question the whole doctrine not only of the Pope's infallibility, not only of the infallibility of general councils, but even more *the infallibility of the Church.* Küng argues this because, in classical (or what Küng calls somewhat deprecatingly "scholastic") Catholic theology, the *ordinary teaching of the Church* is also infallible. This is true. Many doctrines that have never been infallibly defined, at least insofar as anathemas directed against those who deny them, are part of the deposit of faith, such as the resurrection. If a doctrine has not been contradicted, it is usually not necessary to define it; but it is still part of the faith of the Church.

Küng argued that the sinfulness of contraceptive sex had always been taught by the Church down through the centuries. Certainly this was true in confessional practice. It was this ordinary teaching of the Church, Küng states, which finally persuaded Pope Paul VI to reject the majority findings of the Roman Commission, which had recommended that the anovulatory pill was acceptable within marriage, even if the condom and other forms of contraception were not:

> Thus, even according to Roman theory, the prohibition of contraception has not been laid down as an infallible article of faith either by a pope or council. Yet, because, as we have just shown, it had always, or at any rate for half a century before Vatican II, been taught unanimously by the ordinary teaching office of the Pope and bishops, it forms part of the universal, infallible Catholic faith.[63]

From the viewpoint of Roman Catholic teaching, Küng may be right here. There are Catholic moral theologians who argue precisely with Küng (forming an unexpected alliance with him), that the objective wrongfulness of contraception is asserted infallibly by the Church, not in pronouncements of Pope or council, but first and foremost by virtue of its constant teaching. On the other hand, many Catholic moral theologians would categorize the teaching on contraception rather as ordinary but "noninfallible" teaching and therefore as modifiable, because history shows that modification in moral teaching (for example, on the wrongfulness of usury) has taken place before. For these theologians, the question is not as simple as outlined by Küng. However, from now on, Küng goes on to his main argument. He is only using the case concerning contraception in order to question the doctrine of infallibility itself. Abandon the doctrine of infallibility, he claims, and the problem would be resolved. The Pope could then simply admit that the Church was wrong in its teaching, and join the modern world.

The answer, for Küng, is to replace "infallibility" with "indefectibility." Christ's promise that the gates of hell would not prevail against the Church (Matthew 16:18) does not necessarily mean that the Church will not make mistakes in its teaching either on faith or on morals. Rather, for Küng it means that the truth of God will remain in the Church despite the errors of formulae of faith. Even more, Küng stresses, it is neither possible nor required to accept the necessity of propositions of faith that are infallible:

> It is clear from what we said above that it is possible to accept the meaningfulness, utility and in certain circumstances the necessity of summary statements of faith (professions of faith or dogmas) without necessarily accepting infallible and immutable propositions of faith. In other words, the binding nature of statements of faith does not mean necessarily accepting their infallibility.[64]

This is doubtless the key to the whole issue. Behind Küng's change of terminology from "infallibility" to "indefectibility" is a powerful movement in theology that emphasizes the limitation of the words, the propositions, we use to express our faith and our Christian life. Statements of faith, like any statements, are conditioned by circumstances, by our understanding of what those statements mean, by the limitations of our culture and our own personal story. The new *Catechism,* we can be sure, would agree with this. Even more, the *Catechism* points us in the act of faith beyond propositions to the divine reality they only dimly express: "We do not believe in formulas, but in those realities they express, which faith allows us to touch. 'The believer's act [of faith] does not terminate in the propositions, but in the realities [which they express].' All the same, we do approach these realities with the help of formulations of the faith which permit us to express the faith and to hand it on, to celebrate it in community, to assimilate and live on it more and more" (CCC 170).

So far, Küng and Catholic theology would no doubt be in full agreement. But can we accept with Küng that "the binding nature of statements of faith does not mean necessarily accepting their infallibility"? Let us pause for a moment to consider what we are stating here, if Küng is right. We may take the most fundamental proposition of faith, namely "We believe that Jesus Christ is true God become man." All of us would admit that this statement is both an opening toward a mystery, a question as well as an affirmation. We can never fully plumb the depths of what it means to say, "Jesus Christ is true God become man." But, if Küng is right, we would have to say more here. We would have to say, "The Church says that Jesus Christ is true God become man. I accept that statement as binding. *But it might not be true. It is not infallibly true."*

Is that what Christians have meant down the centuries when they have said or sung the Creed week after week at their liturgy? Surely this would be a contradiction of the whole act of faith. Rather, they mean that they are each Sunday "professing the true faith without error" (CCC 890). Karl Barth was presented with the same problem as we saw earlier, regarding the canon of Scripture. At the end of the day, Barth argued (under Question 11 above), we would have to say "it is possible that the church is wrong in saying that book X (e.g., Galatians) is part of the canon of scripture." Otherwise, Barth argued, he would have to accept an infallible Church. Küng seems to have reached a similar position in *Infallible? An Enquiry.*

Curiously, Küng seems to be unaware of the serious arguments for the infallibility of the Church in the writings of John Henry Newman. He even praises "the idea of development introduced into Catholic theology by the great Tübingen theologians (especially Johann Adam Möhler) on the one hand and Cardinal Newman on the other" and castigates Roman neo-scholastic theology for having interpreted this idea of development "intellectually and, instead of the tried and tested methods of interpreting the faith, encouraged dogmatic interpretation and binding definitions."[65] Küng only seems to know that "neo-scholastic textbook theology is also unable to demonstrate from Scripture or the oldest ecumenical tradition either the necessity or the reality or even merely the possibility of propositions that are *a priori* infallible."[66]

But the developmental theologian whom Küng praises, John Henry Newman, made the long and agonizing spiritual journey to become a Roman Catholic precisely because he came more and more to believe in the infallibility of the Church (decades before the infallibility of the Pope was defined at Vatican I), *and that infallibility essentially related to propositions.* Newman began writing his book *Essay on the Development of Christian Doctrine* while still an Anglican. By the time he had finished it, Newman had been received into full communion with the Catholic Church. For Newman, there can be no secure and fruitful development within the Church without an authority being able to make propositions that are infallible:

> Reasons shall be given . . . for concluding that, in proportion to the probability of true developments of doctrine and practice in the Divine Scheme, so is the probability also of the appointment in that scheme of an external authority to decide upon them, thereby separating them from the mass of mere human speculation, extravagance, corruption, and error, in and out of which they grow. This is the doctrine of the infallibility of the Church; for by infallibility I suppose is meant the power of deciding whether this, that, and a third, and any number of theological or ethical statements are true.[67]

Propositions of faith are vital for Newman's whole argument in *Essay on the Development of Christian Doctrine.* That is because his work, carefully argued, of four hundred forty-five pages, is about the development of an *idea,* the idea of the truth of God's revelation in the Church. There are no ideas without propositions. Throughout the history of the Church, for Newman, its doctrine grows in an empirically verifiable way, as an idea that preserves itself, whose principles continue, which is able to assimilate other ideas into itself, which demonstrates logical sequence, which anticipates its future development, which acts to preserve its past, which demonstrates "chronic vigor." These are Newman's famous seven notes of genuine development as contrasted with false developments that he calls "corruptions."[68]

These true developments are expressed for Newman in "dogmas," which emerge progressively in the Church's history. These dogmas eventually are expressed by the councils; but what Newman calls the "dogmatic principle," that total conviction in the truths of faith, was there before such definitions, acting in the great convictions of the first Christian martyrs, before the councils began to meet:

> Councils and popes are the guardians of the dogmatic principle: they are not the principle themselves; they presuppose the principle; they are summoned into action at the call of the principle, and the principle might act even before they had their legitimate place, and exercised a recognized power, in the movements of the Christian body.[69]

It is clearly unthinkable for Newman that such dogmas should admit of fallibility. Why such ideas have such "chronic vigor" is because they are impressed upon the mind of the Church with such total conviction, which allows of no doubt. If we ask how it is that Newman attained such conviction, we must turn to his *Apologia Pro Vita Sua*. In it he argues against Kingsley that far from being given his concept of truth by Jesuits, it was as an Anglican, way back in his Anglican youth, that he first began his journey to an infallible Church: "When I was fifteen, (in the autumn of 1816), a great change of thought took place in me. I fell under the influence of a definite Creed, and received into my intellect impressions of dogma, which, through God's mercy, have never been effaced or obscured."[70]

From this point on, for Newman, the "indefectibility" of the Church would not be enough. There would have to be that total certainty concerning the dogmas of faith that Newman saw as being infallibly testified by the Church. His journey to Roman Catholicism began at that point back at the age of fifteen, when he began more and more to investigate how it was that this "definite Creed" emerged in the Church, and how it was that it was able to sustain itself. This became a more and more urgent question, as Newman saw the Church of England challenged by a spirit of relativism and liberalism, bishops tending to become instruments of the state rather than successors of the apostles.

Newman was increasingly impressed in seeing how the Church of the early centuries resolved the most complex theological issues. Jesus Christ was the Son of God from the beginning. He was not the adopted Son, as claimed Paul of Samosata. Jesus Christ was defined true God, of one substance (*homoousios*) with God the Father, against the Arians. Jesus Christ did have a truly human soul; his human soul was not replaced by the divine Logos, as said Apollinarius. Jesus Christ was only one Person, the Person of the Word made flesh. There were not two Persons in Jesus, as Nestorius seemed to say; and thus Mary could be truly called *theotokos*, Mother of God, and not just Mother of Christ. Finally, Jesus Christ had truly a human and a divine nature. These two natures were not fused into one, as Eutychius asserted.

How did the Church settle all such tortuous issues, Newman asked, and arrive at a totally certain answer? Only, he concluded, through an infallible Church operating through what he called the "external authority" of Pope and bishops. Such has always been required, Newman argued, has always been in evidence even when not called "infallible," and always will be in evidence, in order to fulfill Christ's promise that the gates of hell will not prevail against his Church.

28: Is it not an even greater source of injustice when the faithful are compelled to give "religious assent" to doctrines proposed by the Pope and the bishops in communion with him even when those doctrines are not infallibly proposed? Does not this remove the possibility of theological dissent?

We must first of all make a clear distinction between the *assent of faith* required for decisions of the infallible *magisterium* either of the Pope alone or of the Pope together with the college of bishops, and decisions of the noninfallible teaching authority of the same *magisterium*. Infallible propositions require the assent of *faith*; whereas noninfallible propositions require the lesser assent of *obsequium*, "submission, acceptance." The full text from *Lumen Gentium* is as follows:

> The bishops, when they are teaching in communion with the Roman pontiff, are to be respected by all as witnesses to the divine and catholic truth; and the faithful ought to concur with their bishop's judgement concerning faith and morals which he delivers in the name of Christ, and they are to adhere to this with a religious assent of the mind. The religious assent of will and intellect is to be given in a special way to the authentic teaching of the Roman pontiff even when he is not speaking *ex cathedra*; in such a way, that is, that his supreme teaching authority is respectfully acknowledgd, and sincere adherence given to decisions he has delivered, in accordance with his manifest mind and will which is communicated chiefly by the nature of the documents, by the frequent repetition of the same doctrine or by the style of verbal expression.[71]

Is there in fact a justified complaint that it is unfair that Catholics should be required to follow this teaching, which is admittedly "nondefined" and "noninfallible," but rather should have the right to dissent from it? Moral theologians have, on the contrary, worked out very sophisticated rules as to the legitimacy of dissent in the case of noninfallible teaching. It is permitted for a Catholic to dissent from noninfallible teaching, provided that a great deal of care has been taken by that Catholic to inform his or her conscience beforehand. What is not permitted is *public dissent* from clearly expressed teaching either of the Pope or of the Catholic bishops, particularly on the part of those who hold public office in the Church. The cases cited by Edwards (Charles Curran, Leonardo Boff, Bishop Hunthausen)[72] were instances when the individual concerned had either publicly dissented from current Roman Catholic teaching, or had been carrying out publicly policies that seemed at variance with current Roman Catholic teaching.

Earlier, we discussed the case of contraception, as to whether it was infallible teaching that it was seriously sinful to use artificial means of birth prevention in intercourse. We have already seen that there is a disagreement among Catholic theologians on this matter, Küng and some "right-wing" moral theologians claiming that the teaching is part of constant teaching, and therefore infallible; while others, such as Curran, would put such teaching at the level of "noninfallible" teaching, and therefore open to dissent.

We would have to admit that, in carrying out its disciplinary actions against dissenting public figures, the Roman Catholic Church looks more authoritarian than many other Christian bodies. But, in principle, all Christian bodies will have to discipline those who speak out against its current teaching. Recently, an Anglican bishop suspended from pastoral duties a vicar who declared that he was no longer teaching the traditional God. On a more mundane and regular basis, Anglican clergy, whether they are in agreement or not, must enforce the current divorce laws in their churches.

The principle that there must be obedience within the Church on a day-to-day basis is first evidenced for us in Paul's letter to the Corinthian Christians regarding women covering their heads in church. Paul begins by giving a number of reasons why women should always have their heads covered in church. His reasons appear to us quite bizarre. Paul claims that women should have their heads covered in church because Christ is the head of man, and man is the head of woman. He does not seem very convinced of his arguments, particularly when he adds the argument "this is why it is right for a woman to wear on her head a sign of the authority over her, because of the angels" (1 Corinthians 11:10). No biblical commentator is quite sure, to this day, quite what "the angels" have got to do with it. One biblical scholar even suggested that a woman with her head uncovered might be a source of temptation to the (presumably male) angels looking down on them from heaven! In the end, Paul realizes the dubious nature of his arguments, and falls back on his own clout as an apostle. "If anyone wants to be contentious, I say that we have no such custom, nor do any of the churches of God" (1 Corinthians 11:16). Which bishop, church leader, schoolteacher, or even politician has not fallen back on that last resort: "If you do not like my reasons, do what I say anyway!" All of us will also admit that authority has to be exercised in that way sometimes in any kind of institution, less than ideal though it may be.

We would have also to admit that, in the exercise of this authority, injustice may be possible in any human decision. Disciplinary authority in the Church has tended to become centralized. During the Middle Ages, the universities exercised doctrinal authority through their courts. Theologians would be accused of heresy at the bar of the university, as was Thomas Aquinas. On the other hand, local bishops might often prefer the full resources of Roman authority. Their own resources might be under great strain when a theologian of great talent takes on the Church's teaching in any given area of thought. But there is clearly room for change in this area, of developing structures that might serve ongoing dialogue within the Church (e.g., local theological commissions), rather than the too-frequent use of the heavy hand of the Vatican.

29: The Anglican/Roman Catholic International Commission (ARCIC) attained important agreements on "authority"; but the official response of the Vatican Congregation for the Doctrine of the Faith maintained the traditional position regarding the primacy and infallibility of the papacy. What is the future for such dialogues if the Vatican always overtrumps their agreements?

The ARCIC agreements of 1976 were indeed remarkable, and were one of the main sources for real hopes of visible reunion during those heady days. Anglican (and some Catholic) ecumenists have accused the Vatican Congregation for the Doctrine of the Faith of preventing ongoing progress in agreement on the basics of primacy and infallibility. But, in all honesty, the complexity of the situation does not justify blaming one side or the other.

The agreed statements of ARCIC are indeed extraordinary, coming very close indeed to a Catholic theology of primacy and infallibility — in particular, ARCIC's statement that "when the Church meets in ecumenical council its decisions on fundamental matters of faith exclude what is erroneous."[73] Furthermore, such definitions are not necessarily "the only possible, or even the most exact" way of expressing the faith, so that "the mode of expression" may be superseded. But "restatement always builds upon, and does not contradict, the truth intended by the original definition."

The real difficulty found in the ARCIC statement by the Vatican Congregation for the Doctrine of the Faith was in deciding which statements were, and which were not, free from doctrinal error. ARCIC had insisted that such decisions must be "faithful to Scripture and consistent with Tradition."[74] But who was to decide what was "faithful to Scripture and consistent with Tradition"? After all, Arius the arch-heretic had firmly considered that what he taught was entirely faithful to Scripture and consistent with Tradition.

The real difficulty for Anglicans, I would suggest, is that if they accept an infallible authority, they must accept the authoritative decision of that body when it decides that it *is* speaking infallibly. Otherwise, the gift of infallibility is quite meaningless. Theologians could argue, "Oh, yes, we will accept your definitions when we are sure you are speaking infallibly; but we must be the arbiters of when you are so speaking." This is the importance of the reply of the Congregation of the Doctrine of the Faith to ARCIC:

> For the Catholic Church, the certain knowledge of any defined truth is not guaranteed by the reception of the faithful that such is in conformity with Scripture and Tradition, but by the authoritative definition itself on the part of the authentic teachers. . . . The Catholic Church believes that the councils or the Pope, even acting alone, are able to teach, if necessary in a definitive way, within the range of all truth revealed by God. . . .[75]

As I have argued earlier, infallible teaching must be proposed infallibly, and does not depend upon the democratic decision of the Church *once it has been defined.* This is not to say that discussion and dialogue are not important as part of the process, including not only bishops but also theologians, and indeed all members of the Church. We have already noted *Dei Verbum,* with its beautiful description of the process of developing tradition in the Church; through "contemplation and study of believers . . . through the intimate understanding of spiritual things which they experience"[76] as well as through the preaching of the bishops.

Dialogue, consultation — these are vital in the process prior to a definition. Pope Pius XII sent around to the bishops of the world consulting them before defining the Assumption. Some have argued that, for a definition to be valid, such prior consultation is necessary. But it remains true that, once defined, doctrines so defined are true and require the assent of faith. The truth resides then, not in the process which arrived at the definition, but in the definition itself, as the definition of the infallibility of the Pope in Vatican I states: "Therefore, such definitions of the Roman pontiff are of themselves, and not by the consent of the church (*ex sese, non autem ex consensu ecclesiae*), irreformable."[77] In addition, there has been considerable Anglican protest from the very powerful and by no means diminishing Evangelical wing. Many Evangelical Anglicans would in no way be prepared to accept the primacy of the Roman Pontiff, even in the nuanced way stated in ARCIC-I. They would be equally skeptical regarding the infallibility of general councils even in the terms expressed by ARCIC-I. For them, only Scripture can have any kind of infallible authority, not general councils.

There remains the still deeper question of authority in the Anglican communion. Even if, for instance, the Lambeth Conference seemed able to accept the ARCIC documents, many Anglicans would not accept that the Lambeth Conference, or indeed any other Anglican body, even that of the Convocations of Canterbury and York, which authorized the Thirty-nine Articles of Religion in 1571,[78] has final authority to decide doctrine. Thus, even if the Lambeth Conference accepts the primacy and infallibility of Pope or councils, even in a nuanced way, Evangelicals would not feel bound to those decisions. Finally, there remains perhaps the thorniest question of them all, that of the Church of England Protestant Establishment. Would the present reigning monarch relish submitting to the primacy and infallibility of the Roman pontiff?

All I would suggest here is that not all ecumenical problems arise from Roman intransigence!

Endnotes

1. Tanner, II, pp. 849-855.
2. Ibid., pp. 855-862.
3. Ibid., p. 862.

4. J. H. Newman, *The Arians of the Fourth Century* (sixth edition) (London: Longmans, Green and Co., 1890), p. 466, "There was no authoritative utterance of the Church's infallible voice in matter of fact between the Nicene Council, A.D. 325, and the Council of Constantinople, A.D. 381" (from Note V, *The Rambler,* July 1859). Clearly, therefore, Newman believed that the Nicene Council and the Council of Constantinople were such authoritative utterances "of the Church's infallible voice."

5. J. H. Newman, *An Essay in Aid of a Grammar of Assent* (1903), pp. 224ff.

6. Tanner, II, p. 858, no. 12, line 25.

7. J. H. Newman, *On Consulting the Faithful in Matters of Doctrine,* ed. John Coulson (London: Collins, 1961), p. 63.

8. Tanner, II, p. 862, no. 18, lines 34-36.

9. Edwards, *What Is Catholicism?* p. 39.

10. NJBC, p. 780.

11. NJB translates *anathema sit* as "cursed by God." But the clear context, in both Deuteronomy 7:26 and 1 Corinthians 5:5, is that the offending person is to be cut off from the community. The curse is precisely that cutting off from the community of God.

12. Tanner, II, p. 807, chapter 3, *de fide,* lines 4-10.

13. B. C. Butler, *The Vatican Council 1869-1870: Based on Bishop Ullathorne's Letters* (London: Collins, 1962); e.g., Bishop Dupanloup's position: cf. pp. 102-103.

14. Ibid., cf. p. 61.

15. ODCC, p. 1405.

16. Tanner, II, p. 816, lines 29-35, Vatican I, *Constitutio dogmatica prima de ecclesia Christi,* Session IV, chapter IV.

17. ODCC, p. 692.

18. Ibid., p. 98.

19. J. N. D. Kelly, *Early Christian Doctrines,* p. 339.

20. Tanner, II, LG 25, p. 869, lines 19-26.

21. B. C. Butler, *The Church and Unity* (London: Geoffrey Chapman, 1979), p. 207.

22. R. Brown (ed.), *Peter in the New Testament* (London: Geoffrey Chapman, 1974), p. 17.

23. Raymond E. Brown, *Responses to 101 Questions on the Bible* (London: Geoffrey Chapman, 1991), p. 134.

24. Tanner, II, p. 974, DV, 8, lines 20-21.

25. Ibid., p. 975, DV, 9, lines 5-6.

26. Ibid., p. 812, lines 16-20, Vatican I, session 4, chapter 1, *De apostolici primatus in beato Petro institutione.*

27. Albert Schweitzer, *The Quest of the Historical Jesus: A Critical Study of Its Progress from Reimarus to Wrede,* trans. W. Montgomery (German edition, 1906; first English edition, 1910, third edition, 1956, reprinted 1973), pp. 328-395.

28. R. Brown, *101 Questions,* Q. 76. I would agree with Brown that there is a difference "between a conviction that God would make him victorious (that is not only attested in the New Testament but totally harmonious with the faith and trust of Old Testament psalmists in moments of dire affliction) and a precise knowledge of how this would happen" (p. 103).

29. Ibid., Q. 77. Here, I would like to go further than Brown. Although sophisticated ideas about the "church" and its detailed planning are anachronistic, as Brown insists, it seems to me most reasonable, and entirely in keeping with the Gospel evidence, that Jesus made some provision for his community after his death, including a leader. It would be difficult to imagine a leader such as Peter being able to sustain his position without a clearly understood mandate from the earthly Jesus.

30. NJBC, p. 783.

31. I realize that there are many historical problems related to Acts 15, particularly regarding Peter's acceptance early on of Gentiles without circumcision. How ironically reliable is the account in Acts 15? Cf. NJBC, p. 751, 44:80-83. I am not ignorant of these problems. I am only arguing here that we have no solid evidence from the text, which denies the universal primacy of Peter.

32. R. Brown, *101 Questions,* pp. 130-132. Brown accepts this position, arguing that "I think it urgent in Christianity today that we recognize there can be matters of legitimate dispute among Christian theologians and even among Christian leaders."

33. ODCC, p. 253.

34. NJB, note f to John 21:21, p. 1790.

35. Rudolf Bultmann, *The Gospel of John: A Commentary,* trans. G. R. Beasley-Murray (Oxford: Basil Blackwell, 1971), p. 706.

36. Charles F. D. Moule, *The Origin of Christology* (Cambridge: Cambridge University Press, 1977), p. 2.

37. B. C. Butler, *The Church and Infallibility: A Reply to the Abridged 'Salmon'* (London: Sheed and Ward, 1954), p. 134.

38. Ibid., p. 135.

39. Ibid.

40. Ibid., p. 157, quoting Jerome, *Ep.* xv, xvi.

41. Ibid., p. 177, quoting from Battifol, *Le Siège Apostolique*, p. 543.

42. E. R. Chamberlain, *The Bad Popes* (London: Hamish Hamilton, 1970).

43. Ibid., p. 243.

44. ODCC, p. 1108.

45. Ibid., p. 268.

46. J. N. D. Kelly, *The Oxford Dictionary of Popes* (Oxford: Oxford University Press, 1986).

47. Edwards, *What Is Catholicism?* pp. 72-76.

48. ODCC, p. 275.

49. Tanner, II, *Dignitatis Humanae*, p. 1002, no. 2, lines 32-38. The question of "within due limits" might seem to take away all which has already been given. But all would recognize that the exercise of individual liberty in any society must be regulated within reasonable limits. The Council document leaves those limits to be decided within a given society or community.

50. Edwards, *What Is Catholicism?* p. 74.

51. CCCC, p. 19.

52. DFT, p. 614.

53. Ibid., p. 618.

54. Tanner, II, LG, p. 869, line 38 — p. 870, line 1.

55. Ibid., p. 870, lines 2-6.

56. Ibid., no. 20, p. 864, lines 18-24.

57. R. Brown, *Responses to 101 Questions on the Bible*, p. 118.

58. Ibid., p. 117.

59. Ibid., p. 119.

60. K. Rahner, *Theological Investigations*, vol. 5, trans. Karl H.-H. Kruger (London: Darton, Longman and Todd, 1966), p. 274.

61. R. Brown, *Responses to 101 Questions*, p. 121.

62. H. Küng, *Infallible? An Enquiry* (London: Collins, 1971).

63. Ibid., p. 48.

64. Ibid., p. 123.

65. Ibid., pp. 122-123.

66. Ibid., p. 124.

67. J. H. Newman, *Essay on the Development of Christian Doctrine* (seventh edition) (London: Longmans, Green and Co., 1890), pp. 78-79.

68. Ibid., pp. 169-203.

69. Ibid., p. 360.

70. J. H. Newman, *Apologia Pro Vita Sua, Being a History of His Religious Opinions* (London: Longmans, Green and Co., 1908).

71. Tanner, II, LG, no. 25, p. 869, lines 7-18.

72. Edwards, *What Is Catholicism?* p. 43.

73. Ibid., p. 81.

74. Ibid.

75. Ibid., pp. 82-83.

76. Tanner, II, no. 8, p. 974, lines 20-27.

77. Ibid., p. 816, lines 35-37.

78. F. L. Cross, ODCC, p. 1368, "Thirty-nine articles: . . . The Thirty-nine Articles are not a statement of Christian doctrine in the form of a creed, nor the exposition of a creed already accepted. They are, rather, short summaries of dogmatic tenets, each article dealing with some point raised in current controversies, and laying down in general terms the Anglican view. Though not ostensibly vague, they avoid unduly narrow definition."

Faith and Reason

30: How far is a Christian committed to orthodox doctrine, and how much can our perception of the ancient Christian truths as expressed in our creeds be changed? Does not life itself demand that we change with changing times and perceptions?

This takes us back immediately to the fundamental question "What is our authority?" Why do we believe as Christians what we believe? Why do we believe in the Trinity, in Three Persons in One God? Why do we believe in the incarnation, that in Jesus Christ God became man? Only then can we ask the further question "Is it possible to change what we believe, or to reexpress it in such a way that it is fundamentally different from what we believe now?"

From the beginning, we have looked at three authorities: the Bible, reason, and the Church. Many Christians look to the Bible as the authority for their faith; but who is to interpret the Bible when there are disagreements? That is why the Catholic Church has always insisted upon the need for a Church to interpret the Bible. There is a third possibility, the liberal possibility, which has very much entered into consideration since the eighteenth-century Enlightenment — namely reason. Liberal Christians have demanded that creeds must be subject to reason. Thus, in nineteenth-century Germany, more and more Christians, under the influence of the critical movement and in particular under the influence of the "Quest of the Historical Jesus," radically altered what was believed. Radical Lutheran Christians tended not to believe in the miracles in the

Gospels, or in the traditional doctrine of the incarnation. Jesus Christ was the epitome of virtue, as the rationalist Paulus claimed; but he was certainly not, as Athanasius would claim, "consubstantial with the Father."

But how does the liberal Christian, or what David Friedrich Strauss would call the "critical"[1] Christian, determine what to believe? Early Enlightenment scholars attempted to found a religion upon rational virtue. Perhaps the clearest concrete expression of that religion was in the Unitarian form of Christianity, quite popular in England, particularly in the Northwest, in the seventeenth, eighteenth, and nineteenth centuries. The Unitarian would move from a rational view of God to construct a rational religion, using rationalist principles to study the Gospels, dispensing with the miraculous Jesus but retaining Jesus as a model of reasonable virtue.

Friedrich Schleiermacher, in the early nineteenth century, saw the inadequacy of a rationalist approach to Christianity, while retaining the critical principles of the radical scholars of his time.[2] Schleiermacher attempted to make theology into an empirical science. Instead of religion being based upon objective knowledge of God, Schleiermacher saw religion as based upon the "feeling of transcendence." Schleiermacher has been called the "father of modern theology." What is right for me to believe according to Schleiermacher is what I sense or experience to be in conformity with my feeling of transcendence, which for Schleiermacher is the essence of religion. Hence there is no way in which we can determine whether this or that Christian dogma is right; only how it conforms to my religious experience.

I only outline Schleiermacher's system of thought because it is an illustration of what happens when we abandon the idea of an objective order of knowledge in religion. It is easy for us to "tinker" with elements of our Christian faith: the virginal conception of Christ, the bodily resurrection, the divinity of Christ. A moderately liberal Christian will consider perhaps that some tinkering at the edges is possible, without radically abandoning Christian faith as such. But when do we stop peeling the onion? What happens when we peel an onion is not that eventually we come to the hard core of the essential onion. On the contrary, what happens is that as we keep peeling the onion, the onion simply disappears. This is what can happen with Christian faith. That is because, as we have described earlier, Christian revelation depends upon a set of mysteries that are beyond what reason can argue. If we depend upon reason alone, therefore, the whole house of cards will eventually collapse.

Some, including the Anglican Don Cupitt, have gone all the way down this road. I applaud at least their honesty. Cupitt rejects completely the idea that religion can consist of objective "truths," and reduces religion to the practice of religion, all theological dogma being reduced to myth:

> The view that religious belief consists in holding that a number of picturesque supernatural propositions are descriptively true is encouraged by the continuing grip on people's minds of a decadent and mystifying dogmatic theology. In effect I am arguing that for the sake of clarity it should be discarded entirely, and replaced by the practice of religion — ethics and spirituality — and the philosophy of religion. Then religion can become itself again, with a clear intellectual conscience at last.[3]

Cupitt strongly affirms that such a view that reduces dogma to myth is the only alternative in order to live as a Christian at the end of the twentieth century. In this chapter, I will attempt to provide a foundation for Christian dogma that is both orthodox and contemporary. But, in my opinion, the alternatives are stark, between Cupitt and atheism on the one hand, and a full-blown Catholicism on the other. I recall Bishop Butler saying that, at one stage on his spiritual journey, the alternatives for him were equally stark, Catholicism or atheism. Tinkering about somewhere in the middle no longer presented a viable alternative; that is because, if God truly and objectively exists, that God must have left us a revelation with adequate credentials. Finally, if there is a revelation, it has to be accepted *as a whole*, not piecemeal, because God who reveals is One. That I shall now attempt briefly to show.

31: How can the First Vatican Council maintain that "God, the first principle and last end of all things, can be known with certainty from the created order by the natural light of human reason"? Does not this go far beyond what the human mind can attain, especially in the light of modern scientific theories of the origins of the universe?

The First Vatican Council, in this definition, paid an enormous compliment to human reason, that it was able to attain to the knowledge of God's existence. Very often, Christians in this day and age have tended to give up on proofs for God's existence, claiming that only by faith do we know that God exists. If a person accepts that God exists by faith, and is not concerned with rational demonstrations, good for him or her. But we have to ask whether ceding more and more ground to our agnostic contemporaries will in the end serve the cause of religion; or whether, in the case of God's existence, we have again to give a reason for the hope that is in us (1 Peter 3:15), and stand our ground.

I must begin by saying that, whether or not we accept traditional proofs of God's existence, they have nothing whatever to do with "modern scientific theories of the origins of the universe." Arguments for God's existence have to do with *metaphysics*, not with *physics*. The world may have begun with a big bang, a mega explosion of particles; but that has nothing whatever to do with whether God exists or not. Where God is concerned, we are not speaking of any part of the process of creation, but what fundamentally precedes, is in, and transcends all creation. Something must have existed prior to the "big bang" in order to explode. What was the mega-handgrenade? We are not, where God is concerned, speaking of any particular cause, but *the Cause* of all things. We may think that metaphysics itself is a pseudoscience. The English mind is traditionally suspicious of metaphysics. But, at least to be fair to proofs for God's existence, we must be aware that they are about transcendental causes, and so are neither nullified nor validated by any particular modern scientific theory of how the *cosmos* came to exist.

To illustrate this point, I will quote what is perhaps the most famous proof of God's existence, that of Aquinas. He observes first that there are things in this world that are moved by something else, an observation presumably as valid in the twentieth century as in the thirteenth when he lived:

> Everything therefore which is moved, must be moved by something else. If therefore that by which it is moved is itself moved, then it follows that that which acts as the mover is also itself moved by something else; and that again by something else. But here we cannot proceed to infinity; because in this case there would be no first mover, and, in consequence, neither would there be anything else moving, because secondary movements do not move unless moved

> by a primary mover, just as a stick does not move unless it is moved by a moving hand. Therefore it is necessary to proceed to some Prime Mover, which is itself not moved by anything; and this everyone understands as God.[4]

The old objection "Who made God?" misses the point of this argument, which demonstrates that something needs to exist *that was not made*. What is also true is that everything in our experience *is* made. Thus we must look outside of our immediate experience to a *Something* that is the Prime Mover, or the First Cause, which we call "God."

Whether we accept the logic of Aquinas's "first way" of five ways that he gives for accepting God's existence, we must at least admit that he is arguing in a way that is not affected by any particular scientific theory or discovery. He is arguing from general observation (something in our experience is moved) to an absolutely general principle, the existence of a Prime Mover whom we call God. Whatever scientific developments there have been since the thirteenth century, when Aquinas proposed this argument, are irrelevant to it. If the first way of Aquinas was valid eight hundred years ago, it is valid today. It operates in the order of metaphysics rather than in the order of physics.

It would be quite misleading if I suggested that all Christian philosophers accept any particular proof for God's existence. There is a continuous debate on the validity of each of the arguments. There is no space here for me to discuss fully the various proofs for God's existence, nor am I a professional philosopher with full competence to do so. There already exist excellent books on this subject;[5] except that I would say that, after thirty or forty years, I still accept the validity of St. Thomas Aquinas's five ways. I still think that the argument above from movement to a Prime Mover is valid, as is the argument from cause to a Prime Cause, and the argument from Contingent to Necessary Being. The finite world in which we live, I would submit, does demand the existence of an Infinite Being we call God. But I cannot go fully into these arguments at this juncture.

What I wish to do in the answer to this Hard Question is simply to suggest that proofs for God's existence should be taken seriously for what they are, not a substitute for scientific reasoning, nor invalidated by scientific reasoning, but a debate within another order of knowledge. This order of knowledge we may call "metaphysics," but in another sense is not so much beyond physics (*meta physica*) as presupposing it.

Professor Michael Dummett, the Catholic philosopher, logician, and mathematician, was once interviewed on television, and was asked concerning his beliefs in God. "How is it," he was asked, "you accept that God exists, and yet you are so skeptical about proofs for God's existence?" Dummett replied, "Philosophers have great difficulty in proving that the external world exists, even that they exist. Yet they still act as if the world exists, and they do, and it does!" That was a profound remark, most relevant to the whole question of proofs of God's existence, and even more relevant to the question of our *knowledge* of God. The question as to whether the external world exists, or whether we ourselves exist, or indeed whether an order of cause and effect operates in the world, cannot be answered by science, *precisely because all scientific knowledge and activity presupposes it.* Any scientific activity presupposes that the scientist accepts his or her own existence, that there is a world external to us human beings, and that there is an order of regular activity, which we call "cause and effect" operating in the world.[6] As the philosopher David Hume argued, no amount of scientific activity can "prove" the order of cause and effect. It can only be accepted as a belief without adequate reason.

Unlike Hume, I do not accept that this must lead us to total skepticism regarding the existence of the world outside ourselves. Rather, it should lead us to realize that at the root of a scientist's activity are presuppositions that are never proved, but that are nevertheless perfectly reasonable to assume. It is simply accepted as the presupposition of all scientific activity. If we do not wish to call the question of the existence of the external world a "metaphysical" question because of fear of that particular word, then we must call it perhaps a "prescientific" question.

The example I have introduced regarding our knowledge of the external world, or of ourselves, and of an order of cause and effect within the world, is also important for this reason. It demonstrates that we can be very certain of something, even if we might find proving it difficult. Vatican I does not assert that we can *prove* the existence of God. But neither does it assert that it is a matter of *faith,* rather of *knowledge.* Now, I would suggest, it is exactly the same regarding our knowledge of the external world. We do not *believe* that we exist, or that a world external to ourselves exists, or that an order of cause and effect exists within the world. We *know* it. But we might find it very difficult to *prove* it. Any proof that we might give ("I stick a pin in myself, and I feel pain") can always be countered with, "But even your feeling pain might be an instance of your dreaming." The French philosopher René Descartes found it so difficult to prove that a world outside himself existed, that he claimed that it was impossible, and concluded that the only reality, to begin with at least, concerning which he could be absolutely certain was his own existence, concluding *cogito, ergo sum:* I think, therefore I am.

What Vatican I claims concerning God's existence as the beginning and end of all things is that we can *know* it, just as we know that the external world exists, and that a world exists outside ourselves. It is a form of knowledge, not of course like scientific knowledge, but it is real. In teaching both children and adults, in a skeptical scientific modern world, I am still surprised how often people say that they have no problem whatsoever in accepting the existence of God, even though they might find it difficult to prove it. This is why I can make a great deal of sense of what the new *Catechism of the Catholic Church* says about this matter:

> Created in God's image and called to know and love him, the person who seeks God discovers certain ways of coming to know him. These are also called proofs for the existence of God, not in the sense of proofs in the natural sciences, but rather in the sense of "converging and convincing arguments," which allow us to attain certainty about the truth.
>
> These "ways" of approaching God from creation have a twofold point of departure: the physical world, and the human person. (CCC 31)

Looking at creation, looking at ourselves, we find "converging and convincing arguments," which may not be for us watertight in themselves, but which together reinforce a *knowledge* in ourselves which is not only rational, but also beyond reason. Vatican I, in claiming that we have a knowledge of God, is quoting a biblical text, Romans 1:18-21:

> The retribution of God from heaven is being revealed against the ungodliness and injustice of human beings who in their injustice hold back the truth. For what can be known about God is perfectly plain to them, since God has made it plain to them: ever since the creation of the world, the invisible existence of God and his everlasting power have been clearly seen by the mind's understanding of created things. And so these people have no excuse: they knew God

> and yet they did not honor him as God or give thanks to him, but their arguments became futile and their uncomprehending minds were darkened.

Paul is arguing here that the pagans, even though unlike the Jews they had no public revelation from God, should have known God from exercising their reason. They were foolish to worship idols, even if God had sent them no prophets. Paul is here only taking up a theme already in the Book of Wisdom, that "yes, naturally stupid are all who are unaware of God, and who, from good things seen, have not been able to discover Him-who-is, or by studying the works, have not recognized the Artificer" (Wisdom 13:1).

Paul takes over in his language the word *knowledge* from the Hebrew, which is more than intellectual knowledge. The Hebrew word *yada'* means more a kind of intimate personal knowledge, and can refer to sexual intercourse: "The man had intercourse (*yada'*) with his wife Eve, and she conceived and gave birth to Cain" (Genesis 4:1). The knowledge of God as our Creator and the End of all our activity is not just an intellectual knowledge, but is itself the beginning of a relationship.

We shall see, answering the next Hard Question, that Catholic theology makes a strict distinction between what we can know of God from our reason, and what we can know only when God reveals himself and his plan to us. But even at the level of what we can know of God by reason, we are challenged to develop this personal love of God, even though we are helpless to do this without God's own grace and help. That is why our knowledge of God through reason is very close indeed to a knowledge by experience. Catholic theology has in recent centuries been nervous of the word "experience" regarding God. During the eighteenth and nineteenth centuries, "experience of God" was often associated with the idea that we have some kind of intuition of God, and that a reasoning process is not necessary in order to come to know God.

Aquinas insisted that our knowledge of God by reason was not immediate, but *mediate,* through created realities. That is why, for Aquinas, the existence of God was demonstrable.[7] The new *Catechism,* in speaking of coming to God *through* created realities and *through* our understanding of ourselves as made in God's image, would tend to support this Thomist tradition that our knowledge of God by reason is mediate, and that we do not have a direct experience of God.

But perhaps there is some kind of meeting of the ways here.[8] The Hebrew concept of knowledge of God is, as we have said, not purely intellectual. It is a personal knowledge of God and of his ways. And a correct understanding of our experience of God can leave open the possibility that this experience is not immediate, but mediate, through created realities, and through an awareness of who we are as made in God's image. To "know God" is not so far from "to experience God." But what our retention of the word "knowledge" ensures is that our knowledge of God through our reason is not a feeling that is turned on when we are on a religious "high." It is a permanent state of certain knowledge, even if a mysterious knowledge, according to Vatican I, and not just a transient religious sensibility.

What is important regarding this knowledge of God by reason asserted by Vatican I (and, if we like, by experiencing God) is that it provides the only sure foundation in our human nature of the knowledge of God by revelation. Again, to quote the new *Catechism*, quoting Vatican I: " 'Our holy mother, the Church, holds and teaches that God, the first principle and last end of all things, can be known with certainty from the created world by the natural light of human reason.' Without this capacity, man would not be able to welcome God's revelation. Man has this capacity because he is created 'in the image of God' " (CCC 36).

32: How can the* Catechism *tell us that faith "is more certain than all human knowledge, because it is founded upon the very word of God who cannot lie" (CCC 157)? Surely, faith leads not to certain knowledge but to stable trust?

Behind this question is the old controversy between the Catholic and Protestant view of faith. Traditional Protestants accused Catholics of being overintellectual in their view of faith, faith being related too much to "truths." Protestants, on the other hand, were accused by Catholics of an overemphasis upon *fiducial faith,* that is to say faith is not based upon propositions but upon trust in God that I personally am saved despite my own total depravity.

In reality, both elements, of intellectual assent and of fiducial trust, are necessary in faith, and are so expressed in the New Testament theology of faith. The Pauline view of faith is very much linked to commitment to Christ: "For I see no reason to be ashamed of the gospel; it is God's power for the salvation of everyone who has faith — Jews first, but

Greeks as well — for in it is revealed the saving justice of God: a justice based on faith and addressed to faith. As it says in scripture: Anyone who is upright through faith will live" (Romans 1:16-17).

Paul's view of faith here links up with the faith of Abraham, who without seeing what was to come simply put his trust in God and went out with his family and his property to the Promised Land (Genesis 12:1-3). The "Abraham" type of faith is trust, personal commitment, with a minimal emphasis upon intellectual truths.

But this should not be seen as contradictory to the intellectual aspects of faith. I cannot trust anybody unless I am sure that such a person is trustworthy. "My friend will not let me down" is a verifiable proposition, verified when my friend does not let me down, or falsified when he does let me down. Trust in God necessarily implies a set of beliefs in God. Faith, in the New Testament, is a form of knowledge, and is related to propositions. Just as Paul is typical of fiducial faith, John is typical of the more intellectual type of faith: "There were many other signs that Jesus worked in the sight of the disciples, but they are not recorded in this book. These are recorded that you may believe that Jesus is the Christ, the Son of God, and that believing this you may have life in his name" (John 20:30-31).

In John's theology of faith, it is necessary to believe *that* Jesus is the Christ, the Son of God; the consequence of such intellectual knowledge is that we have life in Jesus' name. In Catholic theology, therefore, intellectual knowledge is essentially related to salvation. It is because we know who Jesus is, the Son of God, that we put our faith and our trust in him, and so begin to share in his life.

In Catholic apologetics, there is a threefold movement in the act of faith, corresponding to three levels of commitment as a response to God's revelation. These levels do not happen necessarily as a definite "time" in a person's conversion story, which may be much more complex than the following three stages. But, logically, there are the following three levels as orders of knowledge, in relation to God's revelation:

First, the preparation for the Gospel

As we saw in the last Hard Question, there are questions about God, the moral law, and religion that can be dealt with at the level of reason, following from the fact that we are made in God's image and likeness. These questions can be discussed at the level of reason. Yet, the First

Vatican Council states that, even where these questions are concerned, revelation provides enlightenment:

> It is indeed thanks to this divine revelation, that those matters concerning God which are not of themselves beyond the scope of human reason, can, even in the present state of the human race, be known by everyone without difficulty, with firm certitude, and with no intermingling of error.[9]

Second, the criteria of revelation

The first level, the preparation for the Gospel, is at the level of philosophy. The second level is that of what used to be called "fundamental theology"; the study of the criteria whereby we consider revelation. At this level, the value of the Old Testament as a preparation for the New Testament and particularly of the Messiah would be considered. The Church claims that there are adequate *signs* of revelation in the life of Christ, his miracles, and above all in his life, death, and resurrection. We repeat the quotation earlier from Vatican I:

> Nevertheless (although faith is a supernatural gift), in order that the submission of our faith should be in accordance with reason, it was God's will that there should be linked to the internal assistance of the holy Spirit outward indications of his revelation, that is to say divine acts, and first and foremost miracles and prophecies, which clearly demonstrating as they do the omnipotence and infinite knowledge of God, are the most certain signs of revelation and are suited to the understanding of all.[10]

Third, the dogmas of faith

According to Vatican I, the dogmas of faith (the Trinity, the incarnation, the sacraments) can only be known by the gift of faith. They presuppose that the previous two levels are there as foundations, whether or not they have been gone through as stages in the life of the Christian. The truths of faith are accepted on the authority of God who reveals, as Vatican I states:

> Since human beings are totally dependent on God as their creator and lord, and created reason is completely subject to uncreated

> truth, we are obliged to yield to God the revealer full submission of intellect and will by faith. This faith, which is the beginning of human salvation, the catholic church professes to be a supernatural virtue, by means of which, with the grace of God inspiring and assisting us, we believe to be true what he has revealed, not because we believe its intrinsic truth by the natural light of reason, but because of the authority of God himself, who makes the revelation, and can neither deceive nor be deceived.[11]

According to Catholic theology, the two previous stages — the preparation for the Gospel and the examination of the criteria of revelation — have helped the person to come to the point where God is trusted alone as the source of revelation. The Holy Spirit helps necessarily in this act of faith.

Thomas Aquinas described theology as a "subalternate science," a science that depended on another source of knowledge as its principle of knowledge, just as music depends upon mathematics as its scientific source (guitar strings are strung according to logarithmic progressions). Thus dogmatic theology, for Aquinas, depends entirely upon God for its knowledge, being unable to reason fully its truths because they are beyond reason. From this, too, dogmatic theology acquires its certainty, not from the intrinsic reasoning of the dogmas, but simply from the authority of God who reveals.

What then is the purpose of dogmatic theology? Has reason no function whatever? Does dogma simply have to listen to the voice of revelation and then fall silent? Catholic theology sees dogmatic theology as having a many-faceted role. Dogmatic theology can show how the mysteries of faith cohere one with the other, as the new *Catechism* refers to the "symphonic" nature of theology. Dogmatic theology can show that a given doctrine is not contrary to reason (e.g., the Trinity and the Real Presence in the Eucharist). Finally, dogmatic theology has the task of studying the meaning of the dogmas of faith in their historical context, so developing understanding of those dogmas in each era of the Church's history.

There is a danger (which is hardly avoided in answering a Hard Question such as this) of reducing dogmas to individual statements of doctrine. As we have seen, dogmas of faith are more than simply a "shopping list of divine truths." Yet, as we have also seen, words are necessary, and necessary to state God's truth infallibly. The counter to this danger of excessive verbalization is first to realize that our certainty is not in the propositions themselves, but in the reality that underlies those statements of faith. The act of faith is certain, the most certain act of all because it is founded upon what God has revealed; but the act of faith terminates in a mystery, the very mystery of God Three in One.

33: How can God's "absolute sovereignty" as expressed in the* Catechism *be consistent with terrible evils that God apparently permits? Is there not some limitation of God's power resulting from his creation of a universe with its own laws? Does not the fact that God's own Son, Jesus, suffered on the cross and said "My God, my God, why have you forsaken me?" emphasize the weakness of God rather than his "absolute sovereignty"?

Without doubt, the greatest moral problem regarding the existence and nature of God is the "problem of evil." Why, if God exists, does he allow such an enormous burden of evil and suffering in the world? There is a particular problem — or rather there seems to be — in the twentieth century, with two horrific world wars. How could God have stood aside and watched tens of thousands of men go "over the top" at the Battle of the Somme, to be immediately scythed to death by machine guns? "What passing bells for these who die as cattle?" protested the poet Wilfred Owen, himself killed as a young officer in the 1914-1918 Great War. How could God have stood aside while thousands of naked men, women, and children, stripped even of their wedding rings and false teeth, were herded into the gas chambers of the Nazi death camps? Evil has existed before in the world — but not, it seems, on the scale of the degradation and inhumanity that seems to have reached new depths in the twentieth century.

In the face of this evil, some modern theologians have had recourse to an actual denial of the omnipotence of God. God, for these theologians, is part of the "process" of the world, and just is unable to prevent evil. The difficulty here is that to deny God's absolute power and sovereignty is to deny that he is God at all. If God is himself subject to limitation, then he must himself have been created, and so cannot be the infinite Creator.

However, even if we accept fully the omnipotence of God, we can accept that, in creating a finite world, God is to some extent subject to working within the limitations of the world he has created. He allows evil by what is called his "permissive will." This follows from having created beings who are to some extent allowed to run their own affairs. Aquinas defined evil as the deprivation of the good (*privatio boni*).[12] For the scholastics, evil is not a thing in itself. Rather, it is the lack of some good in some being or other. In a created world, there are bound to be some winners and losers. If I win the lottery, that is good for me; but my win means that some others suffer the "evil" of losing their bet. If I have a good meal, that is good for my body, but bad for the lamb or (if I am a vegetarian) for the lettuce and potatoes I have eaten. This Thomist explanation of evil is very "natural," and in a way conforms to the view of the natural sciences. The world consists of finite beings (animals, humans, plants, inanimate objects like stones) that interact with one another in the same world. God, in creating the world, and in creating beings with their own natures, has created necessarily a competitive world, where the good of some is of necessity the evil of others.

But this is by no means the whole story according to Christian revelation. Sin has entered into the world through our first parents. The sum of evil in the world is much more than what would be naturally there through created natures. The human race has a tendency toward evil that arises from what we had seen earlier described as Original Sin, while it leaves us with a "wounded nature," a tendency toward sin. Paul, after many years as a committed Christian, still senses this disordered nature inside him:

> So I find this rule: that for me, where I want to do nothing but good, evil is close at my side. In my inmost self I dearly love God's law, but I see that acting on my body there is a different law which battles against the law in my mind. So I am brought to be a prisoner of that law of sin which lives inside my body. What a wretched man I am! Who will rescue me from this body doomed to death? God — thanks be to him — through Jesus Christ our Lord. So it is that I myself with my mind obey the law of God, but in my disordered nature I obey the law of sin. (Romans 7:21-25)

No story of evil in the world in Christian terms can fail to take account of what the traditional theologians called "concupiscence," of which Paul complains above. Only this, it seems to me, can explain the evils of the twentieth century, which seem to have reached demonic proportions.

This is partly because the technology we have created by our human intelligence has opened up new possibilities of evil as well as of good. It would perhaps have been physically impossible to kill hundreds of thousands of people all together before the terrible ovens of Auschwitz were designed, under contract to the SS, by the local German businessmen.

> Thus while human beings are increasingly extending their power, they are not always able to control it in their own service. They are intent on exploring the depths of the mind, yet they often appear more unsure of themselves. They are gradually uncovering the laws of their life in society, but uncertain about how to give it direction.[13]

And God stands by to let it happen? In a way, he must. He must allow human beings to make their choices, even the worst of choices. This is one meaning of the cross, that Christ did share in the apparent absence of God his Father. "My God, my God, why have you forsaken me?" (Matthew 27:46). In that cry is not only the cry of Jesus Christ himself on the cross, but the cry of every suffering human person. The story goes that in Auschwitz early in the morning a poor man was hanged in the main courtyard. "Where is your God now, O believer?" shouted out a cynical prisoner. "There he is, hanging on that rope" came back the reply.

But that does not mean that God is inactive in his own world. Again, Aquinas's explanation of evil was that "God only allows evil to happen in order to bring out of it a greater good"; or, as Paul put it, "All things work together for good to those who love God . . ." (Romans 8:28, *King James Version*). That same God, in the Easter Vigil terminology, even turns the sin of Adam into a "happy fault." Because Adam sinned, we need a Savior; or, as the old Christmas carol put it, if Adam had not eaten the apple, Mary would not have given birth to Jesus. Christian faith understands the whole history of the world as a kind of drama, in terms of Milton, a Paradise Lost and Paradise Regained. It is a drama in which all human beings on this earth have a special part to play. Each of us has good things happen to us, and each of us suffers some evil. Some are luckier than others, some suffer more than others.

But, whether our life is lucky or unlucky, it can only be understood as part of the Plan, that unified plan of the universe that is in the mind of

God, symbolized finally in the "new heaven and new earth" (Revelation 21:1), the New Jerusalem coming down from heaven. Only that in the end can and will make sense of the horrors of the Somme, and of Auschwitz, and of your little piece of suffering and mine. Then you and I will understand the part we have to play in the whole process:

> If we live by the truth and in love, we shall grow completely into Christ, who is the head by whom the whole Body is fitted and joined together, every joint adding its own strength, for each individual part to work according to its function. So the body grows until it has built itself up in love. (Ephesians 4:15-16)

34: Is not the idea that God is "Three Persons in One God" too bound up with past thought patterns to be sustained today?

I must say that I personally have always found the way the doctrine of the Trinity is expressed as "Three Persons in One God" very difficult to make intelligible. If someone could find a better term than "Persons" to describe the Three, no one would be happier than I. Given our Western perception of "person" as a subsistent intelligent subject, it is very difficult to think of Father, Son, and Spirit as "Persons" without at the same time thinking of them as three independent "people." This would strictly lead to heresy, because then we would be thinking of three Gods, whereas orthodoxy tells us that the Trinity do not make three Gods, but only one God.

This point is perceptively made by Professor Nicholas Lash in his fascinating new book on the Creed.[14]

> This, I think, is the heart of the matter. As Newman put it, we knew "before we began to use [the term "person"], that the Son was God and yet was not the Father . . . the word Person tells us nothing in addition to this." In other words, to say that "God is three persons in one nature" tells us no more about God than would "God is three persons in one thing," or than does "God is three and God is one."

Western orthodoxy tells us that, in calling God the Father, Son, and Spirit "Person," we are only referring to the relationship between them. They are, in terms of scholastic theology, "subsistent relations." They do not have anything in themselves as God that the other two "Persons" do not have, except their relationship with one another. There is only one God, one Infinity, one Eternity, one Almighty, but three Persons. This is very difficult indeed; and every theologian is at this point strongly tempted to duck out of the question by saying, "It is a mystery." We can perhaps take some refuge in higher mathematics, which tells us that three infinite numbers added together make only one infinite number, and that infinity multiplied by three makes only one infinity. But entering into higher mathematics perhaps can only make the doctrine seem even more obscure, even if thereby the Trinity ceases to be illogical.

But one matter at least must be clear in response to this Hard Question: The difficulty regarding the doctrine of the Trinity has nothing whatever to do with thought patterns of today or any day for that matter. It has to do with understanding the God of Christian revelation. Reading the early Church Fathers, among them Origen, Athanasius, and Augustine, makes us realize that it was no more easy for them to understand the trinitarian God of Christian revelation than it is for us in the twentieth century. In some ways, it was more difficult for them, because the Greeks so loved to speculate about divine ideas that it was so much easier for them to become really tied up and involved in the question (usually leading to some heresy or other); whereas we Westerners just tend to leave the whole matter of the Trinity alone.

Would it be better, then, to drop the doctrine of the Trinity, and say that Father, Son, and Spirit are just "ways" in which God shows aspects of his being? Again, if we go back to the controversies of the first four centuries, we will find that this option, called "modalism," was fully available then, and was rejected.[15] Why was the doctrine of the Trinity insisted upon, in spite of the fact that there was no Trinity in Judaism, or for that matter in Greek philosophy? The answer to this question is closely related to the answer to the next Hard Question, namely as to the divinity of Christ. Greek philosophy, so much part of life in Alexandria, one of the great theological centers of Christian life, could easily accept a *logos*, a creative Mind at work in the universe. After all, it was good Stoicism and Middle Platonism. But, for Arius, this *logos* had to be created, because it had its origin from God, and that which came from God, originated from God, had to be created from God.

This was the very sticking point of the Catholic doctrine of Christ, and of the Trinity. The Catholic theologians such as Athanasius and Hilary saw the Tradition as clear from the orthodox interpretation of John 1:1-18, where the author of the Fourth Gospel speaks of the *logos.* The *logos,* the Word, came from God, and became flesh in Jesus:

> In the beginning was the Word:
> the Word was with God
> and the Word was God.
>
> JOHN 1:1

In Jesus, this Word spoke to the Father, was related to the Father, and went back to the Father. The Word came from God, but was not created by God. "Before Abraham ever was, I Am" (John 8:58b), said Jesus.

Christian reflection, from Origen onward, understood that the Word came *from* God; what became clear in the debate with Arius was that the *Word was God coming from God.* The Christian revelation was that, as a result of Jesus coming to earth, we now understood that God is continually, eternally, giving birth to God, not as a created being, but eternally one with God the source of origin. Jesus Christ is God from God, light from light, true God from true God. That is why modalism is not adequate, because when God gives birth to God, the Word, that Word is totally God, and not just a mode of God's being.

I personally find Augustine's explanation of the Trinity in psychological terms the most convincing analogy, particularly because it corresponds to biblical language. God, who is the supreme and infinite Intelligence, like any mind expresses himself in an Idea, a Word, which proceeds from him. That Idea, that Word, is nothing less than himself, infinite God. Words proceeding from our minds are not completely ourselves; but, where God is concerned, his Word, his Idea, cannot be less than himself, one with, yet distinct from, him. Now, regarding the Spirit: Any idea coming from a mind creates Love in that mind, as the mind contemplates the idea. As God views his Word, he Loves that Word. That creative Love between God and God's Word we call the "Spirit." That again is God just as much as God and God's Word are truly God. Here, having made some attempt to explain the Trinity, perhaps I can now leave it, God, God's Word, God's Spirit, as a "mystery."

Western theology has been strongly influenced by Augustine, who finds traces of the Trinity in creation. I myself find Augustine's images most helpful, to make sense of the "three persons" doctrine: "With great speculative power and depth Augustine detects in the human spirit ever new ternaries: *mens — notitia — amor* (mind — knowledge — love), *memoria — intelligentia — voluntas* (memory — intelligence — will). . . ."[16]

If we think of God as the Supreme Intelligence, then it is not too difficult to think of that Intelligence as needing a Word, an Image that is itself, to express itself. Then, that Intelligence will generate Love between itself and its Word. The Christian doctrine is that everything that is created is caught up in that trinitarian love, if we offer ourselves in faith to that Trinity: "O my God, Trinity whom I adore, help me forget myself entirely so to establish myself in you, unmovable and peaceful as if my soul were already in eternity . . ." (Prayer of Blessed Elizabeth of the Trinity, quoted in CCC 260).

35: Surely we do not have to accept the full teaching of the ancient councils of the Church, that Jesus is truly "of one substance" with the Father? Can we not be satisfied with calling Jesus the "Son of God," without calling him actually God?

In what is called the "hierarchy of doctrines," for the Christian faith, the doctrine of the full divinity of Christ has to be at the top of the heap. Again, it was during the first four centuries, and still later into the fifth and sixth centuries, that this doctrine was unambiguously defined. On this doctrine, everything else in the Christian faith depends. Without it, the Christian faith falls to the ground like a collapsing dead man.

Many Christians today, under the influence of the critical movement, wish to call Jesus the "Son of God" without identifying him as actually God from God, as stated in the Creed. But if Jesus is the "Son of God," what do we mean by this? Do we mean that he is created by God, and given a special role on earth? In this case, Jesus would be essentially no different from you and me. He would be a man, fully human like us. He would be the "adopted" Son of God, chosen by God to be his special messenger. In this role, he would communicate God's teaching, and even show us the right way by his life. But would he be in any sense our "Savior" from a personal point of view?

In the summer of 1977, an explosive symposium called *The Myth of God Incarnate*[17] disturbed the peace of the English theological vacation. In this book, the symposiasts claimed that it was no longer necessary for Christians to believe the orthodox doctrine of the incarnation. In particular, all the writers felt that the critical study of the Gospels had rendered outmoded the picture of Jesus the orthodox, miraculous, divine Son of God.

It seems to me that, in this kind of statement, a whole set of issues can be confused together. There is the philosophical problem: Can God be joined with the human nature of Jesus Christ, or for that matter with any created being? There is the theological problem: Did the early Church councils get it right, that Jesus was *homoousios* with the Father? There is the scientific problem of the study of Scripture: In principle, do we need a miraculous Jesus in order to have a divine Son of God? How can we demonstrate that the miracles of Jesus, plus his virginal conception and above all his bodily resurrection, actually happened?

First, as to the philosophical problem, the issue as to whether God can be joined hypostatically, personally, with a human nature, is not a new one. It exercised Arius and Athanasius in the fourth century just as much as the symposiasts of *The Myth of God Incarnate* in 1977. The answer that orthodoxy gave then is, I think, quite adequate now; namely that God, in joining his own nature to a human nature, is bringing about a union of the divine and human, not a confusion of the two. God can unite himself with us in many ways. The incarnation is only the greatest and most wonderful example of the uniting of the divine and human, in a single person of the Word made flesh.

Second, the question as to whether the councils were right in their definitions is bound up with the whole question of the infallibility of the Church. As we have argued earlier, the definitions of faith cannot entirely be argued logically, but are essentially an act of faith based upon the authority of God who reveals. An essential element of that acceptance of the authority of God who reveals is the Church, which infallibly testifies to the truth of the apostolic faith.

However, I have also argued above that dogmatic theology can attempt to demonstrate the way in which the truths of faith cohere together. Reason has an essential part to play in our developing understanding of the faith. So it is regarding our understanding of the central Christian doctrine of the incarnation.

Athanasius, the great champion of the full divinity of Christ, defended to his great discomfort the doctrine that Jesus Christ was of one substance (*homoousios*) with the Father. Athanasius' argument was, against Arius, that in Jesus, God became man in order that we might become divine (CCC 460).[18] For Athanasius, the divinity of Christ was not simply a speculative point. It was the only way in which we as human beings could share in the life of God, if God himself became man.

A theologian who lessens the divinity of Christ down even an iota from Athanasius will in the long run fail to see the full saving, healing, spiritual power of Christ. An important contemporary attempt to understand this salvific nature of the doctrine of the divinity of Christ appears in Edward Schillebeeckx's *Christ the Sacrament.* In this fascinating study, Schillebeeckx manages to combine a deep knowledge of Thomist theology, together with a contemporary understanding of personalist, existentialist theology. Schillebeeckx begins with his understanding of salvation, which for him is personal encounter with God. "Personal communion with God is possible only in and through God's own generous initiative in coming to meet us in grace."[19] This encounter with God, for Schillebeeckx, is "salvation."[20] Furthermore, "Because grace is a personal encounter with God, it 'makes history' and precisely for this reason it is also 'sacramental.' "[21]

For Schillebeeckx, this divine plan of salvation as sacramental encounter with God is fulfilled in the very incarnation of the Word made flesh:

> The dogmatic definition of Chalcedon, according to which Christ is "one person in two natures," implies that one and the same person, the Son of God, also took on a visible human form. Even in his humanity Christ is the Son of God. The second person of the most holy Trinity is personally man; and this man is personally God. Therefore Christ is God in a human way, and man in a divine way. As a man he acts out his divine life and according to his human existence. Everything he does as man is an act of the Son of God, a divine act in human form; an interpretation and transposition of a divine activity into a human activity. His human love is the human embodiment of the redeeming love of God.[22]

We might add here, for clarification, that, in addition, this implies accepting the doctrine of the Council of Ephesus, that Jesus Christ is *personally* God. By virtue of the hypostatic union, that is, the union of the Person of the Word made flesh with the human nature of Jesus, everything that Jesus did on earth he did as a divine-human person. Literally, Christ only had to touch you, and you were touched by God.

This means, according to Schillebeeckx, that Jesus of Nazareth was the "Sacrament of Encounter between God and Man." In traditional Catholic terminology, Jesus' humanity was the instrument of his divinity. The new existentialist language used by Schillebeeckx smoothed the rough edges of this doctrine of "instrumentality." Jesus' humanity was in a sense an instrument, but this made it seem mechanistic and impersonal. Rather, in Schillebeeckx's terminology, Jesus' humanity, all his bodily acts while on earth, were signs, sacramental encounters between us and the very God-become-man. They were, again in traditional theological terminology, *theandric* acts, acts of the God-man: "That evening after sunset, they brought to him [Jesus] all who were sick and those who were possessed by devils. The whole town came crowding round the door, and he cured many who were sick with diseases of one kind or another; he also drove out many devils, but he would not allow them to speak, because they knew who he was" (Mark 1:32-34).

Schillebeeckx would understand the cross of Jesus in the same way, that it was the sacrament of God's love for us. It would have the value of a sign. As a human act, it was the death of just another wretched subject of the cruel Roman Empire. But, as an act of the One who was God-man, it would be an effective sign of God's love for us, and of God's judgment on sin. The incarnation therefore was not, for Schillebeeckx, just the birth of Christ. The incarnation was a total life, a life that was the sacrament of encounter between God and Man:

> The foundation of this is the Incarnation. But this Incarnation of God the Son is a reality which grows. It is not complete in a matter of a moment; for example, at Jesus' conception in Mary's womb or at his birth. The Incarnation is not merely a Christmas event. To be a man is a process of becoming man; Jesus' manhood grew throughout his earthly life, finding its completion in the supreme moment of the Incarnation, his death, resurrection, and exaltation. Only then is the Incarnation fulfilled to the very end. And so we must say that the Incarnation in the Son itself redeems us. The mystery of Christ or of redemption we can call, in its totality, a mystery of saving worship; a mystery of praise (the upward movement) and of salvation (the downward movement).[23]

Schillebeeckx goes on to argue that the same divine-human activity begun in Christ's life on earth continues after the resurrection in the life of the Church. But it all depends upon the divinity of Christ, in its fullest sense. Otherwise, Jesus can be seen as a prophet, as a teacher, as a good man, as a spiritual guru; but he cannot be seen as the Sacrament of the Encounter with God, unless he is acknowledged as truly God from God, light from light, true God from true God, *homoousios* with the Father. Only by being "one in being" with the Father can he also be "one in being" God with us.

36: Is the miraculous in the life of Jesus, his miracles, his virginal conception, his bodily resurrection, really important for our faith in him? How can we accept all this and truly believe in the humanity of Jesus for us?

We now move on to consider the questions above, namely: There is the scientific problem of the study of Scripture. In principle, do we need a miraculous Jesus in order to have a divine Son of God? How can we demonstrate that the miracles of Jesus, plus his virginal conception and above all his bodily resurrection, actually happened? Does modern historical study of Scripture give any support to these beliefs?

The miraculous in the life of Jesus is closely bound up with the question as to who he was, and what he came to do. It is because, in Schillebeeckx's terms, Jesus is the Sacrament of Encounter between God and man, that there must be in his life that which manifests that encounter. If, in Liberal Protestant terms, Jesus is a sublime teacher, even one who in some way manifests the ideal in life, then miracles are not necessary. But if, in terms of the Council of Ephesus, Jesus is personally God, and his acts are *theandric* acts (cf. the question above), then it follows that the acts of Jesus must be the acts of God, and so beyond ordinary human natural activity.

In Scripture, John is the clearest in this. He uses the term *erga*, works (for example, John 5:17), which in context refer to creative works of God. In the Gospel, they refer to Jesus' miracles (the cure of the man at the pool of Bethesda, the Feeding of the Multitude, the Walking on the Water, etc.), which clearly show who he is:

> But my testimony is greater than John's:
> the deeds my Father has given me to perform,
> these same deeds of mine
> testify that the Father has sent me.
>
> John 5:36

If the acts of Jesus were limited to what is purely "natural," then there would be no reason to consider that he was actually God literally in person.

Up to and including the eighteenth century, the argument above would have been accepted by Catholics, Orthodox, and Protestants. All believed in the divinity of Christ, and in the miracles of the Gospels. What changed perspectives was first and foremost a mechanistic view of the universe, which saw miracles as unnecessary in a world where God had created all things in order. From the viewpoint of physics, the world from Newton onward was a well-oiled machine, with interventions casting aspersions on the perfection of what had already been created. Paul Davis puts it excellently:

> The concept of the Universe as a strictly deterministic machine governed by immutable laws profoundly influenced the scientific world view. . . . It stood in stark contrast to the old Aristotelian picture of the cosmos as a living organism. A machine can have no "free will"; its future is rigidly determined from the beginning of time. Indeed, time ceases to have much physical significance in this picture, for the future is already contained in the present (and so, for that matter, is the past).[24]

Theology accommodated itself to this new world by making the Deity a Creator who had set everything off in perfect order. Miracles were superstitions of an earlier age, which wished to be more closely aware of God's activity in the world. But an enlightened view would see miracles as simply natural events whose causes were not understood in primitive times. This theological system became institutionalized in Deism and Unitarianism; but it had a profound influence throughout the established churches.

Perhaps the most famous of all critical theologians was David Friedrich Strauss (1808-1874), who wrote the most devastating *Life of Jesus Critically Examined,* which enjoyed the singular distinction of being translated into English by none other than George Eliot the novelist, who was at that time coming considerably under the influence of rationalist theology. Strauss outlines the consequence of adopting the mechanistic view of the universe as a critical principle of the rejection of the miraculous in the study of Scripture. This is the first principle for him that demonstrates absolutely that a given account is "not historical — that the matter could not have taken place in the manner described . . . when the narration is irreconcilable with the known and universal laws which govern the course of events. Now according to these laws, agreeing with all just philosophical conceptions and all credible experience, the absolute cause never disturbs the chain of secondary causes by single arbitrary acts of interposition, but rather manifests itself in the production of the aggregate of finite causalities, and of their reciprocal action. When therefore we meet with an account of certain phenomena or events of which it is either expressly stated or implied that they were produced immediately by God himself (divine apparitions — voices from heaven and the like), or by human beings possessed of supernatural powers (miracles, prophecies), such an account is *insofar* to be considered not historical."[25]

Strauss here has uncritically accepted the mechanistic worldview of the scientific era in which he was living; and he has quite dogmatically applied that to biblical studies. It is hardly unjust to call Strauss here a critical fundamentalist, since he rejects entirely *univocally* any narrative that is miraculous in his terms; just as uncritically as a conservative fundamentalist will reject any possibility that a given narrative, miraculous in nature, might possibly be a fictional account.

What is also clear from reading the history of the critical movement of the eighteenth and nineteenth centuries is that it was practically impossible for a biblical critic to maintain orthodox belief in the divinity of Christ while at the same time rejecting entirely the miraculous in the Gospels and in the life of the historical Jesus; *and this on grounds of the presuppositions to the historical inquiry*. We have already rehearsed the reasons for such above; that if Jesus can no longer perform miracles, then he cannot act directly as God, and the doctrine of the hypostatic union is abandoned. And, as we see above, Strauss and the others within the German critical movement were *a priori* unable to accept that God could act directly, and not only through secondary causes.

The critical movement was also helped by a developing Christology. From Luther onward, Protestant Christology had shifted from an emphasis upon Jesus as objectively God, the icon of the divine in Catholic and Orthodox Christology, to an emphasis upon Jesus as my Savior. As Protestant theology developed, therefore, it became more and more easy to abandon the doctrine of the divinity of Christ, to concentrate on the work of Jesus, whoever he was from a metaphysical point of view. This approach to Christology is also present in Bultmann, who rejects any kind of ontological Christology, together with continuing to espouse a similarly dogmatically mechanistic approach to the world that we find in Strauss.

How do we respond to this? First, we simply deny what Strauss affirms: "Now according to these laws, agreeing with all just philosophical conceptions and all credible experience, the absolute cause never disturbs the chain of secondary causes by single arbitrary acts of interposition." But why should not God, even if he does not act arbitrarily, act by single acts of interposition if he himself thinks there might be a reason for it, for instance, divine revelation? Strauss has himself arbitrarily rejected the notion of divine direct activity, but for no clearly expressed reason. We would simply say that such is possible.

We also have no need to continue with a rigid notion of the universe as a machine, with the new physics bringing exciting possibilities into play. Whereas the world does usually act predictably, because God has given it laws of activity, these laws are not absolute, and indeed are not always easy to observe. This means, as *Dei Verbum* states, that there is no reason why God cannot directly intervene, especially in the life, death, and resurrection of his Son:

> To see Jesus is to see his Father also (see Jn 14, 9). This is why Jesus completes the work of revelation and confirms it by divine testimony. He did this by the total reality of his presence and self-manifestation — by his words and works, his symbolic acts and miracles, but above all by his death and his glorious resurrection from the dead, crowned by his sending the Spirit of truth. His message is that God is with us, to deliver us from the darkness of sin and death, and to raise us up to eternal life. (DV 4)[26]

What is important here to emphasize is that Jesus is not just an ethical example, he is not even just the most perfect human being who ever lived. He is a manifestation of God himself, the divine dwelling among us. We can no longer remain with a "natural" Jesus in such a scenario. This obviously links with what we outlined earlier concerning "Christ the Sacrament of Encounter with God" *à la* Schillebeeckx.

Recent studies have strongly defended the miraculous in the life of

Jesus. René Latourelle has produced an important work on the miracles of Jesus,[27] as part of a trilogy of books on the whole methodology of studying the historicity of Jesus in the light of modern biblical criticism.[28] For Latourelle, far from playing down the miraculous in the life of Jesus, the miracles authenticate the mission of Jesus, and the use of redaction criticism for Latourelle further vindicates the miracle stories of Jesus, provided that the reader of the Gospels does not have a prior prejudice against the miraculous.

A similar point is made in the work much more widely known in the English-speaking world by Gerald O'Collins, *Interpreting Jesus*:[29]

> It is claimed that *historians* must suppose human history to be a closed system of causes and effects, in which historians should expect things to follow similar patterns (the principle of analogy) and not even allow for the possibility of religious wonders which could express special divine interventions and concerns. To maintain that human history is such a closed system is to accept a presupposition — prior to any particular historical investigation — and to maintain something which can never as such be proved historically. Further, analogy means some degree of similarity, but not identity. So far from ruling out different even strikingly different events, the principle of analogy rules them in, inasmuch as it entails both likeness *and difference*. A miracle, in fact, manifests both a likeness to other (ordinary) religious events and a difference (in being a religious "marvel" which points to God's special intervention). So far from flouting the historical principle of analogy, a miraculous event would maintain it.[30]

The miracles were performed first before unsophisticated and prescientific Jews and Romans of the first century A.D. On the other hand, it is a mistake to imagine that they were credulous. They had as much common sense as we do, and perhaps sometimes more. They would be as skeptical as we would if told of a man who could raise the dead, feed a multitude with five loaves and two fishes, or walk on the water.

Jesus had to win his audience, not by one miracle, but by many, and even more important, miracles combined with sublime teaching and extraordinary personal integrity. The public ministry of Jesus began with miracles, and with an extraordinary claim on his part. Jesus did not immediately say, "I am the Word made flesh, *homoousios* with the Father." This would have been quite incomprehensible to his contemporaries. It was, after all, difficult enough for the Chalcedonian bishops four centuries later to understand. But nevertheless, Jesus did begin his ministry with an extraordinary claim for himself, namely a close identification of himself with the coming kingdom of God. In this text from Luke, Jesus is being questioned by the Jewish authorities regarding the authority by which he performs miracles. The Jews challenged Jesus that perhaps he was performing miracles by demonic power. Jesus answers:

> Any kingdom which is divided against itself is heading for ruin, and house collapses against house. So, too, with Satan: if he is divided against himself, how can his kingdom last? — since you claim that it is through Beelzebul that I drive devils out. Now if it is through Beelzebul that I drive devils out, through whom do your own sons drive them out? They shall be your judges, then. But if it is through the finger of God that I drive devils out, then the kingdom of God has indeed caught you unawares. (Luke 11:17b-20)

New Testament scholars have developed highly sophisticated tools to sift out those words and deeds of Jesus going back to his time, and those elements in the stories that betray the later interest of the community. But a most demanding scholar, Norman Perrin, is convinced that the above text goes back to the claims of the historical Jesus himself. Perrin is most impressed by the claims of Jesus to be the prime agent of the kingdom.[31]

What impressed the contemporaries of Jesus was not only the miracles, but the *context* in which the miracles took place, of the saving power of God. Like any other ordinary people, they were also impressed by the *number* of miracles. They asked, "When the Christ comes, will he give more signs [miracles] than this man?" (John 7:31). The miracles caused the contemporaries of Jesus to ask questions about him: "The words caused a fresh division among the Jews. Many said, 'He is possessed, he is raving; why do you listen to him?' Others said, 'These are not the words of a man possessed by a devil: could a devil open the eyes of the blind?' " (John 10:19-21). This no doubt reflects a debate that actually went on in the actual ministry of Jesus while on earth. The debate concerned *divine causality.* If a man was able to perform extraordinary acts of healing and exorcism, who was he? The question, in terms of O'Collins quoted above, was as to the similarity and the difference between the marvelous acts of Jesus and ordinary human activity. The similarity (using spittle, giving orders to a sick girl — "get up") went alongside the dissimilarity (curing from blindness mysteriously, the girl suddenly sitting up in bed when apparently dead). These raised the questions concerning the identity of Jesus as performing the "works of God."

Stimulating the debate further was the *moral integrity* of Jesus. He was not just a wonder worker. His teaching was "with authority, unlike their own scribes" (Matthew 7:29). The old apologetic, that Jesus could not be just a good man if he made the claims he did, is still valid. He was, as the old apologetic argued, either bad, mad, or the Son of God. This would be the challenge not only to us, but to the very contemporaries of Jesus as they followed the progress of this extraordinary prophet from Nazareth.

All seemed to come to an end, of course, with the condemnation to death of Jesus, and his crucifixion as a criminal. Jesus retained his integrity to the end, so that even the Roman soldier said, "Truly, this was an upright man" (Luke 23:47). But all seemed lost. The miracles, the sublime teaching, the challenging words, the love that Christ had for the poor and oppressed — all seemed now a distant memory.

Everything in Christian thinking depends upon the resurrection. In the words of Paul to the Corinthian Christians, "If Christ has not been raised, then our preaching is without substance, and so is your faith" (1 Corinthians 15:14), Contrary to those who tend to reduce the resurrection to being a subjective experience of the disciples, the new *Catechism* emphasizes the necessity of the resurrection being an *objective historical event,* happening to a demoralized and fearful group of followers of Jesus. There are two essential elements to this happening, both factual events: the discovery of the empty tomb, and the appearances of the risen Jesus to chosen witnesses as risen from the dead.

More and more critical New Testament scholars are prepared to admit the historicity of the stories of the discovery of the tomb empty on that first Easter morning. O'Collins argues strongly for the historical character of this tradition; perhaps the strongest argument to my mind being that if the disciples had not thought that the tomb was empty, there is no way in which they would have believed that Christ was risen from the dead.[32] The new *Catechism* admits that the empty tomb in itself is not a proof of the resurrection: "The absence of Christ's body from the tomb could be explained otherwise. Nonetheless the empty tomb was still an essential sign for all. . . ." It made the disciples reflect that "the absence of Jesus' body could not have been of human doing and that Jesus had not simply returned to earthly life as had been the case with Lazarus" (CCC 640).

But if the tomb was empty, does the resurrection become, in the media debate involving the views of David Jenkins, a previous bishop of Durham, just a "trick with bones"? On the contrary, here is where the genuinely miraculous event of the resurrection is perceived, *when viewed together with the appearances.* For O'Collins, the fact that there was no body there means that the whole of creation has been transformed, with the transformation of Christ's own body into his glorious body in heaven, in which transformation his own earthly corpse of Jesus takes its own part. The corpse of Jesus is not in the tomb, because the whole of Jesus, body and soul, has been transformed into the glorious body that he now has in heaven, as a promise of our own resurrection, body and soul, on the last day.

The event above all that led to faith that Jesus had risen from the dead was the appearances to the disciples, testified by Paul by "five hundred of the brothers at the same time" (1 Corinthians 15:6):

> Given all these testimonies, Christ's Resurrection cannot be interpreted as something outside the physical order, and it is impossible not to acknowledge it as a historical fact. . . . The shock provoked by the Passion was so great that at least some of the disciples did not at once believe in the news of the Resurrection. Far from showing us a community seized by a mystical exaltation, the Gospels present us with disciples demoralized ("looking sad": Luke 24:17) and frightened. . . . (CCC 643)
>
> Even when faced with the reality of the risen Jesus the disciples are still doubtful, so impossible did the thing seem: they thought they were seeing a ghost (Luke 24:38-41). . . . Therefore the hypothesis that the Resurrection was produced by the apostles' faith (or credulity) will not hold up. On the contrary their faith in the Resurrection was born, under the action of divine grace, from their direct experience of the reality of the risen Jesus. (CCC 644)

In this account, the orthodox Christology is underpinned by its only adequate foundation, the life, death, and above all the resurrection from the dead of Jesus of Nazareth. All this is necessary to demonstrate that in Christ "in bodily form (Greek *somatikos*), lives divinity in all its fullness" (Colossians 2:9). It is because, in all these marvelous events, the divinity of Jesus has manifested itself in bodily form, that we now have a certainly true revelation of the One who is the Word made flesh, God from God, light from light, true God from true God.

The reader will notice that we have not used the virginal conception of Jesus as part of this briefly outlined apologetic above. With Raymond Brown,[33] I am totally convinced that this is a dogma of faith for Roman Catholics. I see less difficulty than Brown in accepting Mary herself being the ultimate source of the tradition, and, in this connection, incline more to the views of John McHugh.[34] But, granted the discussion concerning the historical origins of the tradition of the virginal conception, not least among Roman Catholic exegetes and theologians, I have considered it better not to use it as an apologetic initially for the claims of Jesus to be the only begotten Son of God. Once Jesus is recognized for who he really is, God from God and light from light, then the virginal conception itself begins to make sense. "The eyes of faith can discover in the context of the whole of Revelation the mysterious reasons why God in his saving plan wanted his Son to be born of a Virgin" (CCC 502).

The virginal conception is a miraculous sign of both the humanity and the divinity of Jesus, his having no human Father emphasizing that his true Father was God; and his being born of the Virgin Mary being a sign of his true humanity. We could also use fruitfully the doctrine of Irenaeus of Lyons, that the virginal conception is the sign of a new beginning, the miraculous birth signaling the end of the legacy of Adam and Eve, paradise lost being replaced by paradise regained in the womb of the Virgin Mary.

37: If we are to have a religion "for all nations," must we not be more open to different approaches to Christ than appear simply in a narrow orthodoxy?

As we saw earlier, the word "Catholic" means "according to the whole" (*kath holos*). To translate it as "universal" can be misleading if by that we just mean that it is worldwide. As we saw, from the historical viewpoint, "Catholic" in the third, fourth, and fifth centuries meant those Christians who held the orthodox Christology, as opposed to those who accepted a "partial" view of Christ, such as Arians, Nestorians, and Monophysites. The word "Catholic" has an exclusive as well as an inclusive meaning. It is a challenge, a question. Are we prepared to accept the whole of Christ's revelation as handed on in the visible Church that he founded, as opposed to those parts that we in our wisdom, rather than the wisdom of God, choose as acceptable to us?[35]

The only religion that can be for "all nations" is the one true revelation that God has given to us in Christ, and infallibly declared in the Apostolic Church that he founded. This is the whole thesis not only of this book, but of the Roman Catholic Church itself. What alternative is there? It would seem unfair to say that the alternative offered to us in the liberal Christianity of the West (bypassing of course the traditional denominations and Evangelical Christianity, which is very much thriving, but on what we have argued is the unsound principle of individual interpretation of Scripture) is a "pick 'n' mix" combination of Christianity, New Age, and comparative religion; but I cannot think of any other alternative, nor can I see any logical route to follow, granted the principles of liberal theology.

What is positive in the above Hard Question is the recognition that, in order to be Catholic, as well as a dogmatic base, Catholicism must be open to a plurality of approaches and theologies. This has always been the case. In the Middle Ages in particular, there were fierce controversies between the different schools of theology within the one visible Church; more aggressive to one another certainly than the different denominations of Christianity would dare to be today.

But this is to say that within the one faith there will be many different approaches to it, and explanations of it. It is not to deny that there is one faith, expressed definitively in the infallibly guaranteed formulations of faith proposed by the whole Church for our acceptance in faith as members of the people of God. I have also argued that we cannot have one faith unless there are some infallibly guaranteed formulations of faith; and that the only Christian body where there is such an ongoing process of such formulations, as Newman argued a century and a half ago, is in the Roman Catholic Church. This should not stifle theological debate, either before or after the formulation, since there is always progress in understanding involved. But it does mean that there is one faith, which traverses diachronically in history (we profess the same faith as Paul, Athanasius, Augustine, Anselm, Thomas More, Robert Bellarmine, Newman, Rahner), and synchronically (Germany, England, USA, Southeast Asia).

The new *Catechism* expresses this one faith perfectly, quoting the words of Irenaeus, writing before two centuries had passed since the resurrection of Christ:

> "Indeed, the Church, though scattered throughout the whole world, even to the ends of the earth, having received the faith from the apostles and their disciples . . . guards [this preaching and faith] with care, as dwelling in but a single house, and similarly believes as if having but one soul and a single heart, and preaches, teaches and hands on this faith with a unanimous voice, as if possessing only one mouth."[36] (CCC 173)
>
> "For though languages differ throughout the world, the content of the Tradition is one and the same. The Churches established in Germany have no other faith or Tradition, nor do those of the Iberians, nor those of the Celts, nor those of the East, of Egypt, of Libya, nor those established at the center of the world. . . ."[37] The Church's message "is true and solid, in which one and the same way of salvation appears throughout the whole world."[38] (CCC 174)

Endnotes

1. D. F. Strauss, *The Life of Jesus*, p. 757.

2. ODCC, pp. 1243-1244. For a devastating critique of Schleiermacher's Christology, cf. Strauss, *The Life of Jesus*, pp. 768-773.

3. D. Cupitt, *The Sea of Faith: Christianity in Change* (London: British Broadcasting Corporation, 1984), p. 270.

4. ST, I, q. 2, a. 3: Omne ergo quod movetur, oportet ab alio moveri. Si ergo id a quo movetur, moveatur, oportet et ipsum ab alio moveri; et illud ab alio. Hic autem non est procedere in infinitum: quia sic non esset aliquod primum movens; et per consequens nec aliquod aliud movens, quia moventia secunda non movent nisi per hoc quod sunt mota a primo movente, sicut baculus non movet nisi per hoc quod est motus a manu. Ergo necesse est devenire ad aliquod primum movens, quod a nullo movetur: et hoc omnes intelligunt Deum (Biblioteca de Autores Cristianos [Madrid, 1961], vol. I, pp. 17-18).

5. B. Davies, *Thinking About God* (Introducing Catholic Theology, no. 5) (London: Geoffrey Chapman, 1985).

6. This would not be nullified by so-called "principles of uncertainty" in the world of science. These do not invalidate an order of cause and effect. All this means is that some causes and effects act within some parameters of uncertainty. But this cannot deny that some causes produce some effects, and these are observable and predictable. Otherwise, again, science would be impossible as an activity.

7. ST, I, q. 2, a. 2.

8. D. Lane, *Experience of God* (second edition) (Dublin: Veritas, 1975).

9. Tanner, II, Vatican I, Session 3, chapter 2, on Revelation, p. 806, lines 15-19.

10. Ibid., p. 807, lines 10-15.

11. Ibid., Session 3, chapter 3, "On Faith," p. 807, lines 1-9.

12. ST, I, q. 14, a. 10.

13. Tanner, II, *Gaudium et Spes*, no. 4, p. 1071, lines 6-10.

14. N. Lash, *Believing Three Ways in One God: A Reading of the Apostles' Creed* (London: SCM Press, 1992), p. 32.

15. J. N. D. Kelly, *Early Christian Doctrines*, p. 119.

16. W. Kasper, *The God of Jesus Christ*, trans. M. J. O'Connell (London: SCM Press, 1982), p. 272.

17. J. Hick (ed.), *The Myth of God Incarnate* (London: SCM Press, 1977).

18. Athanasius, *De inc.* 54.3: PG 25, 192B.

19. E. Schillebeeckx, *Christ the Sacrament of the Encounter with God* (London: Sheed and Ward, 1963), p. 2.

20. Ibid., p. 3.

21. Ibid., p. 4.

22. Ibid., pp. 13-14.

23. Ibid., p. 20.

24. P. Davis and J. Gribbin, *The Matter Myth: Beyond Chaos and Complexity* (London: Penguin Books, 1991), p. 25.

25. D. F. Strauss, *The Life of Jesus*, p. 88.

26. Tanner, II, DV, no. 4, p. 972, line 38 — p. 973, line 3.

27. R. Latourelle, *The Miracles of Jesus and the Theology of Miracles*, trans. M. J. O'Connell (New York: Paulist Press, 1988).

28. The other two books in the trilogy are *Finding Jesus Through*

the Gospels: History and Hermeneutics, trans. A. Owen (Staten Island, NY: Alba House, 1979), and *Man and His Problems in the Light of Jesus Christ,* trans. M. J. O'Connell (Staten Island, NY: Alba House, 1983).

29. G. O'Collins, *Interpreting Jesus* (Introducing Catholic Theology, no. 2) (London: Geoffrey Chapman, 1983).

30. Ibid., p. 57.

31. N. Perrin, *Rediscovering the Teaching of Jesus* (London: SCM Press, 1967), pp. 64-65.

32. G. O'Collins, *Jesus Risen: The Resurrection — What Actually Happened and What Does It Mean?* (London: Darton, Longman and Todd, 1987). Cf. also O'Collins's critique of Schillebeeckx's position in *Interpreting Jesus,* pp. 121ff.

33. R. Brown, *Responses to 101 Questions on the Bible* (London: Geoffrey Chapman, 1990), pp. 90-91.

34. J. McHugh, *The Mother of Jesus in the New Testament* (London: Darton, Longman and Todd, 1975).

35. Cf. ODCC, art. "Heresy," p. 639: "The formal denial or doubt of any defined doctrine of the Catholic faith. In antiquity the Greek word *airesis,* denoting 'choice' or 'thing chosen,' from which the term is derived, was applied to the tenets of particular philosophical schools."

36. St. Irenaeus, *Adversus Haereses,* 1, 10, 1-2: PG 7/1, 549-552.

37. Ibid., 552-553.

38. Ibid., 5, 20, 1: PG 7/2, 1177.

A Realistic Look at Sexuality

I mentioned earlier that it was a pity to have to focus almost entirely on the question of infallibility when considering the theology of the Church in Chapter 3. It is even more of a pity that, in considering Catholic moral theology, we will have to concentrate almost exclusively on the morality of sexuality. However, we remind the reader that this is not intended to be a manual of Catholic theology, only an attempt to answer some objections to the teaching of the Roman Catholic Church in a book by David Edwards. And it is indisputable that at this particular point in time, at the close of the twentieth century, the most controversial issue regarding the teaching of the Catholic Church is its uncompromising stand on sexual ethics, which controversy, we must admit, does find much echo within the ranks of the Roman Catholic Church itself.

As we have seen already, in the third, fourth, fifth, and sixth centuries of the Christian era, the most controversial subject was the question of the divinity and humanity of Christ. At the time of the Reformation, the most controversial issue was the authority of the Bible related to the authority of the Church and of Tradition. Now, these issues are still important, as evidenced by our Hard Questions; I would say, much more important even than moral questions as a foundation for our beliefs. But in the "real world," it is more usually questions of sexuality that exercise people when they think of religion and religious convictions. In the late 1960s, a TV program was asking famous personalities what their hopes and expectations were regarding sex and regarding religion at the beginning of the New Year. A media star replied, "Regarding sex, I just hope that people enjoy it. Regarding religion, I do hope that Roman Catholics will be able to use the pill." The latter was the sum of her hopes regarding *religion*!

The Catholic Church is often accused of having an obsession with sex. But a read of any number of tabloids, or even often the daily newspapers, a look at the week's programs on television, and an eavesdropping on the conversation at lunchtime at the local office or factory will, I am sure, convince an impartial observer that it is not only the Church that has an obsession about sex.

In 1993, the Pope issued a controversial encyclical entitled *Veritatis Splendor* ("The Splendor of the Truth"),[1] in which he outlines the principles underlying Catholic moral theology. It is a most important encyclical for our time, and I will be using it extensively in this chapter. It is a substantial booklet of some one hundred eighty pages. Only one paragraph deals with the question of contraception, and simply reiterates the teaching of previous popes. But the media, in commenting on *Veritatis Splendor,* concentrated almost entirely on this reiteration of the Church's teaching on a sexual matter, hardly one percent of the encyclical's content.

However, the principles of sexual ethics relate to the principles not only of sexual ethics itself, but of every area of human morality. One particular factor that I find convincing regarding Catholic sexual ethics is not only the positive value of its principles, but that the alternatives seem so inadequate. I have found that the Church's moral teaching, once it is understood and well explained, has a reasonableness that springs not from human wisdom, but from God the source of all wisdom, who sent his only begotten Son to teach us not only the right faith, but the right Way of Life, which is himself.

38: The Roman Catholic Church surely cannot sustain its rigid line in sexual ethics in the face of so much criticism both inside and outside of its ranks?

Before we begin to deal with this question, it might be worth making a general point at the outset. Many speak about the isolation of the Roman Catholic Church in its teaching on sexuality, even among other Christian churches. But it needs to be remembered that, before the 1930s, when differences emerged between the Catholic and Orthodox churches on the one hand, and the Anglican and Reformed churches on the other, there was complete unanimity regarding sexual ethics among mainline Christians.

All mainline Christian churches up to the nineteenth century and into the twentieth accepted that contraception was wrong; and the moral norm that excluded contraception also excluded any act of sexuality that was not procreative, such as homosexuality, masturbation, adultery, and all other forms of extramarital sexual activity. Strongly influential throughout Christendom was the Old Testament attitude to marriage and sexuality, which saw procreation as sharing in the creative work of God, for man and woman to rule the earth in God's place: "Be fruitful, multiply, fill the earth and subdue it" (Genesis 1:28a). Heterosexual marriage was also given a spiritual basis, both by the Genesis text, that the man and his wife "become one flesh" (Genesis 2:24b), and by the Christian view that the relationship of husband and wife in some way mirrors the relationship between Christ and his Church (Ephesians 5:29).

To this positive biblical attitude, after the conversion of Gentiles to Christianity, were added approaches based more upon Greek philosophy. John Noonan sees this essential moral link between procreation and sexuality as at root Stoic, that a right sexual act had to be in conformity with nature.[2] "As the eye is to see, so the generative organs are to generate with," went the maxim.

This was developed by St. Augustine in his attack on the Manichaeans, who thought that all sexual activity was of its nature evil, because matter and the body were evil. Augustine's argument is summarized by Noonan:

> He (Augustine) stressed that the cardinal moral point separating the two was the Manichaeans' abhorrence of procreation and their taking steps to prevent it, while the Catholics believed that only procreative marital intercourse was moral. Augustine, the most influential writer on Western sexual ethics, thus repeated and put in succinct formulae the Christian rejection of contraception.[3]

Noonan points out that Luther and the Reformers accepted this Augustinian teaching without question, as did the philosophers of the eighteenth-century Enlightenment. Even in the nineteenth century, when movements arose to promote contraception, these movements did not attempt to reconcile their views with Christianity, but with some secular philosophy or other.

What is most important to emphasize looking back at the history of the morality of contraception is that even more vital than the condemnation of contraception itself is the principle that the morality of contraception underpinned the whole of sexual morality by giving it a simple basis, namely that if a sex act is not open to procreation, it is "against nature" and so wrong. Many theologians and philosophers today will attack this principle as "simplistic," "biologistic," and "mechanistic." As we shall see later, there are more profound reasons at the basis of sexuality in Christian terms than simply procreation. But it still remains true that the Church in its moral teaching about sexuality has in no way surrendered this necessary principle, going back to the roots of Greek and Gentile Christianity together with Augustine of Hippo, that a sexual act to be morally right must not deliberately prevent conception, but must be open to life within marriage.

A Christian understanding of procreation sees it as a way of collaborating with God in the gift of life from the Creator, who bestows an immortal soul directly on each new human life. In this way, the Stoic concept of obeying nature and the biblical view of our cooperating in God's eternal plan for the human race come together, and bestow on the genital act of man and woman in marriage its basic morality.

That does not mean that the destruction of the seed before fertilizing the egg is murder; although Christian theology was not always clear biologically concerning the difference between contraception and the actual taking of human life. But it does mean that the sexual act is a particularly sacred act, and therefore must not be a matter purely for pleasure, and its natural dynamism must be respected. Eve exclaims after giving birth to Cain her child, "I have acquired a man with the help of Yahweh [God]" (Genesis 4:1b). Its relationship with the giving of human life, as we shall see later, is the grounds for an act contrary to the procreative ordering of marriage being "intrinsically evil."

In recent decades, Church thinking has insisted upon there being a unitive as well as a procreative dimension in marriage. However, what *Humanae Vitae* refused to surrender was that the *sexual act as unitive could be detached morally from the sexual act as procreative.* It also insisted that "it is necessary that each conjugal act [*matrimonii usus*] remain ordained in itself [*per se destinatus*] to the procreating of human life."[4] On the contrary, argued *Humanae Vitae,* each sexual act had to fulfill the moral description of being both procreative and unitive. Only in this way would the sexual act fulfill the beautiful description in Genesis, that the man and the woman "become one flesh" (Genesis 2:24). They become one flesh when the man gives the whole of himself, including his own source of life, his seed, and the woman accepts that seed of life, open to having a child "with the help of God."

This is the traditional reason for the sexual act being limited to that fullness of procreative union between a man and a woman consecrated to becoming two in one flesh. It is that positive reason that excludes all other kinds of genital acts, because they do not come up to that positive norm, whether we are speaking of masturbation, homosexuality, sex outside of marriage, or the more perverse forms such as bestiality and pedophile activity. If this norm is abandoned, it is difficult to find any other sound principle for sexual morality. This is the crisis afflicting Western society today regarding sexual ethics.

39: The changes in the Roman Catholic Church's attitude to war, Vatican II for the first time in Church documents giving positive support to those who are pacifists, are clear evidence that moral teaching can change. Cannot these changes signal similar changes in other areas of morality?

Moral theology, like dogmatic theology, develops through the months, years, centuries, and millennia. Our understanding of the term "Jesus is God from God, light from light, true God from true God" develops, while we can still say with Athanasius that Jesus is *homoousios* with the Father. Likewise, there can be a development of ideas in moral theology, without there being an "alteration" in Vincent of Lérins's terms, or, in terms of C. F. D. Moule quoted earlier (under Question 22), development as in New Testament Christology can be either *evolutionary,* the generation of new species, or *developmental,* the growth, from immaturity to maturity, of a single specimen from within itself.[5]

I would submit that there has been a genuine *development,* and not an *evolution,* in the Church's attitude to war. It is true that the Church gave positive support to those who adopt a pacifist stance, for reasons of the Gospel. But on the other hand, the Church still recognizes the right to self-defense, both on the part of the individual and on the part of the state. The Church has never insisted upon pacifism as obligatory, except for those committed in a special way to the Christian life as priests or religious: "Legitimate self-defense can be not only a right but a grave duty for someone responsible for another's life, the common good of the family or of the state" (CCC 2265).

But how does the Church reconcile the right to legitimate self-defense, while at the same time encouraging its members to recite the commandment "Thou shalt not kill"? The answer is that for centuries the Church has interpreted "Thou shalt not kill" as meaning "You shall not kill the innocent." It is clear that, in the Old Testament, the state exercised the right to capital punishment (cf. CCC 2266). Also, as is well known, the Israelites fought the enemies of God on the battlefield. It seems that the word "kill" in the Ten Commandments (Exodus 20:13; Deuteronomy 5:17) — *rasah* — means "violent or unlawful killing, murder." The Old Testament always condemned the killing of the innocent, as for instance in the story of Susannah (Daniel 13), who was falsely accused of adultery, and who was only saved from death by the intervention of Daniel. Similarly, Naboth, who owned a vineyard desired by King Ahab, was put to death by Ahab's wicked Queen Jezebel; but God sent the prophet Elijah to meet Ahab, to inform him that his royal dynasty would be destroyed by God's punishment for this act of murder (1 Kings 21:17-24).

This is the point of consistency throughout the Church's teaching on the taking of human life; that the killing of those who have done no wrong to deserve death is gravely sinful. This is why abortion and euthanasia are wrong. The new *Catechism* (CCC 2271) quotes the *Didache of the Twelve Apostles,* a first- or second-century document, and follows it up with a quotation from *Gaudium et Spes* ("Joy and Hope"), the Pastoral Constitution of the Second Vatican Council on the Church in the Modern World: "You shall not kill the embryo by abortion and shall not cause the unborn to perish. God, the Lord of life, has entrusted to men the noble mission of safeguarding life, and men must carry it out in a manner worthy of themselves. Life must be protected with the utmost care from the moment of conception: abortion and infanticide are abominable crimes" (CCC 2271).[6]

The Church has enunciated a proposition such as, "The *direct* taking of innocent life is always gravely wrong." In this way, far from the Church being inconsistent in its moral theology, the development of the taking of innocent life has always been consistent. Similarly the Church has always consistently stated that regarding the act of sexual intercourse, there must always be an orientation toward procreation.

This is not to say that there are not gray zones. Regarding euthanasia, the Church forbids the direct killing of a person who is dying, because that is the killing of the innocent. But what of switching off complex machinery, without which a seriously ill patient will not live? The Church's moral tradition has always said that we do not need to use extraordinary means to keep a patient alive, only ordinary means. Does the old adage (originally used as a satire) apply here: "Thou shalt not kill, but needst not strive officiously to keep alive"? The line between killing and allowing to die can be very thin; but the principle remains secure, that the direct taking of innocent life is wrong.

Similarly, there is a point of consistency in the Church's teaching on sexual ethics. *Humanae Vitae* allowed the use of the infertile period as a means of responsible parenthood. Some have seen this as a form of permitted contraception, and the Church is said to have changed its teaching here. But there is an essential difference from the contraceptive act, which would effectively attempt to prevent the bestowal of new life by God, even if God wished to give life at that time. *Humanae Vitae* explains:

> These two situations are essentially different. In the first (the use of the infertile period) the spouses legitimately use a faculty that is given by nature; in the second case (i.e., contraception), the spouses impede the order of generation [*ordo generationis*] from completing its own natural processes.
>
> It cannot be denied that the spouses in each case have, for defensible reasons [*probabiles rationes*], made a mutual and firm decision to avoid having a child; and [it cannot be denied that] each of them is attempting to ensure that a child will not be born. Nevertheless, it must also be acknowledgd that only in the first case are the spouses strong enough to abstain from sexual intercourse during the fertile times, when, for good reasons [*justae rationes*], offspring are not desired. And then, when the time is not apt for conception, they make use of intercourse for the sake of manifesting their mutual love and for the sake of maintaining their promised fidelity. Clearly when they do this, they offer a witness to truly and completely upright [*recti*] love.[7]

We see here an important example of how moral questions are interrelated, depending on principles adopted. In the case both of abstention from even legitimate taking of life (pacifism) and in the use of the infertile period, we have an instance where there is development in teaching, but not an essential alteration of the principles involved. The way in which we handle one moral question will to a large extent determine how another question is dealt with. This takes us on to the whole question of what is "intrinsically evil" in morality, which is related both to the ethics of self-defense and to sexual ethics.

40: Why does the Catholic Church still insist that sexual activities that exclude procreation and are outside of the marriage situation, namely "two in one flesh," are against the "natural law"? Cannot only situations in human relationships determine what is right and wrong, and not absolutes?

The *Catechism of the Catholic Church* expounded the Church's morality in all areas; but *Veritatis Splendor,* the encyclical that followed up the new *Catechism,* may go down as more significant in the history of moral theology. In it, Pope John Paul II saw as his task to concentrate, not on the morality of any particular issue (sexuality, taking of human life, capitalism), but to deal with "an overall and systematic calling into question of traditional moral doctrine, on the basis of certain anthropological and ethical presuppositions."[8] What is so important about this encyclical is that it includes a justification for basic moral principles. In particular, it deals with various kinds of relativist morality that the Pope sees as rife today.

First, it must be emphasized that Pope John Paul II is a professional philosopher who applied personalistic ethical principles to sexual morality while he was Bishop of Krakow in Poland. This means that he has reflected deeply and competently on these issues prior to his becoming Pope. This must be taken into account before his views are too quickly dismissed. Second, in order to appreciate the encyclical, it cannot be taken apart piecemeal, but must be viewed as a whole, and its arguments considered as part of an interconnecting structure. While based upon the theological tradition of scholasticism and Aquinas in particular, it goes beyond Aquinas to penetrate to a renewed understanding of the natural law. In particular, its use of Scripture combined with an understanding of the natural law is striking, and reflects developments in contemporary moral theology.

For the Pope, the natural law is not simply a biological principle (even though, as we have seen above, biology has its importance), but means that:

> The natural moral law expresses and lays down the purposes, rights and duties which are based upon the bodily and spiritual nature of the human person. Therefore this law cannot be thought of as simply a set of norms on the biological level; rather it must be defined as the rational order whereby man is called by the Creator to direct and regulate his life and actions and in particular to make use of his body.[9]

What the word "natural" means in this context is a contrast with "supernatural," the latter being laws that derive from God's positive revelation through Scripture, Tradition, and above all through Jesus Christ. "Natural law" means that the given moral principle derives, not from specific revelation, but from the very creation of the human person as made in God's image and likeness, and prior to any specific revelation.

However, this is not a law that is derivable from natural science, without any consideration of God the author of the natural law; because (and here the Pope quotes Aquinas) "the *natural law* enters here as the human expression of God's eternal law."[10] It can only therefore be discovered when we consider God's perspective on these moral matters, precisely as our Creator. Furthermore, although it is a law that should be discoverable without divine revelation, as the First Vatican Council stated, divine revelation is practically necessary even for those truths that could theoretically be known by reason. Human reason, Vatican I insists, could come unaided to a knowledge of God as the source and end of all things. Yet, nevertheless:

> It is indeed thanks to this divine revelation, that those matters concerning God which are not of themselves beyond the scope of human reason can, even in the present state of the human race, be known by everyone without difficulty, with firm certitude and with no intermingling with error.[11]

From this arises the importance of the Ten Commandments, which Catholic morality always insisted arise from this natural law, from the original constitution of human nature formed in the divine image and likeness. The fact that these Commandments appear in the Old Testament, in Exodus 20 and Deuteronomy 5, and in a context where scholars admit they are central to the whole life of Israel, means for Pope John Paul II that these Commandments must be considered to be revelation, even if based originally upon "nature." They are an example of Vatican I's clarification of what could be known by reason, but which has been made explicit by divine revelation. It then follows, as we have discussed in Chapter 3, that the Church has authority from Christ to interpret this revelation expressed in the Ten Commandments; including the commandment "You shall not commit adultery" (Exodus 20:14; Deuteronomy 5:18).

The Church has always seen the Ten Commandments as absolute prohibitions, based upon the divine command in nature reinforced in biblical revelation. As we have already seen, "You shall not kill" has been interpreted by Tradition as an absolute ban on the direct killing of the innocent. We have seen that, despite the gray areas, and the complex issues on the borderline, this absolute ban is held consistently by Catholic Tradition as applied to abortion, euthanasia, and the direct killing of innocent civilians in an otherwise just war.

Pope John Paul II, in *Veritatis Splendor*, insists that:

> *A doctrine which dissociates the moral act from the bodily dimensions of its exercise is contrary to the teaching of Scripture and Tradition.* Such a doctrine revives, in new forms, certain ancient errors which have always been opposed by the Church, inasmuch as they reduce the human person to a "spiritual" and purely formal freedom. This reduction misunderstands the moral meaning of the body and of kinds of behavior involving it (1 Corinthians 6:19). St. Paul declares that "the immoral, idolaters, adulterers, sexual perverts, thieves, the greedy, drunkards, revilers, robbers" are excluded from the Kingdom of God (cf. 1 Corinthians 6:9). This condemnation — repeated by the Council of Trent[12] — lists "mortal sins" or "immoral practices," certain specific kinds of behavior the wilful acceptance of which prevents believers from sharing in the inheritance promised to them. In fact, *body and soul are inseparable:* in the person, in the willing agent and in the deliberate act, *they stand or fall together.*[13]

The reader will see the way in which, in Catholic teaching, the "natural law" is related to the Commandments of God, which are related in turn to the human person as a body-soul unity, which again in turn make some absolute demands on our moral conduct if we are to respect that nature created by God.

Finally, it links up with what I said earlier about mortal sin in the Hard Question on hell in Chapter 2. We do not believe as Catholics in "once saved, always saved." We quoted earlier, in that answer to the Hard Question on hell, 1 Corinthians 10:12, where Paul warns his readers: "Everyone, no matter how firmly he thinks he is standing, must be careful he does not fall." Falling away from the Christian life is possible if we deliberately choose against the fundamental good of our nature as expressed in the Ten Commandments as interpreted by the Christian Tradition, whose ultimate decision is to be found in the teaching authority of the Catholic Church. But there is no reason to fear rejection by God if we are following the right Way that is revealed to us, and we use all the helps provided by God's grace in the Church.

41: People today cannot accept the Church's prohibition of masturbation, homosexual acts, fornication, contraception, and adultery. Is it not time for a change in the Church's teaching in this respect?

If what we have said above is correct, then there cannot in any way be a change in the Church's prohibition of any sexual act that violates the norm of being an act oriented essentially toward the unitive and procreative meanings of marriage; what we may call the "two in one flesh" norm.

All the above acts in the Hard Question fall short of that procreative and unitive norm. Masturbation is an act of solitary sex. Homosexual acts are not between man and woman oriented toward procreation, and furthermore lack the essential complementarity of the act of coitus. Fornication is a sexual act outside of the context of marriage's lifelong commitment. Contraceptive acts within marriage or outside of it are acts that deliberately prevent the sexual act from reaching its possible goal in the conception of a new life. Adultery is a heterosexual act where one or other, or both, of the parties involved are married to someone else, and so are acting contrary to that "two in one flesh" norm.

Catholic moral theology, with centuries of confessors and spiritual directors dealing with the "sins of the flesh," realizes the weakness of human nature regarding sexual matters. When the Lord saw his disciples asleep on the night of his betrayal and arrest, he said, "The spirit is willing enough, but human nature is weak" (Matthew 26:41). In addition, Original Sin has left the legacy of a wounded nature, a tendency toward sin, called "concupiscence" (see under Question 8).

Sometimes, the strength of temptation to commit sexual sins such as masturbation, sex outside marriage, homosexual acts, any kind of sexual acts according to the inclination of the person concerned, can be enormous. The story goes of a man going to a priest and saying, "Father, same old sin," and the priest replying, "Same old absolution."

For there to be a "mortal sin" in the person committing that sin, there must be *grave matter*, that is, a serious sin in itself, not just an involuntary temptation of thought (cf. CCC 1858); there must be *full knowledge and complete consent* (CCC 1959). That fullness of knowledge and consent is often lacking in an explosive moment of sexual desire, even though perhaps it could have been avoided in hindsight. Particularly regarding sex within marriage, and problems of contraception, it is most important for the couple to discuss this question, either with a priest, or with a local Catholic marriage counselor. On the other hand, we know that we are all affected by the present climate of sexual free-for-all, whether we are married or not; and all of us have at some stage or other to say "no" to our sexual desires, and exercise that self-control that is a gift of the Spirit of love and purity. There is also the wise old advice of "avoiding the occasions of sin." A meal followed by an accepted invitation to "his or her place" is very often predictable as to its result.

Sexual hedonism is not new in the history of the world. When Paul was writing to the Corinthian Christians as early as the year 57, he was writing to a city renowned for its prostitution, inhabited by retired Roman soldiers, and a port for all to visit who wanted pleasures perhaps illicit elsewhere. Paul reproves the Corinthian Christians for a case of an incestuous relationship. Paul condemns the wrongdoer, and orders his excommunication (1 Corinthians 5:13b). But Paul goes on to enunciate a much more general principle regarding sexual conduct:

> Do you not realize that your bodies are members of Christ's body; do you think that you can take parts of Christ's body and join them to the body of a prostitute? Out of the question! Or do you not realize that anyone who attaches himself to a prostitute is one body

> with her, since the *two,* as it is said, *become one flesh.* But anyone who attaches himself to the Lord is one spirit with him.
>
> Keep away from sexual immorality. All other sins that someone may commit are done outside the body; but the sexually immoral person sins against his own body. Do you not realize that your body is the temple of the Holy Spirit, who is in you and whom you received from God? You are not your property, then; you have been bought at a price. So use your body for the glory of God. (1 Corinthians 6:15-20)

For Paul, therefore, the sexual act most of all reflects the body-soul unity of the human person, and in particular the communion in that act between man and woman. That is why union with a prostitute, or any other union apart from that "two in one flesh" that is the will of Creator for man and woman in lifelong oneness, is unthinkable. This was excellently put in an old commentary on 1 Corinthians by the biblical scholar H. L. Goudge, an Anglican Canon of Christ Church, Oxford, writing in 1903:

> Thus impurity is here condemned not merely as inconsistent with the Christian's obligation to seek the highest good of all, and to avoid becoming the slave of external things (v. 12), but on the grounds of the revealed purpose of the human body and its glorious destiny, or the corporate union of the Christian with the Lord, and of the indwelling of the Holy Spirit.[14]

This finds a strong echo in some modern Roman Catholic moral theologians, where there is a new emphasis upon that aspect of sexuality as the fullness of physical/spiritual union between man and woman in marriage. Any act that violates this not only breaks the "natural law" of failing to orient toward procreation, but thereby violates the communion between persons that is the fulfillment of the sexual act within marriage. This act of union, in which the couple are open to each other and to God's new life, is broken when any sexual act violates the two-in-one-flesh norm. What Paul established in A.D. 57 we affirm within the Christian communion two thousand years later.

Only in this context can we understand the traditional teaching on "intrinsically evil acts." I quote again from *Veritatis Splendor:*

> Reason attests that there are objects of the human act that are by their nature "incapable of being ordered" to God, because they radically contradict the good of the person being made in his image. These are the acts that, in the Church's moral tradition, have been termed "intrinsically evil" (*intrinsece malum*): they are as such *always and per se,* in other words, on account of their very object, and quite apart from the ulterior intentions of the one acting and the circumstances. Consequently, without in the least denying the influence on morality exercised by circumstances and especially by intentions, the Church teaches that "there exist acts which *per se* and in themselves, independently of circumstances, are always seriously wrong by reason of their object."[15]

The most controversial teaching of the Pope's encyclical *Veritatis Splendor* is without question that of the existence and the nature of what are traditionally called "intrinsically evil acts." We must admit that there has been a long debate in Catholic moral theology as to what precisely are intrinsically evil acts, and much difficulty has been encountered in formulating a proposition that clearly states what in a given case is intrinsically evil. For instance, Gerard J. Hughes makes the point that often it is difficult to decide what the "object of the action is."[16]

Regarding the object of a moral action, we have seen already the complications in trying to define more clearly what an "intrinsically evil act" is in relation to the commandment "You shall not kill." More precisely understood, this means, "You shall not directly kill an innocent human being." In this way, the killing of unjust aggressors whether individually or collectively (the latter in war) is sometimes allowed, and the allowing to die of a terminally ill person; but abortion, euthanasia, and the killing of innocent civilians in war is absolutely forbidden. However, to reach this position, a great deal of moral debate is necessary, sometimes over many centuries, and even then gray areas remain, answers only emerging after protracted discussion. It is for this reason, it seems to me, that the Church is reluctant to teach infallibly on moral matters. Rather, the popes limit themselves generally to giving authoritative teaching, to clarify moral problems in the light of Scripture, Tradition, and sound reasoning, applying the Gospel to new situations.

Even regarding the question of contraception, there have been borderline cases. There was the whole question as to whether a woman (or indeed a man) being raped could use contraceptives in self-defense, provided that the contraceptives are not abortifacient, and as long as abortion is not used post-coitus. And there has been increasing clarity concerning the use of the infertile period, that this is not a contraceptive act unless it is in the context of an anti-child mentality.

Difficulties of definition there will always be in moral cases. But this must not blind us to the importance of maintaining the principle of the intrinsically evil act, which has great practical effect in real life situations. Abortion, the killing of innocent civilians in war, devil worship, homosexual acts — all these are instances where the Church's "hard line" objectively speaking is based upon this principle of the intrinsically evil act, that these activities are ordered against a fundamental good of human life, "such as bodily life and marital communion."[17] No one can say that such a principle has no practical effect, because it is this that has made Catholic moral theology distinctive, and in many places unpopular.

Cultural taste cannot determine what is morally right or wrong, nor can a democratic vote. The "moral maze" that many speak about is not limited to children at school, but extends to adults. A local authority official, asked in a broadcast interview a question concerning a moral problem related to civic life, remarked, "What is right or wrong is the result of the collectivity of feelings as to what the majority think is acceptable or non-acceptable." In such a relativistic climate, there is a desperate need for clear principles as we find laid out in *Veritatis Splendor.*

42: Why are celibate clergy able to dictate to married or unmarried people what to do or not to do in bed?

As we have discussed earlier, the root of the Christian teaching about sexual ethics is not in Christianity itself, but begins in the Old Testament as the interpretation of the natural law. Leviticus condemns incest (18:6-17), adultery (18:20), homosexual acts (18:22), which are described as a "hateful thing," and bestiality (18:23).[18] This is not a case of mere ritual uncleanness, but matters for which reason a person would be "outlawed from his people" (18:29). We may think that Israelite society of the sixth century B.C. was male-dominated, but it certainly was not celibate. Yet it rejected as a "hateful thing" deviations from a straight marriage.

As we have demonstrated earlier, the standard Christian teaching about marriage and sexuality, including the condemnation of contraceptive intercourse within marriage, was accepted by all Christian denominations up to and including the beginning of this present century. There were nineteen centuries of basic agreement within Christendom on the wrongness of any sexual intercourse outside of marriage. This was whether the clergy of the respective denominations were mainly married, as within the Protestant and Orthodox churches, or celibate within the Catholic Latin rite. Furthermore, the laity of the respective Christian congregations, whether married or single, do not seem to have objected strongly to that teaching, but seem to have accepted it without question. Today, some married people have changed their views, including committed Christians, and have accepted the rightness of contraceptive intercourse within marriage. Why do not the celibate clergy of the Roman Catholic Church follow suit and accept the modern situation? It is argued that celibate clergy can never feel the strength of the desires that married couples experience in bed, and therefore cannot tell them when to abstain from sexual intercourse, or whether or not to use contraceptive methods of avoiding having children.

Before we try to answer that question, it might well be worth putting into parenthesis that in fact some of those who are most strongly defending the Church's teaching at the present time are not priests, but laypeople, including married laypeople. There is also a growing movement, not only among Catholics, in favor of the newer methods of the prediction of the safe period, which are becoming as safe as the traditional forms of contraceptive. We may eventually arrive at a situation where a number of couples for aesthetic reasons will be following more "natural" methods. This will have nothing whatever to do with celibate priests, but will be first and foremost a movement among married people themselves.

But to answer the main question, while celibate priests can be remote, sometimes it is in fact better for a person to give advice who is not in the actual situation. Many excellent marriage counselors of all persuasions are unmarried. People can be swamped by the very situation itself, and an "outsider" is precisely the person who is needed to help. Priests also learn a great deal through living and working in the pastoral situation. It is not true that a priest has no awareness of sexual problems, even of the intense temptations that arise when people are in bed together. He knows how strong temptations to sexual fantasies can be, even where there is no partner beside. It hardly needs great imagination to realize that these temptations could be multiplied many times over if a wife was sleeping next to him.

What is true of the priest is stated in the Letter to the Hebrews: "It was essential that he [Christ] should in this way be made completely like his brothers so that he could become a compassionate and trustworthy high priest for their relationship to God, able to expiate the sins of the people. For the suffering he himself passed through while being put to the test enables him to help others when they are being put to the test" (Hebrews 2:17-18).

Many priests are "put to the test" when sexual temptations are concerned, throughout their lives. The story goes of a young curate who went down to breakfast, and mentioned in conversation with his parish priest how he was tempted by strong sexual desires. "Father," he said, "when do these temptations stop? About what age?" "Well," said the parish priest, "about sixty, I suppose." The next morning at breakfast, the parish priest looked a little sheepish. "You know I said yesterday that sexual fantasies stop at about the age of sixty? Well, you had better make that sixty-one."

When a person goes to a priest for confession, he or she is going to a person like him- or herself, one who is tempted in various ways, according to his own particular sexual orientation, but who recognizes that, and who is coming to terms daily with it in order to be faithful to his vows. In a priest's training and development, it is so important to come to terms with his own sexuality, and be able to react in a mature way to the challenge of relationships of various kinds within his priestly work, and in his times of relaxation. Those who are charged with the training of priests, and with their in-service direction, are fully aware of these challenges, and are developing modern tools of dealing with them. The modern priest does not run away from his sexuality, but deals with it in the whole process of his development. Only then can he be a faithful priest, able to help those who like him are weak and human. There are priests who for a number of reasons no longer continue their priestly ministry; but that applies also to those who are married, and whose marriages have failed.

Finally, of course, the priest will often recommend a person to go to a specialist or counselor of one kind or another who is not a priest, if he feels that this would be better in a particular instance.

43: Jesus himself did not leave a legalistic set of commandments. Why has the Church made Christ's morality seem so restrictive?

It is certainly true that Jesus did not leave a complete list of commandments on every aspect of morality. He also opposed some very strict interpretations of the Law of Moses in his own day. He had a more liberal interpretation of what was allowed on the Sabbath. He allowed his disciples to pluck ears of corn to eat on the Sabbath (Mark 2:23-28); and he was angry when told that he was not allowed to cure a man with a withered hand on the Sabbath. These were strict interpretations by Jesus' contemporaries of the commandment that no work should be done on the Sabbath (Exodus 20:8-11; Deuteronomy 5:12-15).

But Jesus also said, "Do not imagine that I have come to abolish the Law or the Prophets. I have not come to abolish but to complete them. I tell you, till the heaven and earth disappear, not one dot, not one little stroke, is to disappear from the Law until all its purpose is achieved" (Matthew 5:17-18). Many see an inconsistency between these verses and the rest of the New Testament message.[19] They would see a problem in the fact that, while Christians accept that the Ten Commandments retain their significance in the New Law left by Christ, they do not treat all 613 precepts of the Mosaic Law as binding, for example circumcision, and the command to eat meat drained of blood.

But the eminent Talmudic scholar W. D. Davies does not see this necessarily as a difficulty. He quotes rabbinic texts that "reveal an awareness that, even though the Torah was immutable, nevertheless modifications of various kinds, at least in certain details, would be necessary."[20] But this, for those rabbis who held those views, Davies argues, would not mean that "one dot or one little stroke" had disappeared from the Torah. The Torah had been fulfilled in its very development.

We may admit that there were variations of interpretation of the relationship between the Law and the Christian Gospel in the first century of Christianity. But it does seem that there is a basic consistency between the "historical Jesus," Paul, and the later developed Matthew's Sermon on the Mount. Benedict Viviano, in my opinion, provides a balanced presentation of the case:

> *Jesus* probably did not break in principle with Torah but only with Pharisaic *halaka*. Yet he was a free spirit who directly confronted and resolved life situations in his healings and parables without carefully citing texts. *Matthew* remains in the same line of basic fidelity to the Torah but with a concentration on the more important values

> (23:23) and with a lawyerly concern to provide textual support for innovations. *Paul* prefers an ethic of values like faith, hope, love, and walking in the Spirit to a legal ethics, but he does cite the Decalogue as applicable to Christians (Romans 13:8-10) even though the ceremonial laws do not bind Gentile converts according to his gospel.[21]

This means that, however much or little innovative Jesus was regarding the Torah and its rabbinic interpretation, the teaching of Jesus certainly did not have to be complete: *Its roots were already well set in the Old Testament.* Furthermore, we find that this basic acceptance of the Old Testament ethic as expressed in the Ten Commandments, whatever the attitude might be to the observance of certain Old Testament rituals such as circumcision, remains throughout the sixty-year development of the New Testament literature, from the foundation of the Church at the Day of Pentecost right through to the end of the century.

A vital element of the teaching of Jesus was also its *authority.* As expressed in the Gospel testimony, his moral teaching was itself part of his claim to be the new Moses and even higher, the Son of God. "You have heard how it was said. . . . But I say this to you" (Matthew 5:27-28). That would have sounded close to blasphemous among the rabbis, who saw themselves as not able to innovate, but only to interpret. He did not only teach that it was wrong to kill, but also condemned anger and insulting others (Matthew 5:21-26). He not only taught that breaking oaths was wrong, but condemned the careless taking of oaths (Matthew 5:33-37). He did not allow his followers to follow the saying (not in the Old Testament) that they should hate their enemies provided that they loved their neighbor. Rather, Jesus taught his followers to love their enemies (Matthew 5:43-48).

As we saw above, both for Jesus, Paul, and Matthew, we are expected to obey the Ten Commandments. Regarding specifically now the matter of sexual ethics, what strikes us is the strictness of Jesus' interpretation of the commandment "You shall not commit adultery" (Exodus 20:14; Deuteronomy 5:18). He does not want the penalty of the Law to be inflicted on the woman taken in adultery (John 8:1-11). To those who wished to stone her to death he said, "Let the one among you who is guiltless be the first to throw a stone at her" (John 8:7). Jesus forgave her, but he also said to her, "Go away and from this moment sin no more" (John 8:11). Jesus clearly accepts here the ancient teaching that adultery was a sin. But he went even further. He stated that even if "a man looks at a woman lustfully, he has already committed adultery with her in his heart" (Matthew 5:28). This is consistent with the general principle in Jesus' teaching that he *interiorizes* the Commandments. This is an extension of a principle already begun in the last commandment, "You shall not set your heart on your neighbor's house" (Exodus 20:17; Deuteronomy 5:21; called in the older translations, "Thou shalt not covet").

But the interiorization of the commandment in no way means that in Jesus' teaching the original commandment forbidding an external action (adultery) is abrogated. Rather, its application is extended to deal at root with the motivation underlying such an action. Without the evil motivation the external act would not itself have taken place.

It is true that Jesus condemned other sins much more than sexual sins. For instance, his condemnation was particularly hard on those who loved money, and who stored up riches for themselves, "instead of becoming rich in the sight of God" (Luke 12:21). It was, according to Jesus, easier "for a camel to pass through the eye of a needle than for someone rich to enter the kingdom of heaven" (Matthew 19:23-26). In fact, his disciples were so worried about this (realizing of course that everyone has riches of some kind) that Jesus reassured them, "By human resources this is impossible; for God everything is possible" (Matthew 19:26). He was also most angry about hypocrisy, particularly in religious matters: making an outward show of almsgiving (Matthew 6:1-4); or of prayers (Matthew 6:5-6); or interpreting the Law with selfish motives in mind (Matthew 15:1-9).

Therefore, despite the fact that there was certainly development of moral teaching from the historical Jesus through Paul and to the Matthean-constructed Sermon on the Mount, yet there is a basic consistency throughout. There was a rooting in the Old Testament, particularly in the Ten Commandments, and above all we see the *authority* of Jesus, which was accepted in the Church and then interpreted with authority by the Church. The teaching was not legalistic, because it was rooted in the interior love that Christ not only demanded of his disciples but came to give us. Yet it does nevertheless contain specific precepts, in particular the deepening of the moral law contained in the Torah to become based in the heart; but in no way implying that in the new dispensation external actions were unimportant. Jesus says not only to the rich young ruler, but to us in the late twentieth century, "If you wish to enter into life, keep the commandments" (Matthew 19:17b).

What we have seen in the earlier Hard Questions, concerning the authority of the Church to interpret authentically and when necessary infallibly, we find based in the Gospels themselves. Paul himself began this principle of interpreting the teaching of Jesus and applying it authoritatively (cf. 1 Corinthians 7). Later generations have continued this process.

44: Another major problem is the Catholic Church's refusal to allow divorced people to remarry while the previous partner is still alive. Is this not totally unrealistic and insensitive in this day and age?

This aspect of Roman Catholic teaching goes back to Jesus' own teaching regarding marriage and divorce. We will have to repeat what we have already said regarding scriptural arguments. They are hardly ever watertight. But what we can say in this instance is that there are good scriptural grounds, grounds in the teaching of Jesus himself, for the Catholic teaching that a valid marriage between two baptized Christians cannot be "torn asunder" (cf. Matthew 19:6) while the partners are still living, so that a subsequent marriage of either of the partners will be invalid. The Church adds its authority, and the authority of Tradition, to what is a sound scriptural argument.

This again seems to be very tough and uncompromising teaching, particularly in the modern situation where divorce and remarriage is so frequent. This is even more difficult, granted that now in the majority of Western countries, including those with a majority of Catholics, divorce and remarriage is possible in law. But the new *Catechism* does not give an inch on this matter:

> Today there are numerous Catholics in many countries who have recourse to civil *divorce* and contract new civil unions. In fidelity to the words of Jesus Christ — "Whoever divorces his wife and marries another, commits adultery against her; and if she divorces her husband and marries another, she commits adultery" — the Church maintains that a new union cannot be recognized as valid, if the first marriage was. If the divorced are remarried civilly, they find themselves in a situation that objectively contravenes God's law. Consequently, they cannot receive Eucharistic communion as long as this situation persists. (CCC 1650)

This teaching was clearly stated in the Council of Trent.[22] The key text quoted in part above is Matthew 19:3-9, which we now quote in full:

> Some Pharisees approached him, and to put him to the test they said, "Is it against the Law for a man to divorce his wife on any pretext whatever?" He answered, "Have you not read that the creator from the beginning *made them male and female* and that he said: *This is why a man leaves his father and mother and becomes attached to his wife, and the two become one flesh*? They are no longer two, therefore, but one flesh. So then, what God has united, human beings must not divide."
>
> They said to him, "Then why did Moses command that a writ of dismissal should be given in cases of divorce?" He said to them, "It was because you were so hard-hearted, that Moses allowed you to divorce your wives, but it was not like this from the beginning. Now I say this to you: anyone who divorces his wife — I am not speaking of an illicit marriage — and marries another is guilty of adultery."

The background to this discussion is well known. There was a rabbinic dispute concerning the Mosaic Law in Deuteronomy 24:1, where a man was allowed to divorce his wife (note that the woman was not allowed to divorce her husband!), provided that he gave her a writ of dismissal, which would leave her free to marry another man. The rabbis disputed the grounds giving a man the right to divorce his wife. The rigorist Shammai school demanded that the wife had committed some infidelity in order for the man to have the right to divorce her. The laxist Hillel school, on the other hand, claimed that the man could even divorce his wife if she cooked him a bad meal.

The reply of Jesus took everyone by surprise by its strictness. He teaches that there is to be no divorce and remarriage at all. He even reinforces the Genesis text "What God has united, human beings must not divide" with an even stronger statement, "Now I say this to you: anyone who divorces his wife — I am not speaking of an illicit marriage — and marries another is guilty of adultery." No wonder the disciples are shocked, and wonder if marriage is worth it at all! (See Matthew 19:10-12.)

The discussion over the meaning of this statement of Jesus about marriage and divorce has been endless. But, it seems to me, it reduces itself to three main positions:

a. Jesus is not being "legalistic," but presenting an ideal.[23] However, this position is difficult to sustain exegetically. If Jesus was simply saying, "The ideal is indissoluble union, but I am not being legalistic," then all would agree, but it would have no practical effect. No doubt both the Hillel and the Shammai schools would posit lifelong union as an ideal; but it does not answer their question about what reasons would make divorce and remarriage justifiable. Second, the way in which Jesus expresses the matter leads us to think that he is stating a *conditional law* as in the Old Testament. "If . . . then" (cf. Leviticus 5). If . . . then the man is actually committing the crime in Jewish law of adultery.

b. Jesus is stating a law, but provides an exception to the law of divorce and remarriage in the famous "exception clause" "I am not speaking of an illicit marriage." If this view was correct, the translation of the exception clause in Greek *me epi porneia* would be more like "I am not speaking of marital infidelity." This is the Eastern Orthodox position, that divorce and remarriage may be allowed on the grounds of infidelity. But there are two great difficulties with this view. The first is that if Jesus meant the exception was for marital infidelity, then the word here used should not be *porneia*, sexual impurity, but *moicheia*, the actual Greek word for "adultery." The second is the even more decisive objection that Jesus would be saying nothing at all new in his reply. He would be simply adopting the position of Shammai that there had to be serious grounds before divorce and remarriage was allowable. The reply sounds quite radical. The exception clause, in this view, simply takes such radicality from Jesus' reply.

c. The third view, expressed in the NJB,[24] is that the exception clause refers to marriages that are illicit because they are incestuous, falling within the forbidden degrees of marriage in Matthew's Jewish Christian community, as expressed in Leviticus 18. In this case, such marriages would have been considered by Matthew's Christian community as *invalid*, and are not therefore a genuine exception to the rule expressed by Jesus that there is no going back from a genuine valid marriage. This would, of course, support the Roman Catholic rule concerning marriage and divorce. In this case, the exception clause would most likely have been added by the Matthean community as a clarification of the teaching of Jesus.

Paul most certainly seems to take the same absolute line in 1 Corinthians 7, written according to the scholars in the year 57. He says the following to the Corinthian Christians: "To the married I give this ruling, and this is not mine but the Lord's; a wife must not be separated from her husband — or, if she has already left him, she must remain unmarried or else be reconciled to her husband — and a husband must not divorce his wife" (1 Corinthians 7:10-11).

Scholars dispute as to whether the phrase "and this is not mine but the Lord's" refers to a definite body of teaching handed on from Jesus himself forbidding divorce and remarriage (such is not impossible, since the hypothetical document *Q* might well have existed then, or other pre-Gospel collections of Jesus' sayings); or whether "and this is not mine but the Lord's" refers rather to a special vision of Paul himself. The former is much more likely in my opinion; but whatever the origin of Paul's teaching on marriage, it appears identical with that which was eventually transmitted as the teaching of Jesus in Matthew. This surely adds up to a strong argument from the New Testament that the teaching of the Roman Catholic Church on the indissolubility of marriage is well based.

I would add here that, in Catholic teaching on marriage, there are three "goods" (*bona*) of marriage: *fides* (fidelity), *proles* (offspring), and *sacramentum* ("sacrament, mystery"). In answering earlier Hard Questions, we have concentrated on the aspect of procreation (*proles*) as so important in helping to give a moral description of the sexual act. Here it is necessary to balance such obvious but necessary overemphasis on the procreative aspect. The procreative aspect still remains essential, since it is in the coital act that the couple become two-in-one-flesh. But, for this completeness of union, their fidelity together is equally if not more essential (they are not just procreative machines); and finally, their union is a sacramental sign of the "union between Christ and his Church" (Ephesians 5:32).

These reasons make the Church apparently unbending in its teaching on marriage and divorce. There has recently been a development in teaching and canonical practice concerning the granting of nullity, in particular on grounds of defective consent. As Herbert Waddams explains:

> A declaration of nullity in regard to a marriage establishes that there has never been a true marriage, whatever may have appeared to be the case, and however long the parties may have lived together. Various reasons, such as defective consent or other impediments, may make a supposed marriage null.[25]

This presentation appears of necessity impersonal, and unrelated to individual marriage problems. For reasons of time, to answer the Hard Question, I have dealt with the teaching and not with its pastoral implementation. In practice, an enormous amount of time, skill, and patience, together with great compassion, go to make up the marriage service of the Catholic Church today. Perhaps the most important aspect is the starting point, the belief of the couple in the indissolubility of marriage, and their determination to make their marriage work. But, if the marriage does run into difficulties, all kinds of help are available to see what can be done to sustain the relationship. If, on the other hand, despite all efforts, the marriage clearly cannot work, then professional advice from priests and from counselors can help repair and lessen the damage.

The Catholic teaching also has proved itself immensely practical, even if not easy, down the centuries, and again was followed by the Church of England substantially right up to this present century. In today's society, where the institution of marriage itself is under threat, with all the consequent unhappiness, the corrosion has followed the ignoring of these words of the Lord, "What God has united, human beings must not divide" (Matthew 19:6b).

One final note: The present chaotic situation regarding marriage, divorce, and people living together without being married, means that perhaps there is quite a common situation developing where people will not be able to receive Holy Communion at least for a time. Perhaps since the Second Vatican Council there has been an overemphasis upon the act of going to Holy Communion, to counter the very strict attitudes prior to the 1960s. Perhaps people in the Church need to realize that there are great spiritual benefits from participating in the liturgy without receiving Communion. Perhaps also the Christian community will accept more and more that there will be members in the congregation who will not be receiving Communion, for any number of reasons, and will accept that without any comment or judgment.

Endnotes

1. *Veritatis Splendor. Encyclical Letter Addressed by the Supreme Pontiff Pope John Paul II to All the Bishops of the Catholic Church Regarding Certain Fundamental Questions of the Church's Moral Teaching* (London: Catholic Truth Society, 1993).

2. J. Noonan, article "Contraception" in NDCE, pp. 124-126.

3. Ibid., p. 125.

4. J. E. Smith, *Humanae Vitae: A Generation Later* (Washington, DC: Catholic University of America Press, 1991), p. 281.

5. C. F. D. Moule, *The Origin of Christology* (Cambridge: Cambridge University Press, 1977), p. 2.

6. *Gaudium et Spes,* 51, no. 3.

7. *Humanae Vitae,* 16. Translated in J. E. Smith, *Humanae Vitae: A Generation Later,* p. 285.

8. *Veritatis Splendor,* p. 8.

9. Ibid., p. 78, no. 50. Quotation from the Congregation for the Doctrine of the Faith, *Instruction on Respect for Human Life in Its Origin and on the Dignity of Procreation (Donum Vitae)* (February 22, 1987), Introduction, 3: AAS 80 (1988), 74.

10. *Veritatis Splendor,* p. 68.

11. Tanner, II, p. 806, lines 15-18.

12. Ibid., II, p. 667, lines 22-31.

13. *Veritatis Splendor,* pp. 77-78 (emphasis in the original).

14. H. L. Goudge, *The First Epistle to the Corinthians* (Westminster Commentaries; London: Methuen, 1903), p. 50.

15. *Veritatis Splendor,* p. 122. At the end of our quotation, in quotation marks are excerpts from the Pope's Post-Synodal Apostolic Exhortation *Reconciliatio et Paenitentia* (December 2, 1984), 17: AAS 77 (1985), 221.

16. CCCC, p. 347. Gerard Hughes makes this criticism regarding CCC 1751-1756, quoting Aquinas, ST, I-II, q. 18, a. 10, and saying that "in some cases circumstances are more properly to be considered part of the object of the action itself."

17. Cf. the excellent summary of the argumentation of *Veritatis Splendor* in the article by Germain Grisez, "Revelation versus dissent" in J. Wilkins (ed.), *Understanding Veritatis Splendor: The Encyclical Letter of Pope John Paul II on the Church's Moral Teaching* (London: SPCK, 1993), pp. 1-8.

18. Cf. NJB, Leviticus 18a, p. 157: "The chp is to some degree a literary unit. It is more akin to Deuteronomy than the rest of the 'Law of Holiness.' " M. Black (ed.), *Peake's Commentary* dates the Law of Holiness, of which it considers Leviticus 18 a part, between 600 and 570 B.C.

19. NJBC, p. 641, 42:26-29.

20. W. D. Davies, *The Setting of the Sermon on the Mount* (Cam-

bridge: Cambridge University Press, 1964), p. 161. Cf. also W. D. Davies and D. C. Allison, *The Gospel According to Matthew: A Critical and Exegetical Commentary*, vol. I (Edinburgh: T. and T. Clark, 1988), p. 492.

21. NJBC, p. 641, 42:26-29.

22. Tanner, II, Trent, Session 24, Canons on the Sacrament of Marriage, no. 7, p. 754, line 40 — p. 755, line 4. "If anyone says the church erroneously [i.e., erred when it] taught and teaches, according to evangelical and apostolic doctrine, that the bond of marriage cannot be dissolved by the adultery of one of the spouses, and that neither party, even the innocent one who gave no grounds for the adultery, can contract another marriage while their spouse is still living; and that the husband commits adultery who dismisses an adulterous wife and takes another woman, as does the wife dismissing an adulterous husband and marrying another man; let him be anathema."

23. NDCE, p. 161.

24. NJB, Matthew 19:9, note b, p. 1641: "By contrast *porneia* in this context seems to have the technical sense which *zenut* has in the rabbinic writings when used of a union incestuous because within the degrees forbidden by law, Lv 18. Such unions contracted legally between gentiles or tolerated by the Jews themselves between proselytes must have made difficulties in legalistic Judaeo-Christian circles like that of Mt, when people were converted; hence the instruction to break off such irregular unions which were no true marriage."

25. NDCE, p. 428.

CHAPTER 6

Realism About Unity

Cardinal Hume spoke recently of a present "winter" in the movement for church unity. In his position of leadership, he is closer to feeling the temperature of the prevailing ecumenical wind, although all of us have experienced some slowing down of momentum since the ARCIC Reports. A time of taking stock, when there is not a great deal of apparent forward movement, can be a positive development. Our churches have been apart for four hundred years (regarding the Orthodox, even longer, a thousand years) and perhaps we were premature to think that unity could come almost immediately. The season of winter is not a time when nature is dead, only asleep. Like the little girl in the beautiful story of Jesus' healing, nature only awaits the call of the Master, "*Talitha kum!* . . . Little girl, I tell you to get up" (Mark 5:41).

So perhaps it is with the ecumenical movement. This time is given to consolidate what has been already achieved, to continue discussions even when there is no immediate result, to grow together as fellow-Christians in every aspect of our church community life, and to wait for that voice of the Master. Naturally, there is no excuse for complacency. Winter, if it lasts too long, destroys rather than protects what is preparing to grow. But this ecumenical "close" season can be used most positively.

An essential part of continuing discussion will be concerning questions that still divide us, and that may seem intractable. That is surely not the end of ecumenism, but rather the beginning, which faces real mutual difficulties with both honesty and charity. Until we have faced that point, mature ecumenism does not even exist.

45: Has not the change in leadership in the Roman Catholic Church set back the cause of unity in the past ten years? Does not the condemnation of some theologians highlight this intolerance and put back unity still further?

Where a theologian denies an essential doctrine of the faith, or publicly dissents from official church teaching, then the church has no option but to make its own position clear in one way or another. I cannot see how this sets back the cause of church unity. We can only unite over what is essential concerning divine revelation. In a tension between truth and unity, we must serve the truth as we see it. Theologians might speak out strongly against the "official church's" position, in the name of Truth, and in spite of ecumenism. They cannot complain when the Vatican is equally outspoken.

A similar decision was made by the Church of England General Synod in voting for the ordination of women to the priesthood. It was pointed out more than once, and over some years, not only by the Vatican, but by Catholic bishops in England, that if the Synod went ahead with the ordination of women, this would set back the cause of church unity. It was an agonizing decision for the Synod, but, as more than one member pointed out, in this case it was felt that the Church of England must even put ecumenical dialogue with the Roman Catholic Church second in priority to following the Spirit, which seemed clearly to be calling the Church of England to break new ground in ordaining women to the ministerial presbyterate of the Church.

Individuals are not the only ones who make decisions. Communities do also make decisions, for a variety of reasons. We have a long history in our Church of theologians being disciplined by authorities. There is always a tension between the genuine desire on the part of the Church to allow freedom of research, and for theologians to push forward the frontiers of understanding; and, on the other hand, the need for the Church to protect the people of God from error. This tension can arise, not only by a theologian teaching what is explicitly contrary to the Church's teaching, but simply because his or her ideas have not yet been assimilated by the generality, and thus can cause confusion.

We saw earlier how the biblical critical movement, particularly as applied to the Gospels, could lead to a denial of the miraculous in revelation, and ultimately to a denial of the trinitarian God who reveals, in favor of a deistic or pantheistic prime mover. There could be in this case a confusion between methods that were quite legitimate (historical critical research) and much more radical philosophical and theological denial of Christian revelation. A theologian who is at the forefront of such a kind of discussion may suffer from that resultant confusion.

What is such a theologian to do? The classical spiritual advice is for the theologian to take the flak, not to deny his opinions, but to be obedient to authority. It is a hard road, which many have followed, among them Yves Congar, Henri de Lubac (both under a cloud, but subsequently both made cardinals), and Pierre Teilhard de Chardin. These great thinkers were removed from their academic posts, and often suffered from small-minded superiors. In the case of Yves Congar and Henri de Lubac, they were totally vindicated by the Church, and became completely acceptable when their ideas were understood.

Perhaps the happiest story in this kind of instance is of the great pioneer in biblical scholarship Father Marie-Joseph Lagrange, the Dominican rector of L'École Biblique in Jerusalem when it was founded in the nineteenth century. Lagrange, while completely orthodox, was under suspicion by more fundamentalist Catholics for what were seen as dangerous views about the historicity of the Scriptures. As Roland de Vaux wrote in his fascinating biographical article about Lagrange:[1]

> He [Lagrange] saw that some men were taking liberties which, because of their origin, were dangerous, and would inevitably prove fatal; he saw others clinging to conservative views on weak evidence which he could not in honor accept, and knew that this was in fact equally dangerous, but he also saw that there was room between the two for a road which would meet the demands of faith and of reason.[2]

During the modernist crisis, Lagrange was for a while under a cloud, his writings being forbidden for use in seminaries by order of the Vatican Consistorial Congregation dated June 1912. But Père Lagrange kept his cool:

> He had always been unreservedly obedient to the Holy See, and it was sufficient for him to express it. He sent a declaration of

complete obedience to Rome, for which Pope Pius X at once expressed his gratitude. He also asked to be removed for a while from the École Biblique and was recalled to France. Less than a year later he returned to Jerusalem with instructions to continue his course of exegesis.[3]

By no means are all stories of such conflict between theologian and church authority as happy as this. But some responsibility devolves upon the theologian himself or herself to act responsibly, and to listen to such criticisms. Like politics, if the theologian does not like the heat, he must stay out of the kitchen. The kind of conflict with new ideas is part of a healthy church, provided that the theologians concerned (and this was the case with de Lubac and Congar) were not clearly denying a dogma of faith. The same is entirely true of Karl Rahner, who was always pushing out the frontiers of theology, but never knowingly denied a defined dogma of faith.

In any reunited church, it must be fervently hoped that there will always be theologians in advance of the pack. But there are limits to what can be speculated upon (as we have seen, the limit is what the Church has defined for our faith), and the theologian has some responsibility also to be prudent so as not to cause unnecessary confusion in the midst of all speculation. Perhaps, as I suggested earlier, we may need to develop more sophisticated structures (e.g., commissions in which theologians can try out new ideas with their peers). But nothing can take away the responsibility of church authority to state unambiguously what is the truth, even if such a statement causes anger among the theological community, or challenges the ecumenical movement; provided of course such unambiguous statement of the truth is joined with sensitivity and charity.

46: Cannot there be some flexibility in the question as to what doctrines need to be believed in a future united Church? Is this not taking seriously the "hierarchy of truths"?

Anyone who studies Catholic theology knows that there is a great deal of flexibility in the whole spectrum of doctrine. The limits are placed on those doctrines to which the *magisterium*, either ordinary or extraordinary, has committed the faith of the Church. Furthermore, even regarding these defined doctrines to which we are committed in faith, ecumenical dialogue will enable us better to understand the context of these doctrines. But enough has been said so far to emphasize the fact that the truth cannot be compromised, in this case the revealed truth of apostolic faith clarified by the ultimate teaching authority of the Church, the bishops in union with the Bishop of Rome, the successor of Peter.

When the *Catechism of the Catholic Church* speaks of the "hierarchy of truths," it does not mean that some doctrines, the lesser ones in the hierarchy, are optional, but rather that the doctrines of the faith all interconnect with one another: "The mutual connections between dogmas, and their coherence, can be found in the whole of the revelation of the mystery of Christ. 'In Catholic doctrine there exists an order or "hierarchy" of truths, since they vary in their relation to the foundation of the Christian faith' " (CCC 90).[4]

The doctrines of the Immaculate Conception and of the Assumption of Mary are in no way as central to our faith as is the doctrine of the Trinity and of the incarnation. But we have seen earlier how the doctrine defined at Ephesus, of Mary as *theotokos,* "Mother of God," protected the Church's doctrine of Christ from Nestorianism. Mary was the mother, for orthodoxy, of the Word made flesh, who was a single divine person (*hypostasis*). If one is able to say that Mary is the "Mother of God," then at the same time one is able to say that Jesus not only possesses a divine and human nature, but acts "theandrically." Everything that Jesus does, even his dying as a man, he does as God, the Word made flesh. All this was defended by the statement that Mary is *theotokos.* So it was said that Mary in herself had destroyed all heresies.

The doctrines of the Immaculate Conception and of the Assumption are less central again even than Mary as *theotokos,* which is close to the center of the doctrine of the incarnation. Yet they are doctrines that help to adorn the radius of the Christian mystery. No one could argue that it was impossible in the schema of revelation for Mary to have been born as a sinner, and that her body like ours remained corrupt until the general resurrection. God could have so arranged matters, even with Jesus being born in the normal way. We cannot limit the providence of God, even when considering the possibilities of revelation.

Even more, Aquinas argued that God could even have saved us without the incarnation. God could have saved the world with a prayer. The cross was not absolutely necessary. Aquinas argued that the cross was necessary as the most fitting means of our salvation (with the necessity of *convenientia*),[5] God expressing and manifesting his deepest love for us by the incarnation and redemption. God freely chose to save the world in what God himself saw as the best way. We believe as Catholics that part of that best way was that the Mother of God, the Mother of Jesus, should share in the full glory of Christ by being free from sin, and by rising body and soul immediately to be with her Son, and not to wait for the general resurrection.

This is expressed beautifully by Pope Pius XII in the beginning of the text defining the Assumption in 1950:

> From all eternity and by one and the same decree of predestination the august Mother of God is united in a sublime way with Jesus Christ; immaculate in her conception, a spotless virgin in her divine motherhood, the noble companion of the divine Redeemer who won a complete triumph over sin and its consequences, she finally obtained as the crowning glory of her privileges to be preserved from the corruption of the tomb and, like her Son before her, to conquer death and to be raised body and soul to the glory of heaven, to shine refulgent as Queen at the right hand of her Son, the immortal King of ages.[6]

Curiously, the doctrine of the Immaculate Conception had a much more difficult time to be accepted within the development of doctrine than did the Assumption. From very early times, tradition accepted that Mary the Mother of the Son of God did not commit an actual sin during her life. This was seen as necessary for her to be the Second Eve, a fitting Mother for the Redeemer. There was nothing in Scripture to make absolute Paul's statement that "all have sinned and lack God's glory" (Romans 3:23). His statement refers only to the generality of the human race, arguing explicitly that both Jews and Gentiles indiscriminately need God's grace, and would not rule out an individual exception. The medievals thought that not only Mary but also Jeremiah and John the Baptist were free from actual sin during their lives, because they were filled from their mother's womb by the Holy Spirit (cf. Jeremiah 1:5; Luke 1:15b). Whether or not we agree with their exegesis, the medievals certainly saw no incompatibility with a sinless life in an exceptional case, by a special mandate by divine grace.

What was difficult was not Mary's sinlessness — that had been accepted for a long time — but precisely her sinlessness *from the first moment of her conception.* This, for Aquinas, caused a problem regarding redemption. How could Mary have been redeemed if she was free from sin from the very first moment of her conception? Duns Scotus provided the answer: that Mary was free from sin from the very act of redemption itself. Mary was like us redeemed by Christ her divine Son; then and only then could she be truly immaculately conceived.

Regarding the Assumption, this had never been questioned, even though we must admit that the doctrine was not well known until the second half of the first millennium.[7] What is significant is that, despite the enormous industry of relics during the Middle Ages, no one ever claimed to possess any part of the body of Mary, even though for instance they advertise the body of St. Mark buried in Venice Cathedral. The real difficulty concerning the Assumption is the lack of explicit Scripture reference. But here it is important to reemphasize the Catholic doctrine of Tradition. Certainly there is nothing contrary to the Assumption contained in the pages of Scripture. The development of doctrine, which understands Scripture in a dynamic and ongoing way, is well expressed again in the papal definition of the Assumption by Pius XII to which we referred originally above. The biblical reasons are presenting us with the whole thrust of the message of salvation, in which Mary plays an essential part in the divine plan. Her conception, birth, life, death, and above all her resurrection mirror that of her divine Son, to whom she gave her bodily life in her birth, but from whom she received physical/spiritual grace through that total and immaculate union that lasted through her life on earth, and continues now in heaven. She is the prototype of redemption, that "woman robed with the sun, standing on the moon, and on her head a crown of twelve stars" (Revelation 12:1b).

47: If baptism is the sacramental source of unity among Christians, then why does the Roman Catholic Church still continue to refuse to give Holy Communion to, and refuse to receive Holy Communion from, those it considers "separated Christians"?

This is a very complex question, but we must begin by saying that it is not entirely true to say that we "continue to refuse Holy Communion to, and refuse to receive Holy Communion from, those it considers 'separated Christians.' " There are something like one hundred fifty million Christians, referred to usually as Eastern Orthodox (called in our official documents "Separated Eastern Christians"), Greek, Russian, and of various kinds and nationalities, who are welcome to receive Holy Communion from us "if they spontaneously ask for them and are properly disposed";[8] and our Church allows us to receive Holy Communion from their churches provided there is not a Catholic church within reasonable distance. Unfortunately for us, the Orthodox themselves vary as to how welcome they make us at their eucharistic celebrations! But there is now no barrier on our side, as the new *Catechism* clearly expresses:

> The Eastern Churches that are not in full communion with the Catholic Church celebrate the Eucharist with great love. "These Churches, although separated from us, yet possess true sacraments, above all — by apostolic succession — the priesthood and the Eucharist, whereby they are still joined to us in closest intimacy." A certain communion *in sacris,* and so in the Eucharist, "given suitable circumstances and the approval of Church authority, is not merely possible but is encouraged."[9] (CCC 1399)

We are not yet in full communion with these Eastern churches, particularly regarding their nonacceptance of papal primacy and infallibility, which means that Orthodox and Catholic priests concelebrating is, as far as I am aware, entirely unknown thus far in the ecumenical movement. But there is a *reciprocity* allowed by our own Church discipline, whereby we may receive Holy Communion from them, and they from us, under specified but not infrequent occasions.

Why do the Orthodox enjoy a privilege that the Anglican churches, and the churches of the Reformation, do not enjoy? The problem is always concerning the *doctrine of the Eucharist* where these churches are concerned. We turn to the *Catechism of the Catholic Church* once more, integrating quotations from the Decree on Ecumenism (UR):

> Ecclesial communities derived from the Reformation and separated from the Catholic Church "have not preserved the proper reality of the Eucharistic mystery in its fullness, especially because of the absence of the sacrament of Holy Orders." It is for this reason that Eucharistic intercommunion with these communities is not possible for the Catholic Church. However, these ecclesial communities, "when they commemorate the Lord's death and resurrection

in the Holy Supper . . . profess that it signifies life in communion with Christ and await his coming in glory." (CCC 1400)

We do believe as Catholics that we are one with other Christians in a special way by virtue of the sacrament of baptism. But in our sacrament of initiation, there are three sacramental parts to it: baptism, confirmation, and Eucharist. The Christian is not fully initiated until he or she has received Holy Communion. As the Decree on Ecumenism, already quoted, of the Second Vatican Council states:

> Thus baptism establishes a sacramental bond of unity existing among all who have been reborn by it. But of itself baptism is only a beginning, an inauguration wholly directed toward the acquisition of the fullness of life in Christ. Baptism, therefore, is oriented toward the complete profession of faith, complete incorporation into the institution of salvation such as Christ willed it to be, and finally the completeness of unity which eucharistic communion gives.[10]

The churches of the Reformation did not accept the Roman Catholic doctrine of transubstantiation, that the bread and wine in the Eucharist are changed completely into the body and blood of Christ. While not using the term "transubstantiation," the Orthodox accept the core of the doctrine, as we shall see in the answer to the next Hard Question. The Reformers differed in their eucharistic doctrine from both Catholic and Orthodox Tradition.

The Swiss reformer Zwingli held the "lowest" doctrine of the Eucharist, that the bread and wine remain just bread and wine, only a sign of Christ's presence as a ring is a sign of the presence of a husband for his wife when he goes away on a journey from her. Luther held a much "higher" doctrine, that of consubstantiation, namely that the bread and wine after the consecration remain, but coexist *with* the body and blood of Christ, analogously with the divinity and humanity of Christ coexisting in the being of the person of Jesus. The Anglican formularies are ambiguous, but the most we can say is that the Church of England does not clearly teach the doctrine of transubstantiation, and many Anglicans would be horrified to think that it did.

We must consider more deeply this doctrine in answer to the following Hard Question. But what is important to realize is that it is this insistence upon what the Roman Catholic Church believes to be the orthodox doctrine of the Eucharist that is at the heart of all the ecumenical problems concerning intercommunion and the sacrament of orders. There can be no intercommunion as there is with the Orthodox until the Roman Catholic Church recognizes in the ecclesial community concerned their doctrine as fully compatible with the Catholic doctrine of the Eucharist.

However, even before our communities come together in intercommunion, before that blessed day when our doctrines of Eucharist are compatible, we could allow *individuals* on specified occasions to our Holy Communion, *even where their ecclesial community does not enjoy the same intercommunion as do the Orthodox.* It is worth quoting in full from the Code of Canon Law in this respect:

> Can. 844, §4. If there is a danger of death, or if, in the judgement of the diocesan Bishop or of the Episcopal Conference, there is some other grave or pressing need, catholic ministers may lawfully administer these same sacraments to other Christians not in full communion with the catholic Church, who cannot approach a minister of their own community and who spontaneously ask for them, provided that they demonstrate the catholic faith in respect of these sacraments and are properly disposed.[11]

Roman Catholic priests will always be generous in giving Holy Communion to Christians of all denominations who are in imminent danger of death. We would most liberally interpret the statement of the Code that those Christians of other denominations in danger of death and wish to receive the Eucharist from us "demonstrate the catholic faith in respect of these sacraments and are properly disposed." There is no time in such a situation for a detailed investigation of that person's disposition to accept the doctrine of transubstantiation! Rather, the grace of the sacrament will be given to one who needs that sacrament on that final journey to God that we must all take in due time, and the benefit of theological doubt.

This area, of giving Catholic Communion to those of other denominations under special circumstances, does leave scope for development. Recently, the Catholic Episcopal Conference of England and Wales has issued some special guidelines whereby Catholic priests may give Holy

Communion to those of other denominations in such special circumstances.

Where there does not seem to be scope for flexibility is concerning the possibility of Catholics receiving Holy Communion from those ministers whose priestly orders are not recognized, and whose ecclesial communities do not hold a doctrine of the Eucharist compatible with the Orthodox and with ourselves. Catholics cannot receive a Eucharist that is adjudged invalid viewed in the spectrum of our own doctrine. This leads us without delay to the question of our understanding of the Catholic dogma of transubstantiation.

48: Why does the Roman Catholic Church still insist upon the doctrine of transubstantiation, which seems to be a formula from a dead scholasticism? Why does not the Catholic Church accept the agreements of ARCIC in this respect?

We must begin by rejoicing that ARCIC-II, the Second Anglican/Roman Catholic International Commission, seems to be drawing ever closer together regarding the doctrine of the Eucharist as held by our two churches, Roman Catholic and Anglican. In a letter dated March 11, 1994, Cardinal Cassidy, the president of the Vatican Council for Promoting Christian Unity, stated to the ARCIC-II Co-Chairmen that, as a result of some clarifications, "The agreement reached on Eucharist and Ministry by ARCIC-I is thus greatly strengthened and no further study would seem to be required at this stage."[12] However, perhaps we ought still to be cautious, since, in that same letter, the cardinal still asks for further clarification concerning the use of the reserved sacrament of Communion in the Anglican Church. He asks whether Anglicans actually *adore* the Blessed Sacrament; and that brings us to the heart of the problem.

What the Roman Catholic Church insists upon is not first and foremost the word *transubstantiation* as such, but rather the doctrine of the *real conversion* of the whole reality of bread and wine in the Eucharist into the body and blood of Christ *that is aptly termed transubstantiation.* The term expresses the deeper reality, the reality of the marvelous and mysterious conversion of ordinary bread and wine into the sacrament of Christ's true body and blood, making the sacrament itself worthy of the adoration.

The scholastic term "transubstantiation" serves the doctrine, just as the term "consubstantial" is a technical term describing another deeper reality, the doctrine that Jesus Christ, as the Word proceeding from the Father, is equally God in being with the Father. The latest English version of the Creed now translates *consubstantialem Patris* with "*of one being* with the Father," avoiding the term "consubstantial" while attempting to fully express what the term "consubstantial" means.

It is most important to realize this order of priorities because, while we would freely admit that the doctrine of transubstantiation developed within the framework of scholastic philosophy, the underlying doctrine preceded scholastic philosophy and does not depend upon it.

It is not true to say that the Church simply takes philosophical categories, particularly Greek ones, and fits its doctrine into those categories. Rather, the opposite is true. The Church is confronted by a stupendous mystery, the incarnation, the Eucharist, and attempts to use philosophical insights to help understand this mystery. In doing this, the philosophy is stretched to the breaking point. Aristotelian philosophy knows of no instance where the whole reality of something actually changes, its "matter and form," its total conversion. It only knows of a substance changing into another substance, while the underlying "matter" remains throughout that change; as when one substance (e.g., a pig) is replaced by another substance (the human being who has eaten the pig). Total conversion as in the Eucharist is entirely unknown in orthodox Aristotelianism, but the term serves the developing theology.

It is worth quoting in full the Tridentine definition:

> But since Christ our redeemer said that it was truly his own body which he was offering under the form of bread, therefore there has always been complete conviction in the church of God — and so this holy council now declares it once again — that by the consecration of the bread and wine there takes place the change of the whole substance of the bread into the substance of the body of Christ our Lord, and of the whole substance of the wine into the substance of his blood. And the holy catholic church has suitably and properly called this change transubstantiation.[13]

The Council of Trent defines the doctrine of transubstantiation before it uses the word. What is being defined is the *conversion* of the bread and wine into the reality of the body and blood of Christ. That can be stated in any philosophy; or, rather, it is so mysterious that it is baffling to any philosophy. In attempting to explain it more coherently a whole philosophy of transubstantiation was developed by the scholastics.

The starting point of the doctrine, as Aquinas explains, is not Aristotle but Scripture. Aquinas deals in his usual masterly way with "the conversion of the bread and wine into the body and blood of Christ" in Question 75 of the Third Part of his *Summa Theologiae.* What Aquinas was concerned to insist upon was that the change is *real* and not *figurative:*

> I answer saying that the true body of Christ and his blood is in this sacrament, not in a way, which can be grasped by the senses, but only by faith which is based upon divine authority. Therefore concerning Luke 22:19, *This is my body which is given up for you,* Cyril states: *Do not doubt that this is true, but rather accept the word of the Savior in faith: for since he is truth he does not lie.*[14]

Aquinas for his sources goes back long before the scholastics, to Cyril of Alexandria in the fifth century and elsewhere in that same Question 75 to Hilary of Poitiers in the fourth. If the reality is mysterious, and it is not just symbolic, then it is not only the scholastics who are struggling with terminology. We really do eat Christ's flesh and drink his blood, according to Scripture and the Tradition of the Church.[15]

Biblical scholars see this precise problem also in John's Gospel, chapter 6, when the Discourse on the Bread of Life leads on to the Eucharistic Discourse, John 6:52-58. Many are of the opinion that here John is presenting his own version of the institution of the Eucharist.[16] The realism of John is quite startling. Jesus tells the multitude: "In all truth I tell you, if you do not eat the flesh of the Son of Man and drink his blood, you have no life in you. Anyone who does eat my flesh and drink my blood has eternal life, and I shall raise that person up on the last day. For my flesh is real food and my blood is real drink" (John 6:53b-55).

Naturally, Jesus' hearers are shocked, and he replies: "Does this disturb you? What if you should see the Son of Man ascend to where he was before? It is the spirit that gives life, the flesh has nothing to offer. The words I have spoken to you are spirit and they are life" (John 6:61-63).

This does not take away the force of 6:53b-55, about eating Christ's flesh and blood. The "flesh which has nothing to offer" can in no way refer to the eucharistic eating and drinking of Christ's flesh and blood, which profits a great deal. Rather, many scholars say today, it refers back to 6:36, which refers to the Jewish listeners' lack of faith: "You can see me and still you do not believe."[17] Nothing therefore can take away from the scandal of the realism of the words of Jesus that "my flesh is real food and my blood is real drink."

What prevents eucharistic eating of Christ's flesh and blood from being cannibalistic is that we are speaking here of the real but sacramental presence of Christ in the Eucharist. When we eat the flesh of an animal, we divide the piece that we eat. But according to the traditional doctrine of the Eucharist, Christ can never be divided in the eucharistic species. He is present *totus in toto et toto in qualibet parte* (wholly in the whole and wholly in every part). Having died and risen again, Christ can never again be divided, but is totally present wherever he is present in the eucharistic species, changed into his body and blood.

Pope Paul VI found expressions such as "transignification" and "transfinalization" inadequate precisely for this reason, that they were not sufficiently unambiguous regarding the substantial presence of Christ in the Eucharist. Some argued that the concept of Eucharist as "sign" was of sufficient value to express the Real Presence.[18] But a sign is a distinct reality from what it signifies. A road sign is not a road, still less is it the destination to where we are going. A ring that, in Zwingli's eucharistic theology, a man gives to his wife as a sign of his love is not the man himself. Likewise, "transfinalization" would be inadequate, because the bread and wine is not only used for the finality of being Christ to us, it actually is Christ substantially.

Another word for "sacrament" is "mystery." Moses, standing before the burning bush that burned without consuming the bush, took his sandals off his feet before the awful presence of Yahweh (Exodus 3:1-6). Like the bush that burned without being consumed, the bread and wine become totally the body and blood of Christ in the Eucharist without ceasing to be in the form of food and drink for our salvation, in fact with no perceptible change whatsoever in their appearance. May we too have the faith of Moses to remove our shoes before this wonderful mystery and sign of future glory.

49: Why does the Vatican still insist upon refusing to recognize the validity of Anglican orders?

The current position of the Roman Catholic Church today remains as stated in the papal encyclical of Pope Leo XIII *Apostolicae Curae* in

1896, namely that Anglican orders are "absolutely null and utterly void." This is because, according to that Pope, there is in the Anglican ordination service a defect of intention and of form, which makes that service less than what would be required for a valid Catholic ordination to the priesthood.

The reason for this is linked to the other great aspect of the Catholic doctrine of the Eucharist, perhaps even more important than transubstantiation, namely the Catholic doctrine of the sacrifice of the Eucharist. The Protestant theology of the Eucharist is that it is first and foremost a remembrance, a commemoration, of the one true sacrifice of Christ for our salvation. The Catholic faith is that each celebration of the Eucharist is a re-presentation of the one sacrifice of Christ on Calvary, but offered again truly in an "unbloody" manner, with Christ victorious in heaven making intercession for us, but being present in the person of the priest celebrating Mass, offering that one sacrifice now for the living and the dead.

If Anglican orders had been considered by that Pope even as possibly valid, then the possibility of the conditional ordination of Anglican presbyters would have been opened up. The formula would have been something like, "If you were not ordained priest in the Anglican Church, then you are ordained now." Rather, the Pope required the subtext of such a Catholic ordination of an Anglican minister to be the much sharper: "You were certainly not ordained in the Anglican ordination service. I therefore ordain you now as a Catholic priest."

The objections of Pope Leo XIII to the Anglican ordination service relate to the form of the service itself, and to the intention of those who perform that service. The Pope argues that the rite itself was composed by those who did not accept the teaching of the Council of Trent on the sacrifice of the Mass, and that those who performed the Anglican service of ordination from the Elizabethan Settlement onward had an intention clearly contrary to that doctrine of the sacrificing priesthood. The Pope expressed himself thus:

> The efforts (made to vindicate the validity of the amended form) have been [fruitless], we say, and remain fruitless. And they are fruitless for this reason also that, even if some words of the Anglican Ordinal as it now stands may present the possibility of ambiguity, they cannot bear the same meaning as they have in the Catholic rite.

For as we have seen, when once a new rite has been introduced denying or falsifying the sacrament of Order and repudiating any notion whatsoever of consecration and sacrifice, then the formula "Receive the Holy Spirit" — the Spirit, namely, who is infused into the soul with the grace of the sacrament — is deprived of its force; nor have the words "for the office and work of a priest" or "of a bishop" and similar expressions any longer their force, being now mere names, voided of the reality which Christ instituted.[19]

These are strong words. What the Pope is saying is that if a seriously defective notion about the priesthood is being communicated in the ordination rite, and in the intention of those performing that rite, then the ordination must be invalid. It would be similar to a canonist deciding that a given marriage was invalid, for the reason that the couple had no intention to have children throughout their marriage, and had expressed that intention in a marriage service that they had performed.

To understand the Pope's objections to Anglican ordinations, the relevant history must be understood. Henry VIII broke with Rome in 1534; yet there was no change regarding the sacramental beliefs of the country. But after his death in 1547, his son Edward VI became king, and was more and more subject to Protestant ideas. In 1549, the First Book of Common Prayer was produced, and then in 1552 the Second, which "was an accurate embodiment, in the dignified English of which Cranmer was a master, of the radical Protestant conception of the Eucharist, as opposed to the Catholic doctrine of the Real Presence and the Eucharistic Sacrifice."[20] The Reformers, in insisting upon the priesthood of all believers, denied that there was a specific priesthood with a genuine sacrifice in the Christian dispensation, but rather held that the minister was a preacher of the Gospel. The new rite ordained ministers of the Gospel, but not Catholic priests offering the sacrifice of the Mass.

Trent provided its counter-blast in Session 23, on July 15, 1563, when already the new form of religion had been established in England under Elizabeth I:

Sacrifice and priesthood are so joined together by God's foundation that each exists in every law. And so, since in the new covenant the catholic church has received the visible sacrifice of the Eucharist from the Lord's institution, it is also bound to profess that

> there is in it a new, visible and external priesthood into which the old has been changed. The sacred scriptures show, and the tradition of the catholic church has always taught, that this was instituted by the same Lord our savior, and that power was given to the apostles and their successors in the priesthood to consecrate, offer and administer his body and blood, as also to remit or retain sins.[21]

All recognize that from the Elizabethan Settlement onward, there has been a variety of doctrinal positions within the Anglican Church regarding the Eucharist; from the Zwinglian doctrine of the eucharistic bread and wine as sign only, right across the spectrum to those within the Anglican Church who accept the full Catholic doctrine of the Sacrifice of the Mass and of the eucharistic Real and Substantial Presence. Also, particularly since the growth of the Anglo-Catholic movement in the nineteenth century, Old Catholic bishops whose orders are certainly recognized as valid have taken part in Anglican ordinations. Many would argue that this changes the situation, and that the intervention of these bishops means that Anglican orders are *possibly valid* from the Catholic viewpoint.[22]

At the time of the ARCIC reports, there were great hopes that the question of Anglican orders would be reopened.[23] A most commendable attempt was made in those reports to discover a new theological language that would bring the two traditions, Anglican and Roman Catholic, together. Perhaps ecumenists have been too discouraged by the responses of the Sacred Congregation for the Doctrine of the Faith, which have commended those attempts at finding a common language, but asked for more clarification in the ongoing process of dialogue. The Sacred Congregation for the Doctrine of the Faith, in its *Observations*, required further clarifications from ARCIC regarding this question of the sacrifice of the Eucharist:

> It would have been helpful, in order to permit Catholics to see their faith fully expressed on this point, to make clear that this real presence of the sacrifice of Christ, accomplished by the sacramental words, that is to say by the ministry of the priest saying "in persona Christi" the words of the Lord, includes a participation of the Church, the Body of Christ, in the sacrificial act of her Lord, so that she offers sacramentally in him and with him his sacrifice.[24]

The ordination of women in the Church of England has not helped in the process of reopening the question of Anglican orders. But we must be very careful to distinguish between the two issues, that of the ordination of women, and that of the validity of Anglican orders. For example, if the Orthodox churches agreed to ordain women (which is in fact even less likely than the Roman Catholic Church ordaining women!), the Catholic Church would not recognize those women as validly ordained because of the rule that only a male (*vir*) can be ordained. But that would not invalidate the Orthodox rite of ordination, and validly ordained male priests could still be ordained within the Orthodox Church using the same rite as that used to ordain women. Thus theoretically Anglican orders could be recognized while the ordination of women was not.

In fact, there is no immediate prospect of Anglican orders being recognized, not first and foremost because of the ordination of women, but much more because the doctrinal issues of the eucharistic presence and the eucharistic sacrifice still remain unresolved. It is along those lines, to discuss further our eucharistic faith, that dialogue still has some way to go.

50: Does not the future unity of the Church mean also a legitimate diversity?

From the answers to the Hard Questions raised in this book, the answer to this particular question will be predictable to the reader. The future unity of the Church will mean also a legitimate diversity; but there can be no compromise where the essential faith of the Church is involved: "Through the centuries, in so many languages, cultures, peoples, and nations, the Church has constantly confessed this one faith, received from the one Lord, transmitted by one Baptism, and grounded in the conviction that all people have only one God and Father" (CCC 172).

Furthermore, we have argued in this book the Catholic position of the infallibility of the Church, namely that where it states a matter to be believed as from divine revelation, it cannot be wrong in this. Thus there can never be any compromise regarding the defined content of faith; even though we would admit that not all defined dogmas are of equal importance. How doctrines are mutually balanced and interact is a matter of developing understanding and of doctrinal diversity.

However, having argued for the "bottom line" of infallibly guaranteed dogmas of faith, together with the acceptance of the ordinary *magisterium* of the Church and of the ongoing primacy of the Pope, there remains an enormous area for legitimate diversity within the one visible Church. As the Decree on Ecumenism puts it:

> All in the church must preserve unity in essentials. But let all, according to the gifts they have received, maintain a proper freedom in their various forms of spiritual life and discipline, in their different liturgical rites, and even in their theological elaborations of revealed truth. In all things let charity prevail. If they are true to this course of action, they will be giving ever better expression to the authentic catholicity and apostolicity of the church.[25]

It is difficult to say much more about areas of legitimate diversity without discussing at length some practical examples. But, during the last decade, the Vatican has shown itself most flexible where accommodation can be made. For instance, in its willingness to allow Anglican clergy who are married to become Catholic priests, it has been accused possibly of indecent haste even within the ranks of the Roman Catholic Church. Also, in the United States, whole communities of Episcopalian Christians have been admitted into full communion with the Catholic Church, and have retained their distinctive liturgical and pastoral culture.

There is a tension between the need for the universal Church to be enriched with diverse elements of religious culture, for the process of inculturation to go forward, and at the same time the need for those received into full communion with the Catholic Church to be integrated with the local already existing church. That is why paradoxically it may sometimes be that the Vatican will occasionally be prepared to move faster than the local church, because it will not see, or not view as sufficiently important, local difficulties that people on the ground will see looming much larger in their view. What has not happened so far is the movement toward actual visible unity of sizable whole communities with their bishops. It is difficult to establish ground rules when that wonderful eventuality has not yet occurred, except the most general principles that we have just outlined. But the general pattern as agreed in ecumenical dialogue is not that of absorption by one ecclesial community of another, but of integration, leaving legitimate diversity within the one faith.

51: For how much longer will the Roman Catholic Church insist upon its priests being celibate?

Regarding Catholic priests being celibate, it should be clear to everyone that this is only a disciplinary law, not a question of doctrine. In fact, there always have been married priests in the Catholic Church, in particular in those parts of the Catholic Church that do not follow the Western discipline, but are for example Russian, Greek, or Syriac in their discipline (called "Uniate," i.e., united with Rome, in distinction from the "Eastern Orthodox" separate from Rome). In those communities, the same rule applies as in the Orthodox churches, namely that a married man can become a priest, although a priest cannot marry after ordination.

Furthermore, in England and in the USA recently there have been a number of married men whose wives are still alive, ex-Anglican ordained presbyters, who have been ordained as Roman Catholic priests. Nothing in theory would prevent such a practice spreading wider. The Church acknowledges that many married priests act faithfully and well in their priestly ministry. Particularly those of us who live in countries where the churches of the Reformation tradition are strong will testify to excellent ministers of the Gospel whose wives and families share with them in their pastoral ministry.

However, when the question of changing the law of priestly celibacy was raised at the Second Vatican Council, the bishops strongly agreed to retain the present discipline that the Western Church would continue to ordain to the priesthood only those who were prepared to make a promise of perpetual celibacy. It is at least worth looking at one paragraph of the Decree on the Ministry and Life of Priests to note the reasons why the bishops were so firm in their conclusion to retain priestly celibacy:

> Celibacy is in very many ways appropriate to the priesthood. For the whole mission of a priest is a dedication to the service of the new humanity, which Christ who triumphed over death brings into being in the world by his Spirit, and which draws its origin "not of blood nor of the will of the flesh nor of the will of man, but of God" (John 1:13). Through virginity or celibacy preserved for the sake of the kingdom of heaven, priests are consecrated to Christ in a new and exalted manner, and more easily cleave to him with singleness of heart; in him and through him they devote themselves with greater freedom to the service of God and people; they are more untram-

meled in serving his kingdom and his work of heavenly regeneration; and thus they are more equipped to accept a wider fatherhood in Christ. By this state they make an open profession to people that they desire to devote themselves with undivided loyalty to the task entrusted to them, namely to betroth the faithful to one husband and present them as a pure bride to Christ, and so they appeal to that mysterious marriage, brought into being by God and to be openly revealed in time to come, in which the church has Christ as her only husband. They become, indeed, a living sign that the world to come, in which the children of the resurrection will neither marry nor be given in marriage, is already present among us through faith and love.[26]

I offer this paragraph from *Presbyterorum Ordinis* for the reader's reflection, to make up his or her mind as to whether priestly celibacy is pastorally worthwhile. For many of us priests, while the above words from the Decree sometimes seem to be impossibly idealistic, it does represent a pastoral vision that is inspiring, and has inspired us throughout our priestly lives. In sum, therefore, the Council argues that, while celibacy is not of the essence of the priesthood (its *esse*), nevertheless it is of its well-being (its *bene esse*).

However, being only the *bene esse* of the priesthood, clearly it could change as a law, since the Church could conclude in another situation that although abstractly celibacy might be for the well-being of the Church, in other circumstances it might be better to have married priests. Thus, it concluded, regarding the ex-Anglican married presbyters, that because they had exercised a good ministry in the Church of England, it would be good for the Church that they should exercise their ministry in the Roman Catholic Church. It might similarly conclude that, even if celibacy is for the *bene esse* of the priesthood, yet the circumstances of life today suggest that it might be better to have at least some married priests. For example, priests might be too isolated in some situations, or be too strongly tempted to break their vows of celibacy, or even that insufficient celibate priests were available and needed to be supplemented with married priests.

Church policy is far from such considerations at present. Recent events have made it clear that, while the Vatican is prepared to allow the ordination of married clergy from other denominations, that is not intended to be a general opening up of the celibacy discipline at present.

The convert clergy situation is somewhat unique in that those men were exercising a ministry already in their own denomination prior to being received into full communion with the Catholic Church. The Vatican is determined to retain the general policy of Vatican II throughout the Western discipline, which in Roman Catholic terms is most of the Roman Catholic Church numerically. It may be well worth adding that, apart from in the secular West, for the past year or two the number of Catholic priests worldwide has been increasing, most of them celibate. The Vatican intends to hold on to its policy, which generally is holding its own in terms of ordinations.

May I make some personal observations here, as a celibate priest now for more than thirty years? I am not a "natural celibate," in that when I was ordained an Anglican deacon, I fully expected to fall in love with a girl committed to the Christian faith and to my ministry, and to have children by her to bring up as a Christian family. I have the excellent example of my own sister and brother-in-law, who have just retired from active ministry after many years of first-rate pastoral service for the Church of England. I would never have made a private vow of celibacy had I been left free to do so. Thus it was quite a painful process of growth to accommodate myself to being a celibate priest as I began my training for the priesthood. I needed, and received, a great deal of spiritual counseling. Having, however, become a celibate priest (I must speak honestly, because being a married priest was not an option for me in the Catholic Church) I can see the reasoning behind the above quotation from *Presbyterorum Ordinis*, and the enrichment of my pastoral ministry through priestly celibacy.

I would therefore personally be in favor of the retention of the *law* of priestly celibacy. I would see a real danger (agreeing with Father Keith Barltrop of Allen Hall, Chelsea) of a situation developing where, if celibacy were no longer a law of the Church, those who chose celibacy would very much be seen as second-class citizens within the priesthood. Why did this man choose celibacy? Are his inclinations homosexual? Does he not want the responsibilities of marriage? There would be also peer pressure on him from his fellow-ordinands to marry, and peer pressure from his congregation (in particular, the young single ladies among them!). The law is a challenge, a demand of the Church to the future priest. Moreover, I do not see any change in the discipline operating in both the Roman and the Eastern disciplines not to allow men to marry *after ordina-*

tion; even if there may be some more exceptions of older married men being ordained, as is already happening with married permanent deacons in the Roman Catholic Church. But the discipline that does not allow ordained men to marry seems to be almost universal throughout the history of the Church. The Church has always felt that there is something about the commitment to the priesthood, itself a kind of marriage to the Church, which precludes marriage between a man and a woman.

It may in fact be that the crisis of priestly celibacy is more related to the priest's own self-confidence in his own ministry and life as a Christian. The uncertainties that afflict Catholics, and are reflected in the Hard Questions that I have attempted to answer in this book, have inevitably affected the priest as well as the people. In recent years, the catechesis of Catholic young people has not taken them through Hard Questions such as are posed in this book, as they grow to maturity. "Apologetics" has to a large extent gone out of the Catholic school curriculum, and young priests themselves have perhaps been affected by this gap in Catholic upbringing.

In this context of inadequate catechesis, marriage can be seen as a panacea, which of course it is not, judging from the number of failed marriages that we have in the West at this time. A priesthood that is confident of its mission (and, I would add, confident about the moral teaching of the Church) may find itself with at least slightly fewer problems about celibacy. What this does underline, of course, is the need for priestly training in growth of understanding about the commitment of celibacy, and growth in understanding in particular about one's own sexuality and the ability to handle relationships with both sexes.[27] Celibacy, abstention from sexual activity, does not mean that one has no feelings for people, and that one has no friends.

The dedication of this book was to St. Dunstan, Archbishop of Canterbury. During the time of his ministry, in the second half of the tenth century, he undertook the reform of the clergy, and in particular enforced the law of celibacy.[28] That was a thousand years ago. Whenever the Catholic Church has renewed its faith and life, the renewal of the gift of celibacy among its priests has always been a vital part of such renewal. As the same Decree on the Ministry and Life of Priests already quoted says, "The synod asks not only priests but all the faithful to cherish this precious gift of priestly celibacy, and to beg of God that he will ever lavishly bestow it upon his church."[29]

52: For how long will the Roman Catholic Church persist in its refusal to ordain women to the priesthood?

This has been, in the past few years, a most contentious issue, particularly with the growth of the feminist movement worldwide. We may begin by quoting what the *Catechism of the Catholic Church* states about the question:

> "Only a baptized man (*vir*) validly receives sacred ordination."[30] The Lord Jesus chose men (*viri*) to form the college of the twelve apostles, and the apostles did the same when they chose collaborators to succeed them in their ministry. The college of bishops, with whom the priests are united in the priesthood, makes the college of the twelve an ever-present and ever-active reality until Christ's return. The Church recognizes herself to be bound by this choice made by the Lord himself. For this reason the ordination of women is not possible. (CCC 1577)[31]

The *Catechism* is explicit in quoting Canon Law that only a male (Latin *vir*, as opposed to the Latin *homo,* which would mean "a human being of either sex") can be validly ordained. It is worth noting first of all that there is no suggestion, as is sometimes thought, that the Church only accepts men for ordination to the priesthood because of their inherent superiority. Nor is it a question of whether men or women make better preachers or better pastors. It is a question of what is the will of Christ for this particular sacrament of order.

But what if women "feel the call" to ordination? This is where the *Catechism of the Catholic Church* brings into play a particular theology of vocation to the order of priesthood: "No one has a *right* to receive the sacrament of Holy Orders. Indeed no one claims this office for himself; he is called to it by God. Anyone who thinks he recognizes the signs of God's call to the ordained ministry must humbly submit his desire to the authority of the Church, who has the responsibility and right to call someone to receive orders. Like every grace this sacrament can be *received* only as an unmerited gift" (CCC 1578).

The best biblical testimony to this particular theology of vocation is provided by the call to become one of the Twelve in the Gospels. In Luke's Gospel, we read that, before Jesus chose the Twelve, "he spent the whole night in prayer to God," then "when day came he summoned his disciples and picked out twelve of them" (Luke 6:12b-13). Jesus, as far as we know, did not ask his followers, "Which of you feels the call to be one of my Twelve?" Rather, he made the choice. Thus the Roman Catholic theology of vocation sees the actual call of the bishop to the man to be ordained as the moment of his vocation; although, we must say that what the *Catechism* calls the man's "desire" is often very much more like an interior call, often persistent over many years. Ultimately all the *Catechism* is saying is that such an interior call cannot be the final criterion for ordination, only the actual choice of the Church itself in the person of the bishop.

But could the Church ever reconsider its ban on the ordination of women? It says that it cannot, but how absolute is that *cannot*? All the responses so far have been strongly negative from the Vatican. Pope John Paul II made a most authoritative declaration to the effect that not only could women not be ordained in the present time, but they never would be in the future either. In saying this, he used his full authority as "the successor of Peter." Most theologians, however, agree that he drew back from making this an infallible declaration; and that the Pope is referring to what he sees as the infallibility of the ordinary *magisterium* forbidding women's ordination, not making an infallible pronouncement himself. As Father Avery Dulles says, "Not even the Pope is protected by the charism of infallibility in acts of this kind";[32] although, we would have to add with Dulles, the Pope is making the most powerful assertion of the Tradition in this instance.

This raises the question as to how disciplinary laws relating to the sacraments can be themselves related to the "deposit of faith." The Church does not allow any food but bread and wine to be used for the Eucharist; even though for many people all over the world, and many Catholics, bread and wine is not a staple diet, rather rice and tea, or yams and coconut milk. The Church insists upon bread and wine for the Eucharist because Christ himself used bread and wine at the Last Supper. This is, for the Church, an essential part of the tradition regarding the Eucharist; even though in theory nothing would have prevented Christ from stipulating rice and tea, presuming that he knew of the existence of these commodities. But the Church can still refuse to allow any other food but bread and wine for the Eucharist, if the Church considers that Christ only allowed that particular category of food and drink to be a eucharistic sign. After all, what is consumed at the Eucharist will not actually satisfy the needs of a staple diet.

What is called the "matter" of the sacraments (their material elements, for example water for baptism) does not relate to metaphysical necessity, but simply to what Christ did historically concerning these sacraments. Regarding the sacrament of orders, the "matter" of that sacrament is a "baptized man (*vir*)." Christ could no doubt have ordained it otherwise. Historically, there is no evidence whatsoever that Jesus ordained women to the apostolate, but rather that he did not, and all the evidence we have in the New Testament gives us no evidence that the early Church ordained women to the episcopate nor to the presbyterate, but rather that the early Church only ordained men. But again, why could this not change?

There is an argument of what the theologians used to call an "argument of fittingness" for this. Many Christians who argue for the ordination of women see the priest celebrating the Eucharist as first and foremost representing the Christian community. Then, the argument would naturally go, in these days of equality between men and women, women should equally as well as men be able to represent that Christian community.

But the Catholic doctrine of the priesthood is different. In the theology of Vatican II, reiterated in the new *Catechism* (CCC 1563), priests "are sealed with a special mark by the anointing of the holy Spirit, and thus are patterned to the priesthood of Christ, so that they may be able to act in the person of Christ the head of the body."[33] The priest does not first and foremost represent the Christian community, but Christ to the Christian community. Thus there is some argument (although certainly not an absolute one, since absolute arguments do not exist in this kind of context) that it is more fitting for the priest to be a male, just as Christ was a male. Some have ridiculed this argument saying that if that particular logic was followed, then the priest should be Jewish because Christ was Jewish, or even have a beard because most likely Jesus had a beard. But that is quite facetious. The maleness or femaleness of a human being is an essential dimension of our creation, indeed as part of being the image of God (Genesis 1:27). The same does not apply to the color of our hair, or even of our race.

53: In a future united Church, there must surely be more democratic structures operating within Roman Catholic hierarchical institutions?

There is certainly room within the ecclesiology of the Roman Catholic Church for more decentralized structures. The tendency during the past centuries has been increasingly for power to be centralized in the Vatican. This attained its high point after the definition in Vatican I of the primacy and infallibility of the Pope. But the Second Vatican Council emphasized the collegiality of the bishops, and the fact that each diocesan bishop, as a member of the apostolic college, has authority directly from Christ to teach and pastor his flock. He is not merely a legate of the Pope: "The bishops, therefore, have undertaken along with their fellow workers, the priests and deacons, the service of the community, presiding in the place of God over the flock, whose shepherds they are, as teachers of doctrine, priests of sacred worship and ministers of government."[34]

In fact, since the Second Vatican Council, more power has devolved to the local national bishops' conferences. The new Code of Canon Law, issued by the Pope in 1983, has a number of regulations for the episcopal conferences "to foster cooperation and common pastoral action in the region."[35] Thus programs of religious education, implementation locally of Vatican directives, pastoral plans, media contacts, are increasingly dealt with by such bishops' conferences and the conference staffs that have grown up to serve them. The advantage is clearly the possibility of responding to local needs with the full resources of a number of dioceses working together within a national structure. The dangers are also obvious: the development of a new bureaucracy, the loss of the individual bishop's power in the interests of the unity of the national conference, even some isolation from Rome. There are also diocesan and parish structures: pastoral councils, councils of priests, deanery councils (groups of parishes within a diocese). The modern Church is developing all the sophisticated organs of consultation that exist in the modern world, and the constant complaint among priests and bishops is that there are too many meetings.

Whether this is democracy is a moot point. Ultimately, the Church is a hierarchical institution, even if consultation is a genuine part of the process. The Bishop of Rome has primacy over the whole body of bishops, and the bishops themselves have authority to teach and to pastor their own flocks. Bishops are at present chosen by consultation at local level, but the final say is very much that of Rome. Unlike a democracy, neither a priest nor a bishop can be unseated by popular vote but remains in post with authority until a higher authority decides. If the Church is *apostolic,* then some hierarchical element of necessity follows. But that does not mean that changes, even radical changes, cannot occur, and in the Roman Catholic Church, even sometimes with surprising rapidity.

At the end of the day, the Church is not a democracy, but neither is the Church a dictatorship. Rather, it is a *theocracy,* ruled by the Holy Spirit. As we approach the third millennium, we pray for a liberal dose of that Spirit, and especially a closer union between Christians of various denominations. That is only to continue work already well begun.

Endnotes

1. R. de Vaux, O.P., *The Bible and the Ancient Near East,* trans. Damien McHugh (London: Darton, Longman and Todd, 1972), ch. 15, pp. 270-284.

2. Ibid., pp. 277-278.

3. Ibid., p. 278.

4. Quotation from UR no. 11.

5. ST, III, q. 1, a. 2.

6. ND, p. 206, § 713, no. 3902.

7. ODCC, pp. 98-99, "Assumption of the BVM."

8. CCL, Can. 844, §3.

9. UR no. 2: cf. CCL, can. 844, §3.

10. Tanner, II, UR, p. 919, lines 33-39.

11. CCL, p. 157.

12. *Clarifications of Certain Aspects of the Agreed Statements on Eucharist and Ministry of the first Anglican-Roman Catholic International Commission together with a Letter from Cardinal Edward Idris Cassidy, President, Pontifical Council for Promoting Christian Unity* (London: Church House Publishing/Catholic Truth Society, 1994), p. 12.

13. Tanner, II, p. 695, Session 13, chapter 4, lines 17-23.

14. ST, III, q. 75, a. l: Respondeo dicendum quod verum corpus Christi et sanguinem esse in hoc sacramento, non sensu deprehendi potest, sed sola fide, quae auctoritati divinae innititur. Unde super illud Lc. 22, 19, *Hoc est corpus meum quod pro vobis tradetur,* dicit Cyrillus: *Non dubites an hoc verum sit, sed potius suscipe verba Salvatoris in fide: com enim sit veritas non mentitur.*

15. Controversy about this doctrine goes back centuries before the Reformation, to Berengarius, an eleventh-century Canon of Tours. The heavy hand of ecclesiastical authority came down on Berengarius, and

eventually he agreed to a statement as to the Catholic faith in the Real Presence devised specially for him by the Council of Rome in 1079: "I, Berengar, believe in my heart and confess with my lips that the bread and wine which are placed on the altar are, by the mystery of the sacred prayer and the words of the Redeemer, substantially changed into the true and proper and life-giving body and blood of Jesus Christ our Lord; and that, after consecration, they are Christ's true body, which was born of the virgin and hung on the cross, being offered for the salvation of the world, and which sits at the right hand of the Father; and Christ's true blood, which was poured forth from His side; not only by way of sign and by the power of the sacrament, but in their true nature and in the reality of their substance (*in proprietate naturae et veritate substantiae*). . . ."

16. R. Brown, *The Gospel According to John*, vol. I (*I-XII*) (The Anchor Bible; London: Geoffrey Chapman, 1971), pp. 287-291.

17. Ibid., p. 299.

18. ND, pp. 436-437: Paul VI's Encyclical Letter *Mysterium Fidei*.

19. ND, p. 501, §1726, no. 3317b.

20. F. Clark, *The Catholic Church and Anglican Orders* (Do 337) (London: Catholic Truth Society, 1962), p. 11.

21. Tanner, II, p. 742, lines 4-12.

22. E. Yarnold, *Anglican Orders — A Way Forward?* (C284) (London: Catholic Truth Society, 1977), pp. 8-9.

23. ND, p. 499: "In the new ecumenical climate created in recent years, it is felt that the question of the value of orders derived from the Anglican hierarchy should once more be reexamined."

24. Sacred Congregation for the Doctrine of the Faith. *Observations on the Final Report of the Anglican-Roman Catholic International Commission*, B. I. (1).

25. Tanner, II, UR no. 4, p. 912, lines 10-15.

26. Tanner, II, p. 1062, line 28 — p. 1063, line 5.

27. Cf. D. Rees (ed.), *Consider Your Call: A Theology of Monastic Life Today* (London: SPCK, 1978). The chapter on celibacy, pp. 154-188, is relevant to all who have taken a vow of celibacy, and perhaps even to those who are married!

28. M. Walsh (ed.), *Butler's Lives of the Saints: Concise Edition* (Tunbridge Wells: Burns and Oates, 1956, 1985), p. 149.

29. Tanner, II, PO, p. 1063, lines 26-30.

30. CCL, can. 1024.

31. The CCC quotes as authority John Paul II, *Mulieris Dignitatem* 26-27 and the Declaration of the Sacred Congregation for the Doctrine of the Faith, *Inter insigniores* (1977).

32. Avery Dulles, "Women's ordination and infallibility, no. 2: Tradition says no," *The Tablet*, vol. 249, no. 8105 (December 9, 1995), p. 1572.

33. Tanner, II, PO, p. 1044, lines 5-7.

34. Tanner, II, LG, p. 864, lines 15-17.

35. CCL, can. 434, p. 77.

Bibliography

Raymond E. Brown, *The Gospel According to John,* vol. I (*I — XII*) (The Anchor Bible; New York: Doubleday/London: Geoffrey Chapman, 1971).

Raymond E. Brown (ed.), *Peter in the New Testament* (London: Geoffrey Chapman, 1974).

Raymond E. Brown, *Responses to 101 Questions on the Bible* (New York: Paulist Press/London: Geoffrey Chapman, 1990).

Rudolf Bultmann, *Existence and Faith: Shorter Writings of Rudolf Bultmann,* sel., trans., and intro. Schubert M. Ogden (London: Collins, 1961).

Rudolf Bultmann, *The Gospel of John; A Commentary,* trans. G. R. Beasley-Murray (Oxford: Basil Blackwell, 1971).

B. C. Butler, *The Church and Infallibility: A Reply to the Abridged 'Salmon'* (London: Sheed and Ward, 1954).

B. C. Butler, *The Church and Unity* (London: Geoffrey Chapman, 1979).

Dom Cuthbert Butler, *The Vatican Council 1869-1870: Based on Bishop Ullathorne's Letters* (London: Collins, 1962).

Henry Chadwick, *The Circle and the Ellipse* (Oxford: Clarendon Press, 1959).

B. Childs, *Introduction to the Old Testament as Scripture* (London: SCM Press, 1979).

F. L. Cross and E. A. Livingstone (eds.), *Oxford Dictionary of the Christian Church* (Oxford: OUP, 1983).

Oscar Cullmann, *Peter: Disciple — Apostle — Martyr* (English trans.) (London: SCM Press, 1953).

Don Cupitt, *The Sea of Faith: Christianity in Change* (London: British Broadcasting Corporation, 1984).

Paul Davis and John Gribbin, *The Matter Myth: Beyond Chaos and Complexity* (London: Penguin Books, 1991).

John de Satgé, *Peter and the Single Church* (London: SPCK, 1981).

Avery Dulles, *The Catholicity of the Church* (Oxford: Clarendon Press, 1985).

David L. Edwards, *What Is Catholicism? An Anglican Responds to the Official Teaching of the Roman Catholic Church* (London: Mowbray, 1994).

David L. Edwards, "Prejudice unmasked, no. 6: Roman Catholics as others see them," *The Tablet* (April 8, 1995), pp. 452-453.

John Hick (ed.), *The Myth of God Incarnate* (London: SCM Press, 1977).

Walter Kasper, *The God of Jesus Christ,* trans. M. J. O'Connell (London: SCM Press, 1982).

J. N. D. Kelly, *The Oxford Dictionary of Popes* (Oxford: Oxford University Press, 1986).

Hans Küng, *Infallible? An Enquiry* (London: Collins, 1971).

Nicholas Lash, *Believing Three Ways in One God: A Reading of the Apostles' Creed* (London: SCM Press, 1992).

René Latourelle, *Finding Jesus Through the Gospels: History and Hermeneutics,* trans. A. Owen (Staten Island, NY: Alba House, 1979).

René Latourelle, *Man and His Problems in the Light of Jesus Christ,* trans. M. J. O'Connell (Staten Island, NY: Alba House, 1983).

René Latourelle, *The Miracles of Jesus and the Theology of Miracles,* trans. M. J. O'Connell (New York: Paulist Press, 1988).

Peter J. McCord (ed.), *A Pope for All Christians?* (London: SPCK, 1976).

John McHugh, *The Mother of Jesus in the New Testament* (London: Darton, Longman and Todd, 1975).

James J. Megivern (ed.), *Official Catholic Teachings: Bible Interpretation* (Wilmington, DE: McGrath, 1978).

Charles F. D. Moule, *The Origin of Christology* (Cambridge: Cambridge University Press, 1977).

John Henry Newman, *Essay on the Development of Christian Doctrine* (seventh edition) (London: Longmans, Green, and Co., 1890).

John Henry Newman, *Apologia Pro Vita Sua; Being a History of His Religious Opinions* (London: Longmans, Green and Co., 1908).

Gerald O'Collins, *Interpreting Jesus* (London: Geoffrey Chapman, 1983).

Gerald O'Collins, *Jesus Risen: The Resurrection — What Actually Happened and What Does It Mean?* (London: Darton, Longman and Todd, 1987).

Karl Rahner, *Theological Investigations,* vol. 5, trans. Karl H.-H. Kruger (London: Darton, Longman, and Todd, 1966).

Karl Rahner, *Theological Investigations,* vol. 22 (London: Darton, Longman and Todd, 1991).

Edward Schillebeeckx, *Christ the Sacrament of the Encounter with God* (London: Sheed and Ward, 1963).

Albert Schweitzer, *The Quest of the Historical Jesus: A Critical Study of Its Progress from Reimarus to Wrede*, trans. W. Montgomery (German edition, 1906; first English edition, 1910; third edition, 1956; reprinted 1973).

Janet Smith, *Humanae Vitae: A Generation Later* (Washington, DC: Catholic University of America Press, 1991).

David Friedrich Strauss, *The Life of Jesus Critically Examined*, trans. George Eliot, ed. Peter C. Hodgson (London: SCM Press, 1972).

Index

Note: This specialized index does not strictly conform to conventional styles. For example, some entries may be derivations of other entries or are part of a "family" (for instance, "ecumenical movement" may come under "ecumenism," "Arians" under "Arius," "Nestorians" under "Nestorius," and the like; still other entries will include page references defining, explaining, or otherwise clarifying them). Other entries, because of their perceived importance, may be limited, that is, not every instance of a particular entry may be included. Other modifications and deviations from standard indexes are self-explanatory.